Vanessa Gorman
Layla's Story

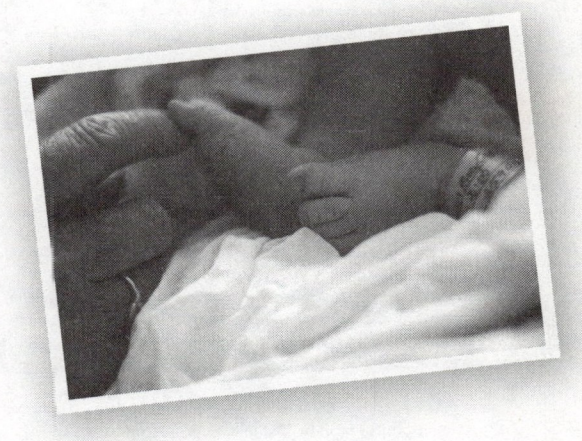

VIKING
an imprint of
PENGUIN BOOKS

Vanessa Gorman's website is: www.vanessagorman.com

VIKING

Published by the Penguin Group
Penguin Group (Australia)
250 Camberwell Road, Camberwell, Victoria 3124, Australia
(a division of Pearson Australia Group Pty Ltd)
Penguin Group (USA) Inc.
375 Hudson Street, New York, New York 10014, USA
Penguin Group (Canada)
90 Eglinton Avenue East, Suite 700, Toronto, ON M4P 2Y3, Canada
(a division of Pearson Penguin Canada Inc.)
Penguin Books Ltd
80 Strand, London WC2R 0RL, England
Penguin Ireland
25 St Stephen's Green, Dublin 2, Ireland
(a division of Penguin Books Ltd)
Penguin Books India Pvt Ltd
11 Community Centre, Panchsheel Park, New Delhi–110 017, India
Penguin Group (NZ)
Cnr Airborne and Rosedale Roads, Albany, Auckland, New Zealand
(a division of Pearson New Zealand Ltd)
Penguin Books (South Africa) (Pty) Ltd
24 Sturdee Avenue, Rosebank, Johannesburg 2196, South Africa

Penguin Books Ltd, Registered Offices: 80 Strand, London WC2R 0RL, England

First published by Penguin Group (Australia), a division of Pearson Australia Group Pty Ltd, 2005

3 5 7 9 10 8 6 4 2

Text copyright © Vanessa Gorman 2005

The moral right of the author has been asserted

Cover and text design by Debra Billson © Penguin Group (Australia)
Cover photograph by Danielle Smith, *Herald Sun*
Typeset in 12/18 pt ITC Legacy Serif Book by Post Pre-press Group, Brisbane, Queensland
Printed and bound in Australia by McPherson's Printing Group, Maryborough, Victoria

National Library of Australia
Cataloguing-in-Publication data:

Gorman, Vanessa, 1961– .
Layla's story.
ISBN 0 670 02898 3.
1. Infants (Newborn) – Death – Psychological aspects.
2. Bereavement – Psychological aspects. I. Title.

155.937

www.penguin.com.au

For Layla, and all children lost to us

slow surrender to softness

no longer solely your own

also her   wonder and

creating   new life. The tend

being round and soft in a

am in love with the

kes and secretly steal

the mirror, both all

enormous swell

prologue

I thought of calling this book *Lucky Middle-class Woman Writes Sob Story*.

Unless you are a beggar in India or some stratospherically wealthy heiress, you, like me, have probably been raised with the notion that while there are many more privileged than ourselves, there are millions worse off – those facing war, starvation, dispossession, the tsunamis of life. I have not had my family slaughtered in front of me, or my lands possessed. I have not been starved or tortured. I am nobody from nowhere with my small human story. I know I am lucky, even though I have faced what felt like the deepest grief.

Perhaps it is my good fortune that leads me to lay this tale before you. Some readers may find parts of it confronting. I don't mean to offend. I have greedily and thankfully consumed the stories of others to guide me in this life. To give thanks I offer my own, mindful of the slings and arrows this process inevitably invites. So let's cut out the middle man: *Lucky Middle-class Woman Writes Self-indulgent, Narcissistic Sob Story*. Ah! It feels better to have that out in the open. I can relax now.

When a Masai traveller sees another across a distant ridge, they raise a hand to say, *I see you*. When deep grief strikes us, we plunge into what seems like another world, the underworld of howling pain, anger, frustration and despair. Often, our only solace is found in hearing or reading the stories of others who have walked the same brambled path, faced the same despair. In exposing my own experience, I raise my hand to others on their lonely ridge and call out, *I see you*.

My hope for this book is that it might serve as a map of the sacredness and profanity lining the hard road through sorrow and back, hopefully, to peace.

This book is also a letter to the children of my heart, so they will know where they came from and be released to travel to wherever they are going. Having children, like life itself, is all about the letting go, a relinquishing that, when done with grace, will honour their soul's path to freedom.

Dear Layla

If I could sing you back into existence, I would. If I could speak words that would make you whole, somehow breathe you back to life, I would. If I could turn back the clock to make you safe, I would give anything. If I could sell my soul to any devil for your life, I would not hesitate.

But the world turns and you have dissolved back into the place from where you came. All I have left is your urn of bone shards and ashes. And these words. The story of your existence. A scrapbook of love, desire, death, grief and new beginnings.

You came into my life like a lightning bolt and I am not the same since that searing. I love you for striking me open, yet can sometimes hardly bear the wound you left.

I write so you will not be forgotten. I write to sing you back into existence.

All my love, my darling.

part One

Vanessa (owner of the Key t...
..... catty chakras)
..... can't get you ou...
...in or mind..... Yes It's definitely addi...
     How to have U & not ow...
...how to be secure in this love & not be
jailed ..... How to have love & li...
...on the same bush .....
          the space / intimacy dance
one & it feels easy to trip over...
     I'm so proud of who you are
on my love for you tonight .... even
you prancing around in a white dr...
ether........   ♡ Michael)

Blueberry Cheesecake and the Nature of Consciousness

. . . the soul cannot range freely, cannot realize more
than a particle of itself in the hopelessly cramped field that
is a single existence . . . the best solace for the unfinished,
untidy business of being human is the company
of another human being.

Edwin Dobb

Sometimes life has a curious way of bringing you to your knees and then throwing hope in your face.

I got sacked on the Friday and met someone who would change my life on the Saturday. I like the drama of that, *I got sacked*. The more boring truth is that the television program I was working on got axed. To apologise for being a big corporate arsehole and only giving us four hours' notice and one week's severance pay, the network shouted myself and twenty suddenly jobless colleagues to a boozy lunch – a wake for a broadcasting stillbirth that became more hysterical as day slid into the hazy hours of night.

The next morning I was going to a meditation weekend.

The six a.m. alarm pierced a monumental hangover. My hand clawed for the snooze button as a dispute began between my slothfulness and my desire for upward spiritual mobility. Above it all I could hear my father's voice, *Engage with life, follow every opportunity* . . . An exhausting creed to follow.

I first saw Michael in the foyer of the meditation centre.

We registered each other. I thought, *He looks nice . . . I wonder if they've still got that cheesecake here,* and kept on my trajectory to the toilet. At lunch he passed by my table and I thought, *Mmmm, one of those nice high-set arse*s. *Was that shredded carrot dangling from my mouth?*

On the second day I sat next to him at lunch, trying to look at once friendly and coolly detached. Like I wasn't a 33-year-old woman with a biological clock at twenty to midnight, desperately searching for a soul mate.

'I sometimes sit in meditation and all I can think about is if they'll have the blueberry cheesecake,' I confessed.

'Cheesecake's a valid thing to contemplate. Blueberry cheesecake is a fairly exceptional form of consciousness.'

'Blueberry cheesecake is God!' I said with mock reverence, taking the piss out of the meditation teacher, and we both laughed.

I took a few mouthfuls of the chickpea curry. It was troublesome, too liquid. I concentrated on not dribbling it down my shirt. It pooled instead in my sleeve.

'What do you do out in the world?' he asked.

Because I was partial to his high-set arse, I told him what I did in a tone of, *Ahh, it's nothing, I just fly around the world with film crews and stuff like that,* like my job was no more interesting than your average sales rep position.

'Wow, that sounds fascinating.'

'Yeah . . . What do you do?'

'I'm a sales rep.'

He hurriedly added that he ran his own sales agency, did it just for the money, and what he was really passionate about was how the creative arts intersect with therapeutic work, or something like that. He said later that he had been a bit partial to my high-set arse and wanted to put his best cheek forward.

I was listening, but I was also noting the way his crop of silky wheat-coloured hair was swept back from his face in an annoyingly perfect way. I sensed a nervous naivety mixed with deep kindness in his huge blue eyes, the blue of the water nearest the shore. I was also trying to surreptitiously excavate the chickpeas from my sleeve.

Whereas most of my meditating time that weekend had been spent contemplating the cake selection, during the last session I engaged in improbable sexual fantasies, sneaking peeks at him through the gloom of the meditation hall.

I hadn't told him I'd just lost my job. Instead I did something profoundly unspiritual. Profoundly sneaky. Later that day, at the close of the meditation intensive, when people were sharing their deep and meaningful experience of the teachings, I stood and proclaimed my own, fake insight. The contemplation for the weekend had been the pat-sounding but deep truth 'everything happens for the best'.

So I said something like, *I just lost my job on Friday and came here feeling like nothing much is happening for the best but after contemplating the message I can accept that perhaps things happen for a reason and I just have to trust that things are unfolding perfectly, blah blah blah . . .*

If I was being honest with God and all those in the room, I would have stood up and said, *I just lost my job on Friday but I don't really give a stuff and I'm just telling you this because I quite like the look of that blond guy over there with the high-set arse and I want to give him an excuse to talk to me again, if only to offer his sympathy, because I'm longing for love in my life and I'm ready to have babies and I'm too scared to make the next move . . .*

'You didn't tell me you'd just lost your job,' he said later.

Bingo. I had sensed him loitering near the exit as I retrieved my shoes. He'd followed me out into the night air and caught up with me down the path.

We exchanged numbers in the carpark. 'Would you . . . um . . . like to have dinner some time?' he stammered.

'I'd love to,' I replied, thinking, *And I wouldn't mind having your children either*. 'You made the first move,' I said, 'so I'll ring you. That's only fair.'

At home I stood for a while in the park across the road, watching the pulsating yellow moon rise from the ocean, smiling at her beautiful pockmarked face. 'What about this stranger?' I asked her. I had asked questions of her all my life and she had never done more than hang like Mona Lisa's smile in the night sky. I raised my water bottle to her, toasting the possibility that at some time in the future I might know the mysteries of Michael as well as I knew myself. Or I might not.

I waited three days and then nervously called, relieved to get his answering machine. I left a quote from David Malouf's novel, *An Imaginary Life*. '"What else should our lives be but a continual series of beginnings, of painful settings into the unknown, pushing off from the edges of consciousness into the mystery of what we have not yet become".'

I hoped it might be a mating call for a brave heart but when I put down the phone I nearly puked at my pretentiousness. Months later, he admitted that none of my efforts had worked. As he'd walked me to the car after meditation, he got a hard on – all *he* needed to continue the pursuit.

The Wrong Crowd

I fell in with the wrong crowd early. Sleeping Beauty, Rapunzel, Snow White. At six, my drug of choice was Cinderella. I would sit beneath my father's chair and liberate the Little Golden Book from my banana-scented Globite case, waving it in the air to short-circuit the political talk of my parents.

'Cinderella again!' my father would exclaim. 'That's only the third time this week.' I can hear the playful irony in his voice now, but back then I was oblivious to all but getting my fix – and he was my supplier. I would settle against his lounging frame, my head bobbing against his Adam's apple as I waited for the story to unfold. Waited for the rush.

'And at the ball, all the other noblemen wanted to dance with Cinderella, but when they would ask, the prince would shake his head and say, *No, she's my partner.*'

'Read that bit again,' I would cry, the romance mainlining through my system, and he would read it again with just the right upward inflection on the *no* and a beautiful downward inflection on *my partner*, and I would snuggle against him and shiver with joy as the prince scoured the county for the maiden who had lost her glass slipper.

This longing for union would become almost shameful in its intensity – creeping through my life like ivy, feeding on my imagination. And so I began looking for this partner, *this other*, long before I knew how to navigate, long before I could imagine sex or anything of adult life. All I knew was that somewhere out there dwelt another soul that might one day be joined to mine.

Of all the precious gifts I have been granted in this life, the most enduring is my happy childhood. My sibling and I made up a feral posse of five, our playground a thousand acres. Older sister Alex and big brother Austin led the pack. My younger brother, Henry, was the family's wild child, and little Rebecca ran faster than all of us to keep up. At our worst we were unruly, untamed; at our best, innocence set free.

Fairfield, as our property was perhaps too grandly called, sat in the Riverina District, halfway between Sydney and Melbourne. We ran sheep and cattle and farmed broadacre crops like wheat, oats and barley. The land was lush and verdant in the winter, parched brown to grey in the summer, broken only by the yellow waves of ripening crops and the line of green willows that fringed the creek. It was just one tiny pixel on a satellite photo, but to me it was and always will be the land of my Dreaming.

Still now, I do not have to close my eyes to conjure the moods, colours and contours of that ancient, undulating land. It is burnt into every cell of my body. The Wiradjuri people had walked it for centuries, living by the complex rhythms of their Dreaming and ceremonial cycles. Then they were pushed from it by the straggling army of mostly Irish settlers who came to make a new life under these vast skies.

My brothers and sisters and I looked out for each other and fought in that fierce sibling way, but we were wrangled from above with the sternish, wholehearted love of my parents, the care of a sprawling extended Catholic family, and the benevolent regard of the Yerong Creek community.

Blink and you'll miss it, was how we described our town's insignificance in the wider landscape, but it was here I first saw the way community works best. There was the usual bickering and gossip but mostly an unspoken support and acceptance, as well as an amused celebration of the eccentricities of the townsfolk. The city lived in our imagination as a place of alienation, where you could hear your neighbour's toilet flush and yet, incredibly, not ever get to meet that neighbour.

My mother was a radical in a conservative town – ten years younger and she might have been manning student barricades. Instead, she was stuck on a farm with five children. When she wasn't busy wiping bottoms and spooning mash into mouths, she was busy with projects to change the world. Once we could fend for ourselves, her parenting style became one of benevolent neglect. As she cheerfully admits, she'd open the door in the morning, shoo us out, and close it behind us again at night. We loved the freedom.

To my father, we were the workforce. We roamed on horseback and motorbike, in the ute, by truck or foot, turning every task into a game, although the sheer hardship of some of the work could leave us grim-faced and exhausted. Whenever possible, we would wage war on each other with clods of earth and pats of cow dung – a crusty shell and liquid centre the most satisfying missile.

It is my father's presence that figures large in my memory, the smell of his Drizabone and work clothes a heady mixture of sweat and sheep shit. Away from the paddocks, the mix of Sunlight soap and tweed jacket followed him, a warm and reassuring scent. A gentle man of high integrity, he could still terrify us with the force of his foul language when a mob of sheep headed off in the wrong direction. But most of the time he was the nurturer, leaning over the bath to wash our cuts and scrapes, taking the time to show us how the world worked. At night I would sometimes find him in his study, poring over farm accounts. Pleased to have him to myself, I would lean into him, soaking up his warmth as he explained the figures before setting me the task of entering stock numbers into a leather-backed ledger, mournful lowing from the home paddock occasionally breaking the silence.

I didn't know it at the time but my father was dying. When his children ranged in age from two to eight, he was diagnosed with a rare form of abdominal cancer and given about a year to live. Determined to watch us grow up, he outlived the predictions. Knowing he was to be robbed of a long life, he invested himself in us – teaching and guiding, admonishing, encouraging. He gave us a lifetime of parenting in the seven years he defied his sentence.

I was oblivious to his dying, but the cycle of birth and death was as familiar to me as the ground I walked on. The smell of decay, of animal carcasses rotting in the paddock, was a familiar sting to my nostrils. I saw the stiffening and then the bloating, the slow oozing of flesh as it melted back into the earth. Bleached by sun, skin became a grotesque leather stretched over brittle bones. Eventually, all that distinguished these random gravesites was a patch where, nourished by decay, the grass grew tall and lush.

Birth held its own fascination. Cruising mobs of sheep in the old ute, the sheepdogs salivating on our shoulders from their perch on the cabin shelf, we'd hunt out problem cases, indicated by the comical sight of a ewe wandering around with a lamb's head protruding from what I thought was the mother's bum hole. We would catch the ewe and my father would help her give birth. His hand would disappear up the pink, slippery passage leaking fluid and blood. He would ease the front legs out and then the body, gently turning the lamb to the distressed and urgent bleats of the ewe, who I would try to soothe as I held her firmly to the ground.

Every so often, the lamb would be blue. My father would place the stillbirth underneath the mother's nose. I would watch her lick it, nudge it and make noises, trying to wake it up, and my heart would break a little at her distress. Sometimes the ewe would fret for days near her dead lamb, until eventually she would understand enough to join the rest of the mob. Much later, only a tiny tuft of greener grass remained to mark the loss.

January 1972. Vietnam was on the news every night, the radical youth of Australia were turning on, tuning in and dropping out, and for the last time my father was leaving the house where he had lived his entire fifty-four years. My mother was driving him to the air ambulance for the trip to Sydney, which sounded like an exciting way to travel. Earlier that day we had played outside as he sat unmoving, head bowed with pain, enduring in his garden chair.

I remember feeling unease at our carefree state, even while we shrieked in the delight of our usual games. I wanted to comfort him, but kept my distance because I could not take away the pain. I remember, too, the strange, helpless shame I felt. As my mother lined up suitcases near the door, I could see he needed to be in hospital. Breathless, moving slowly, he sat at the long table and wrote lists of instructions. We girls loitered as he talked to the boys about looking after the dogs and which mobs of sheep needed to be moved soon. I wished again that I was a boy.

'You're the man of the house now,' he said to my older brother, only thirteen years old, who rose from the table taller now under his new mantle.

I was shrinking from the unspoken truth, innocence threatened but intact. Still, I remember the resigned sadness on Dad's face as he looked at us while my mother bundled him out to the car.

He will be home soon, I told myself as we waved the tail lights off into the night. After all, my father's fluctuating health was the background to our lives. And there was a pattern. Every year or two he would travel to Sydney for an operation. A month or two later, he would arrive back, frail but full of life and optimism, laden with interesting gifts that only doubled our delight at having him home. And life would be normal again. *As it would soon.*

Sydney was sweltering when I went with my mother to the city to buy school uniforms. I was twelve and preparing to join my older sister Alex at boarding school. Nervous excitement overwhelmed me; daggers of sunlight reflected from tall buildings stabbed at my eyeballs. Crowds hurried by with purpose. But the hospital was a different kind of alien land. The long corridors were cool and gloomy, nurses and patients moving like spectres across the shiny linoleum floors.

The room where my father lay was veiled in afternoon shadows. When my mother pulled back the curtain, I wanted to jump on the bed and throw my arms around him in a joyful reunion but instead I retreated to a corner in shock. All the colour had drained from his cheeks. A small blue vein throbbed weakly at his temple. His face was sunken, submerged. Tubes snaked from his arms to machines making noises like something from an episode of *Dr Who*.

My mother quietly talked to him as his eyelids fluttered with fatigue. I dutifully told him about preparations to begin school and then slunk back to my corner and watched.

This must be what happens when he comes to Sydney for his operations,

I reasoned. *This must be what he's like until he gets better.* I would wait to see him when he was up and about again, when he could leave behind this sad, wilted figure in the bed and be Dad again, buoyant with energy and plans for our future.

I suddenly wanted to escape the gloom for the heat and the bustle and the new life I was walking into. Nobody told me that this brush of my lips against his parched and grey skin was to be my last kiss. That it was time to say goodbye.

A month into my new life at school, I was pulled from class. Alex met me in the corridor and before I could even whisper a question we were ushered into a sitting room next to the principal's office. My Auntie Joan moved to embrace us, and we stood with our arms around each other in silence. I had no idea why we were standing like that, why we weren't speaking, and why she had tears rolling down her face.

'It's your father,' she said after a long time. And still I had no idea what she meant. All I knew was that my heart was beating hot blood around my brain and back down to my feet and my breath was trapped in my throat.

'What?' I croaked.

He's got a bit sicker, he's getting out early, he wants to see you. What? What?

'He died at four thirty this morning,' she said, and I looked over to Alex in helpless confusion, hoping she might question the truth of this. But she was looking down with a resigned sadness, like she had been expecting this monstrous news.

I remember the rush: trying to breathe properly and hearing the word *no* come from my throat and my aunt holding me tighter as huge sobs of disbelief choked me. And my sister standing quietly on her own, outside the circle now, hardly making a sound.

There was no church in our town big enough to hold the funeral. We knew everyone and everyone knew us. Put a sprawling Catholic family into the mix, and a lifetime of friendships from Sydney and Melbourne, and suddenly the funeral was to be a gathering of several hundred people. The men of the town mowed the cemetery lawn and set out chairs under the huge pines, and on a warm day in March we celebrated his life and buried him.

For some strange, twelve-year-old reason I had resolved not to cry that day, and I almost made it – until we stood above the grave and they started to lower in his coffin and ex-servicemen began to file past and throw red paper poppies into the grave and someone picked up a shovel and threw in the first load of dirt, which landed with a sickening thud on the glazed wood. Then it dawned on me that my father's body in that coffin would soon start to decay. Except I could still feel the texture of his hand in mine, still picture him above my bed, blessing me while I was supposed to be sleeping. I could still smell the sweat and soap.

It seemed unbearable that both the source and object of my love was being lowered into this deep dank place to rot. I wanted to shout to the men to stop throwing in those ridiculous poppies, for someone to let him up for air. But all I did was bite my lip to stifle my sobs as my childhood came quietly to an end.

In the months afterwards, under no illusion about the putrid process of decay, I tortured myself with the image of my father slowly rotting. I told no one this, just as I was not invited to share any part of the grief that shook me from the inside. It was not a time or place where the violent storms that can rent a heart were spoken about, even within our family. In a sense it felt like we had been orphaned, since my mother's energies were taken up with running the farm and forging a career to keep a roof over our heads and school bills paid.

This first big death in my life did two things. It made me understand, somewhere deep in my bones, the impermanence of existence, the frailty of all life; it obliterated the blind trust that had graced my childhood. And, slowly and imperceptively, it shut down my heart.

I resumed my place at boarding school amongst a class of girls who had no idea what to say to me, so said nothing. The teachers' condolences were hurriedly offered but I was not encouraged to speak of my pain. My heart was bursting with love for someone who no longer existed. I was desperate to feel love from someone who could no longer give it.

In a way I could not articulate at the time, I felt abandoned not so much by my father but by love itself.

A few months after he died, I took myself out into a paddock one night and screamed at God to give me ten more minutes with him. Just ten minutes. To say the things I had not been adult enough to say, to tell him how much I loved him, how much I appreciated his love. To say goodbye.

Slowly my heart went underground and I hid it behind a brittle shell of humour, a kind of larrikin despair at life's haphazard brutality. I understood now that life was short and it could all end in a heartbeat, so you might as well squeeze the marrow out of the bones before it was time to rot. And so I went on a wild ride for the next twenty-one years, careening through school and university and a career in documentary television.

I was like a speedboat skimming across the waves, my heartbeat lost in the wash of ceaseless activity.

I wanted my heart back. But I had no idea how to find it.

Shopping for a Soul Mate

To some who associate 'romantic' with 'irrational',
romantic love is a temporary neurosis, an emotional storm,
inevitably short lived, which leaves disillusionment and
disenchantment in its wake. To others, romantic love
is an idea that if never reached, leaves one feeling one
has somehow missed the secret of life.

Nathaniel Branden, 'A Vision of Romantic Love'

A 33-year-old woman is in her prime. Experience animates her beauty, the earliest signs of wisdom are etched onto her face.
My 33-year-old self was both fulfilled and desperate – fulfilled by career and the adventure of life, but also desperate for intimate union and children. I hungered for a deeper, more authentic existence, but had no idea what form that might take. I kept hoping I'd meet someone who would show me a new way of life. I was shopping for a soul mate.

Dating in my early twenties had been an adventure in guy land. It seemed too early to have a serious agenda for rest-of-life-union so I was happy to take what life threw up. I'd been trained to listen, trained to *give*, and dutifully I would coax and laugh, providing a warm receptacle for the tall tales and true of mundane lives. It seemed some men thought I'd be so damn grateful that they talked incessantly about themselves, I'd fall into bed with them.

A seven-year relationship in my twenties ended a few months before my thirtieth birthday. Now dates were becoming more like job interviews, trying to sniff out the long-term union. And I'd become fed up with self-centred pricks.

On our first date, Michael began asking questions about me as soon as we were in the car. About five questions in, I laughed and called a halt.

'That's usually what I do,' I said, 'and the blokes are happy to talk about themselves all night.'

'All right,' he said, 'let's say I get to ask you three questions and then you get to ask me three questions and we take it in turns.'

I was charmed.

And so it was that we began not so much a date as an excavation, delving into each other's past, present and dreams for the future. Michael had been deeply influenced by the New Age quest for emotional healing and freedom of expression, and he'd been on a decade-long exploration of spirituality. But he was earthy, too, and I was struck by his self-deprecating honesty.

Around dessert, he suggested another game. 'You tell me something you don't want me to know and I'll tell you something.'

I laughed hard. This was thrilling stuff – how to think of something that sounded bad but might actually be quite good. How to avoid putting him totally off on the first date but still throw in an appallingly honest wildcard.

I thought for a while, eyeing off his crème brûlée. 'Sometimes I can be bossy,' I said hesitantly. I'm not sure why I said that. I come from a bossy family, but outside the fold I find it difficult to assert myself. I wore the times I'd been bossy like badges of honour. I think what I was trying to say was that inside my wimpy heart I had a hugely bossy bitch just itching to get out. Months later he let slip that he didn't like bossy people. It was a dangerous game.

'Your turn,' I said, leaning over and helping myself to a spoonful of his crème brûlée. He flushed red, reached for the sugar dispenser, knocked it over, righted it, pushed his chair backwards and took a deep breath. In the moment of that breath, I blanched. *Fuck, something big. Fuck, he's gay, he has a girlfriend, fuck, fuck . . .*

'Gosh, it's sort of hard to talk about,' he stammered, stringing out my suspense.

HIV-positive, motor neurone disease, leaving tomorrow for two years in Zimbabwe . . .

'You're the first woman I've dated for seven years.'

Temporarily gay, been in a monastery . . .

'I'm just three months out of a seven-year marriage,' he blurted. I breathed out. *Single . . . available . . . fuck . . .*

Because I knew that state. That wounded, not ready to love another, time to sow some wild oats and reassess your life state. As he told me the story, I projected empathy but felt the joy in my heart contract. As he talked about this woman he had just separated from, I understood that if we kept seeing each other I would get to know more about her than I knew about my closest friends. I would get to know her unreasonable demands, her selfish behaviour. Her annoying habits and shocking failures as a human being. She would become a character in my life that I would have to hear about ad nauseam while he unravelled the knots of their union.

The night had suddenly turned serious. The anticipation that had hung in the air between us settled like a grimy dew as we made our way back to the car.

'Um, I haven't done this in a while,' he fumbled, 'but would you like . . . I've got a joint on me. Do you ever smoke?'

'That was one of the things I didn't want you to know about me.' I laughed, and we headed for home.

I put on the kettle for herbal tea, produced the dregs of a port bottle and picked out an Ayub Ogada CD. We perched at either end of my old black leather chesterfield, toes almost touching, as my housemates made their way discreetly to bed. We went in deeper then, speaking all the stuff that usually lurks between the lines in a meeting still so new.

'I'll tell you where I'm up to in my life right now,' he said, sucking back a nervous toke, 'and then you can tell me.'

I liked this equal time business. 'Go ahead.' I wiped my palm across my skirt and fortified myself with a swig of port.

'I'm sort of at a place where I want to explore sexuality with different women. I don't mean to be offensive but I'm needing to sleep around a bit. I never really got a chance to do that in my teenage years, when it was acceptable.'

My eyes had begun to narrow, but I forced them open into an accepting gaze as he continued.

'You know, it's sort of difficult to talk about this stuff but I don't want to pretend with you. Umm . . . I'm not really looking for another relationship, monogamous commitment and all that. I've been shut down emotionally and sexually in a marriage for a long time and it's a big thing just to ask a woman out. I mean I'm interested in getting to know you and everything but I'm not ready for anything big. So that's me. How about you?'

I smiled to stop my face from falling. 'Um, you know, I'm ready for a committed relationship, marriage, children, that sort of thing.'

We erupted with laughter – at least it was out in the open. With all our cards now on the table, I felt suddenly close to him. 'If I was to go out with you,' he ventured, 'how would you feel if I was with you and also with other women?'

Non-monogamy. My objections weren't so much moral, but I didn't want to open my heart to such an unsafe bet. 'Oh, look, if I felt like I was becoming attached to you and you wanted to be off with other women, I would probably bow out gracefully.'

We argued the toss for a while and suddenly he stopped. 'How would you feel if I kissed you?'

'Umm, maybe a kiss goodnight at the door?' I offered, suddenly coy. Even now I can't tell you how it happened, but about five minutes later I was leaning towards him and kissing him. And I didn't only kiss him. I hoisted my skirt, climbed on to his lap and began to devour him – face, neck, hair – my groin pressing into his hard cock straining through his jeans. Embarrassment at my unsexy winter tights served as a deterrent. I pulled myself up and awkwardly climbed back to my end of the couch, murmuring some fake apology. All I knew was that I hadn't felt like this for a long time. And that I wanted more. But it was two a.m., so I called a halt like a bossy bitch. But he got that kiss at the door.

Even now, in the midst of the rampant cynicism and despair of modern life and notwithstanding the attacks on romantic love by intellectuals, people continue to fall in love. The dream dies, only to be reborn. Moved by a passion they do not understand for a goal they seldom reach, men and women are haunted by the vision of a distant possibility that refuses to be extinguished.

Nathaniel Branden, 'A Vision of Romantic Love'

Missionary Callings

ack sometime in the 1980s, the SNAG emerged. The Sensitive
New Age Guy had been encouraged by women, seen as a great
leap forward. The men had gone into the forest, banged their drums
and got in touch with their feelings. Sociologists lurked behind
trees studying them, journalists wrote stories. But no sooner had
the men learnt to fold a fitted sheet and say 'I feel' instead of
'I think', than women turned on them, complaining now of a limp-
ness to their masculinity. They had empathised so well with the
feminine, they were swallowed whole by it. To their dismay, they
discovered that women wanted the thrill of opposites after all.

Michael was one of the new breed, the second-generation
SNAG who had learnt that the best way to get a shag was to hold
on to their masculinity. He could be found as easily at a New Age
workshop as in a footy crowd yelling abuse at the umpire.

Michael was part urban hippy, part businessman, part ordinary
bloke, a passionate and obsessive supporter of his AFL team, the
Melbourne Demons. He was emotionally centred, a twist on what
men are usually good at. He had a boyish energy but this lightness
was animated by a compassionate understanding of the human
condition and a willingness to laugh at his own frailties. To use
the term 'average build' sounds slightly denigrating. In my eyes,

he was a perfectly proportioned Adonis, with honey-blond hair that behaved itself, a lower lip that looked like it might not, and ridiculously huge blue eyes – windows into what appeared to be a startlingly beautiful soul. Luckily his nose was just a tad larger than appropriate because, *goddamit*, something needed to mar all that perfection. Or perhaps the perfection lay only in the eye of his beholder.

If Michael was a second-generation SNAG, I was a second-generation feminist. I had a more masculine take on sexuality. I was ambitious, independent, living off the fruits of feminism but often falling on its sword.

'You're good at sex, aren't you,' he said the night we first made love.

'Well, I've never been damaged there in any way.' I was trying to walk the line between nice girl and slut.

'God, it's been such a long time since I did anything like this with someone new.' He nervously ran his fingers through his hair and reached out to roll a Drum. 'And it's not as if I've done it all that much in my life, even.'

I smiled at his honesty.

'You know, I'm feeling that we are probably going to make love tonight, right?'

'Um, yeah, probably,' was all I could manage.

'But I have no idea where to start,' he stammered. 'Should I just lean over and start, or what?'

We burst out laughing, tension slithering from the room.

'Look, let me handle it, okay?' I said. 'You make a herbal tea and I'll set up with some cushions and candles on the floor.'

We didn't set the world on fire that night. My intuition whispered 'speed kills'. I unwrapped him slowly, savouring all of him.

I unwrapped myself and offered my skin to savour. His tentativeness allowed me to feel the power of my artistry, painting the canvas of his skin with my warm wet mouth, brushing his limbs with nipples pulled tight with excitement.

'I think I have to make my acquaintance,' I whispered, sliding down his body until my head rested on his inner thigh. His beautiful penis was erect, bobbing up and down with enthusiasm. I stilled the generous shaft with my hand and placed it wholeheartedly in my mouth. His groans told me all was well in his world. I came up for air and a sip of tea, enjoying the languid pace. I offered him my cup.

'You know, I have to confess something,' he said, staring into the cup. I haven't enjoyed blowjobs very much in the past . . . And I know this will sound weird, but I haven't enjoyed fucking much for a long time either.'

It was an alarming admission.

'Should we go back a step or two?' I asked, worried that we had rushed things.

'No! What you just did felt fantastic. I mean, I'm open to the possibility of liking it all again.'

Salvation my mission, I rose up and straddled him. 'I'm fairly certain this will feel good.' I slid along his penis so that it quivered against my clitoris. I lowered myself a little at a time over him, savouring that euphoric rush of invasion. Closing my eyes against the beautiful spectacle before me, in favour of the magnificent sensation within.

'Oh my God, that feels fantastic,' he whispered, breathing hard.

'Oh my God, that feels fantastic,' I echoed, no longer able to form an original sentence.

The heat spread down my legs and up my spine. New dance partners, we stumbled as we moved to find our rhythm.

'Be careful!' he gasped, and I stopped.

'Do you need to think about football scores?'

'I plan the entire team line-up usually, but right now I need that gorgeous sensation to stop.' He rolled me over. Before I could protest, he slid between my legs and I tensed.

Yes, there was the thrill of a hot tongue on the rosebud, but there was also the sense of affront. That this person who was still mostly a stranger was suddenly exploring my most intimate juncture. I watched with a kind of shamed wonder as his golden head bobbed and weaved in search of the clitoris.

'Go softly and you'll be okay,' I whispered.

He relaxed and nuzzled me gently. The thrill of the new, my Catholic shame, the enthusiasm and heat of his tongue – it was unbearable, exquisite, and I felt that familiar hot flush rise in my belly. I surrendered to his soft probing until my breath and groans lifted to meet the wave of ecstasy that broke over my body. He rose over me triumphantly and pushed into me again. My body had melted in ecstasy's wake and his penis slid easily inside.

'Oh Christ,' he moaned, and I wrapped my legs tightly around him, pulled him deeply into me. We moved together, our groans a shared breath.

'Oh God, I'm coming.'

I felt his cock buck once, twice, three times as he exploded inside me and I thrust to meet his thrusts until he was spent.

We did not set the world on fire that night but we had lit the fuse of a slow-burning desire that would take me to heights I had never dreamed a body could go.

Love's Revolution

Occasionally in life, a relationship comes along that is like a revolution, an unforgettable turning point. For some lucky ones, chaos can settle and deepen into lifelong union. For others, the heat of passion is scorched into the soul, and while future relationships promise a more sensible life, the memory burns with a power that is perhaps never truly extinguished.

Michael and I were the same and we were opposites – it was our differences that held us in thrall. This relationship was a revolution.

I was pursuing my career full tilt. I had travelled the world with a film crew a dozen times, working in some of the most remote places on the planet. My travels had given me a physical confidence that allowed me to feel safe as I walked through life. But inside, I stumbled. What wisdom I owned had been gleaned from self-help books or occasional conversations with those wiser than myself.

Michael's ambition had centred on his inner life. His teaching career had gone by the wayside in the eighties as he travelled through Europe and America exploring the emotional and spiritual pathways that had opened in the wake of the countercultural explosion of the sixties. The power I brought to the relationship was intellectual and sexual, his emotional. We shared a fascination with the spiritual.

I was as wounded emotionally as he was sexually, and our coming together felt like broken shards had finally been glued back in place so we could drink from the same cup.

It was a year that exploded through my life, upending everything. A year that ran on the rails of love, a big dipper of out-of-control emotions that I welcomed, eager to be both terrified and exhilarated by the lunacy. I understood that to love Michael was a dangerous and probably foolhardy proposition. But I had a heart bursting at the seams.

'I'm not a person offering any long-term safety or security,' he would warn, 'but I am a safe person to open your heart to.'

That was enough for me, and I breathed out, laying my whole sorry bundle before him, feeling wild enough to take a chance and wildly grateful to be given it. I thought myself brave in taking the risk to love, but truth was, love crept up on me like a stalker. Before I knew it, I was in its lair, a willing, confused, joyous victim.

And I believed in love's power, that if two people loved each other enough, it would carry them over all obstacles.

When I look back at that time, I sometimes question my judgment. What if, accepting he was not available for committed union and children, I had called a halt right then and there, found the solid man and issued progeny from behind a picket fence? But even in my darkest time, I don't regret meeting Michael and I can't find it within myself to regret even a moment of the time we spent together. Because finally the tough, funny, brittle shell could be peeled away. I wanted my heart back, and if it meant risking everything, then bugger the consequences. What I didn't know was that I would one day have to pay. And, of course, so would he.

I have a saying on my fridge, half joking, half serious: 'It may be that your sole purpose in life is to serve as a warning to others'.

JOURNAL JULY '94

This relationship has such an air of unreality, yet it is the most real thing in my life. I need to face that he is not ready for a committed monogamous relationship. In another sense, the impermanence, the lack of expectation, the celebration of the present is what makes it so special, two butterflies copulating on the wing. A relationship outside of life, going nowhere, everywhere, who knows where?

As far as my friends and family are concerned, Michael's a phantom lover. We're hunkered down exploring the terrain of the other. Hours spent with others mean I don't have him to myself.

We've fallen into this haphazard pattern of what we call 'twelve-glass evenings and a damn good shag'. Preparing for these nights is like training for some perverted marathon. The day before, I do laps at the pool to get the blood circulating and apply a conditioning pack in the sauna. At home I rub in fake tan, smear the blue facemask on and try to get a good night's sleep. On the big night I shower, shave, pluck and primp, moisturise, mousse and daub cover-up on the pimple that bloody well always erupts. I scrounge for decent underwear, discard a large pile of clothes, give a quick critique of myself in the mirror and head out the door. Apparently he has a training regime no less rigorous but involving less product.

And then I'm sitting outside his apartment in my car,

scrunching my unruly hair into place, applying lipgloss and accusing my face in the rear-view mirror of letting the whole side down. Wiping my sweaty palms, I wonder in which emotional territory I'll find him. Shut down, opened to love, or somewhere in between.

Inside, candles and incense are burning, something funky's on the CD, dinner's on the stove. (I mean for all the bad press, you have to love a New Age guy.)

After dinner we bring our glasses of wine down to a nest of cushions on the living-room floor, making room for mugs of herbal tea, water, a beer for him, this Ayurvedic port called Amrit he found. We roll a joint and pass it back and forth and down we go.

'We two form a multitude,' wrote the poet Ovid, and what a bloody racket we make. Into the space come ex-lovers, parents, families – the population of our past lives, the dreams of our future and the intricate workings of our present selves. There's a mutual fascination with exploration. We range through the spiritual realms, our emotional and sexual paths, the political, environmental and sociological state of the world and the changing states of men and women in these dying days of the twentieth century. As well as discussing the ups and downs of his beloved Melbourne Demons.

I feel like I'm living the best moments of my life, that there will never be more joy than this. We might be going nowhere but I love him so much I want wherever he is going to be a happy place.

Twelve-glass Evenings and a Damn Good Shag

Michael was and always will be a teacher, his gift to me and the world his willingness to be transparent – letting his messy bits, his vulnerability, his needs and dark spaces hang out for exploration. This honesty exhilarated and liberated me. With a thumping heart I would lay my own self bare, lifting away the weight of years of hiding, a new future opening up with every layer peeled back. Each shameful or less than perfect part of myself I revealed seemed to burn up in the fire of his understanding and compassion. My number was up and it was time to risk.

Honesty was the game we were playing, its title the only rule. And it could move us to tears or leave us heaving with laughter. Michael would reveal his wounds the way other men talked about a fishing trip.

'Yeah, she was my first girlfriend. I lost my virginity with her. She wasn't a virgin; she'd had older boyfriends. She was a stunning-looking creature and I was this wide-eyed fifteen-year-old. Her parents were away and she took me upstairs and we kissed and she let me enter her. It was glorious. It seemed to go on forever.'

'But you probably came in about a minute, right?'

'Thirty seconds tops.' He laughed. 'We smoked a cigarette and I thought, *God, here I am in bed with a beautiful woman I've just made love to and we're smoking a post coital Craven A.* And finally I felt like a man, you know? I think we did it about four times that night.'

'Did she come?'

'God, no. I was hopeless. I think she just accepted the lack of orgasm as normal. But I fell so in love with her, it hurts to think about. After a while she began sleeping around with other men but she would come back and climb into my bed in the middle of the night and drive me wild and I felt like I was drowning in all this repressed jealousy and hurt. I had no authority over her. I was ashamed and bewildered, and it's sort of sick but I actually admired her for it. Every time she hurt me, I loved her even more.'

'Your first taste of the sickness of love.'

'Totally. But it left this legacy. I was so fraught with jealousy, if it had gone on I might have ended up hurting her. Eventually, the only way I could shut down to her was to shut down my own sexuality, so she had no control over me. By the time I was eighteen or nineteen I was a bit of a mess and celibate for the next four years. From then on I ended up in relationships that were safe. I stayed in my marriage because there was a lot of intimacy and safety, but I made it so safe that I sacrificed any freedom until I completely shut down. I was feeling, like, "Oh my God, I'm trapped in this dead place forever now." I mean, it feels like a miracle I'm even here.' He stood and moved to the CD-player to put on Keith Jarrett, our current musical obsession.

Michael's fear of suffocation and my fear of abandonment were two sides of the same coin. He wasn't that cliché of a guy who perennially shies from commitment. In fact he had been the opposite, a man too committed to a marriage that no longer made him happy. Our paths crossed at the time when he needed to discover who he was, outside of any union. To be in a relationship now, he had to feel completely independent, unrestricted. His earnest candour in expressing his wounds and needs taught me to accept my own fear of abandonment and not be shamed in my desire for deep and lasting love.

Both of us were walking new territory. Michael was as alarmed to be back in a relationship with a woman wanting deep commitment as I was to enter into a relationship with a man who could offer no more than his company in the present moment. Certainly he was not ready to quieten the ticking of my biological clock.

We were both flinging ourselves into the unknown and when we let go, we found a depth of feeling that gave us a code to love by.

Oh, but I forgot the sex. After hours of talking, around two or three a.m., we would move into the second shift.

Reaching out, unwrapping the other with our hands and lips, exploring the soft contours of a wordless union. My turn now to be the teacher, my pupil as enthusiastic and skilled a student as any woman could want.

Our bodies were constantly surprised by the permutations of our coupling. In showing him my wanton slut, slowly he let his own wanton beast out to play – learning to talk dirty, to experiment, to push at our boundaries until we reached that state of liberation when all decorum is abandoned.

JOURNAL SEPTEMBER '94

Great lovemaking is like a freeform dance for two, pure improvisation, a fleeting live performance.

Great lovemaking is all about freedom and communication. Freedom to give way to lust, letting sexual energy thrill you and take you on a dynamic or languorous ride, all five senses speaking and listening, the breath getting deeper, the genitals swelling, releasing pungent juicy smells and tastes. Voices more urgent, crying to higher and higher powers, 'Oh Jesus, Oh Lord, Oh God . . .'

Breathy silence after the applause of orgasm.

The high-minded part of myself enjoys a bit of literary, understated erotica, but what works in bed is the language of the lewd – the short, sharp shock words of porn, including the great 'c' foursome: cock, clit, cunt and cum. You lick and suck and thrust and push and pound and buck . . . In short, you fuck.

So great fucking . . . great lovemaking – it's all about losing yourself in ecstasy, the merging of flesh and spirit. (Or having a quickie in the morning to relieve a little tension before you rush to get the kids to school.)

Michael and I take it in turns now to exert or relinquish control. The other night, all he did was plant his mouth on my breast and I was gone, lost in the land of lust. We sank to the floor and I stretched out like a cat being caressed. He pulled my head back and I arched my neck, my mouth ready to be devoured.

Instead, he begins touching my clitoris, softly, so softly, but it is extraordinary – the tiniest brush, and electric jolts sear my body so my legs fall wantonly open.

Then he clamps his mouth down over mine like he is trying to suffocate me and I abandon myself to his probing tongue and lips and teeth until I try to cry out and with a rush of breath we part. He maintains control of me by pushing his finger into my swollen pussy and I rise towards him. Another finger is being inserted into my anus and his tongue is like fire on my clitoris and I am lost to all but sensation.

My turn and I almost bend him in half, licking the smooth muscle leading to the balls. My wet finger penetrating him also, his cock bobbing frantically until I lasso it into my mouth and devour it. His helpless moans like music, the throb of my own pulse the bass beat.

And there comes that point when the bodies plead for union and I take hold of him, tease him towards me. My other hand finds my opening and I slide inside, releasing a reservoir of velvet fluid, shuddering as my finger moves around the delicate hood of my clit.

Red-hot flesh melts into red-hot flesh. He thrusts, I absorb, pushing against one another, whispering our desire, his moans resonating through me, our mouths shared until we are only one breath. And we rise above ourselves, pleasure mounting towards a single explosion.

We shudder and quiver, waiting in that agonising, ecstatic place until his moans tell me he is beyond control. I grasp his arse and pull him against my clitoris. He pushes against me in strong thrusts of release and some great energy picks me up and crashes inside my body. We are dying and calling out in a lament for this fleeting vision of eternity, the bliss of another realm. We pant and exclaim our way down to earth, coming back into consciousness, flesh tenderised, boundaries dissolved.

'Oh my God, oh my God, that was incredible!' sighed Michael, emerging from the melted tangle of limbs after our very first simultaneous orgasm.

'Mmmm,' I mumbled. 'Amazing.'

'Absolutely fucking amazing. But listen, we can't expect that to ever happen again.'

'It'll happen again, don't you worry,' I said languidly. 'If we keep having sex, we can re-create that.'

'You don't know that, Vanessa. You can't be sure. So I'm just going to think it was some incredible one-off and if it never happens again, that's okay. At least I've experienced it once.'

I laughed, triumphant that I had found another reason for him to draw closer. Another reason to love me.

Raised in a Catholic girls' school, with the Virgin Mary as primary role model, it was inevitable that on discovering sex I would develop a split personality. I call this split the 'prefect/slut'. The prefect is responsible, mindful and generously involved in the welfare of others. She cares about the environment and social justice issues and picks up litter, cursing the animals who threw it. In short, she can be self-righteous and insufferably convinced of her moral superiority, while priding herself on being open to new ways of thinking. A version of this prat is the one I show to the world.

And then there's the slut. Rediscovering my perverted underside – reclaiming the wild child who ran free in nature and pissed standing over the edge of the treehouse – was a welcome relief. It felt good to sometimes throw off the shackles of morality, to be mischievous, adventurous, licentious. Surely it behoves us all to run with the wolves, if only for brief, occasional sprints.

I'd kept my wild child hidden from all the right people, but sometimes stayed up late and laughed with my brother Henry, another wild child, about all the things people didn't know about us.

Now I had fallen so hopelessly in love with Michael, I was

desperate for him to love me back and I worked hard on my lovability. Except here was a man who appreciated the prefect but was falling in love with the slut. Would egg her on. Gradually I allowed her to emerge from the shadows and merge more honestly with my understanding of who I was. And under his emotional tutelage, slowly I came to understand the psychology of the good girl, how she acted out of the wound of abandonment. As the New Age cliché has it, our wounds can be our greatest teacher.

Michael constantly expressed his need for freedom, for space. Although I did my best to honour this need, in my heart I often felt powerless. My vulnerability tempted me to employ a strategy. So when he said, 'I need a lot of space', I said, 'That's okay', and he came a step closer.

And when he said, 'I need to see the exit sign right there', I said, 'It's right there', and he came a step closer. And when he said, 'I may not want to be sexual tonight', I said, 'There's no pressure, it's fine', and he embraced me hungrily. I made it so safe for him, he couldn't help falling in love.

But Michael was no fool and always I ended up having to confess my wiles, my guises, my sneaky attempts to be unbearably lovable, standing naked and shamefaced in my need to be liked. Feeling the wound heal as I did so.

And the truth is, I also needed a lot of freedom and space. Binding myself to someone who didn't really want to be there was not my idea of a good relationship. Love to me was not about ownership but meeting in mutual respect, witnessing the other into self-fulfilment. At least that's the theory.

Repulsion

*Y*es, we had fallen in love. But love came with the terms and conditions of our duelling needs. Always my romantic soul hoped Michael would have some sudden conversion, be struck by a thunderbolt that would sweep aside all doubts so we could move freely into love's true realm (wherever that was).

I am waiting by the airport gate, a mysterious romantic figure, immaculately groomed, ten minutes early. I watch the plane taxi into congress with the black squeeze box. The early evening passengers scurry toward luggage carousels and suburban homes. I scan the faces and wait, breathless, until I see him coming towards me, eyes enraptured, his smile welcoming my soul. We embrace, tender and fierce.

'I've been a fool,' he whispers. 'I want you now and always. Be mine forever.'

Actually, by the time I found a park, the plane had landed. I streaked along the corridors, dragging a brush through my hair. He was pacing near the gate.

'Michael!' I yelled, stuffing the hairbrush into my bag. He smiled and waved. Our kiss was inelegant and when we drew back, his arm got caught in my handbag. His eyes searched for the exit and we made our way toward the escalators. Something, it seemed, had closed down in him while he was in Melbourne. Clearly he'd had no joyful epiphany about our future.

It was not a twelve-glass evening, but at least six sat between the pillows on the floor. We had smoked a joint to ease the unpalatable. My heart pounded.

'Look, I've been talking about it for a while now, but I need to take some space and I have no idea how much I'll need.'

I was barely hearing him.

'It might be a week, or a month. You know . . . it might involve seeing other women. Maybe I'll just keep right on going.'

I wasn't sure if it was his longings or his fears that had caught up with him. 'Uh-huh,' was all I could manage.

He breathed out, softened. 'I was thinking about you in Melbourne. Thinking you deserve to be loved. Remembering you saying you'd never had someone you could love in a complete state of trust, and that it wasn't safe to love me either. I just think you really need that. and if I do care for you, I should get out of your life. At least until I could come back more clearly.'

'Is that what you want?'

'Oh, I don't know.' He flung himself back on the cushions, ran his fingers through his hair and pulled at a clump, like he could release the truth if he pulled hard enough. 'I feel like I want to do it, and then all this panic comes up, because I think, Will I blow it with you? Will you still be available when I need you again? Is it even fair to expect that? I'm scared to not take the space and so scared of losing you if I do.'

The frantic thrumming of my heart had calmed a little. 'Listen, take whatever time out you're needing, no question. But it doesn't have to be the big dramatic "now I have to go" thing. It feels like part of your lesson is how you can be in a relationship but also feel free to do what you have to do.'

'I just need to acknowledge it, because if I don't, it sours the love.'

'I'm not interested in suffocating you, Michael. I'm interested in freeing you to be the biggest person you can be, because it feels like that's what you're doing for me.' I leaned forward and cupped his knee. 'The trouble is, I'm too in love with you to go off somewhere else. You take your space. What the hell!' I laughed. 'I'll be waiting here like a helpless doormat. Come back and trample all over me.'

Freedom versus security. Intimacy versus solitude. A constant duel of the human spirit. Do we always have to give up one to have the other?

I wanted a life with space for both, and so did Michael. But I wanted to give my heart in safety and feel the freedom that comes with that. Such had been the suffocating intimacy of his family ties and previous relationships that freedom shone as the brightest beacon on his horizon.

He took some space. A whole week.

JOURNAL MAY 1994

The world looks different when you are in love. I guess that's what love does – lets you loose in a place where more things seem possible, where the senses are alive to mystery. Love makes me ecstatic, fearless, perverse, and laughter and tears are closer to the surface.

When I think back to the adult relationships I knew

in my youth, most seemed so simple and straightforward. I'm sure they weren't. But sometimes I feel like everything's become too complicated – like we're all looking for this impossible relationship that somehow gives us *everything*. I'm no different – I want the passionate embrace that provides security *and* freedom. Searching, too, for sexual experiences that are safe *and* intense.

I've seen a lot of marriages reach the end of the road. But does this mean love's dying? My elders growl that they knew how to stick it out even when they hated each other's guts, that people my age don't know what it means to be married. And I guess they have a point. But even so, love's still the drug. We still want to be exalted by it. We are still willing to be blinded, bewitched and besotted by it, even if it wounds us.

People aren't staying out of relationships. They lick their wounds and head back into the fray, ready to give the whole monogamous thing another spin. But the way we understand partnership is still shackled to the gold standard of permanency. *My marriage failed, my relationship failed*, people say – when the couple might have raised a family, lived a life together. It might have been a happy experience for years before it seemed best to dissolve the union.

But I sometimes wonder what it would feel like to be in a relationship when I didn't have to think about the possibility of it ending – didn't have to feel like it could all finish tomorrow. Or next week, next year . . .

The dream of lifelong commitment still beats in my heart. It's still an idea we're all in love with. But I have no idea how to make the dream real.

I want to respect Michael's need to pull away. But I want

him to love me so much, he can't stay away. And what to call our relationship? It's nothing like my childhood dream of marriage. More like a hair-raising voyage of discovery, an imperfect joy. The adventure of the heart I was craving.

Notions of God

I Am

I am the specks of dust in the streams of light
I am the shining sun
To the dust I say 'be still'
To the sun I say 'keep spinning'

I am the mists of morning
I am the breath of twilight
I am the windsong in the treetops
The waves upon the rocks
I am the ship you sail in
And I am the reef that sinks you

I am a talking parrot alone in the wild
A silent thinking voice
In the flute I am the breathing
The spark of flintlock
The flash of steel
The flame and the moth together
The sweet fragrance that unites the nightingale and the rose

I am every detail of creation
the orbit of the stars
the evolving cosmic thought
the rising and the falling
I am what is and what is not

You who truly know me
You the unity in my world

Tell me who I am
Tell me I am you

RUMI

In any life, in any relationship, the search for who or what God is can give a deeper perspective to the small, egoistic self. In his essay 'A Vision of Romantic Love', American psychotherapist Nathaniel Branden talks about romantic love as a 'passionate spiritual-emotional-sexual attachment between two people that reflects a high regard for the value of each other's person'. Scott M. Peck, in *The Road Less Travelled*, defines love simply as 'The will to extend one's self for the purpose of nurturing one's own or another's spiritual growth'.

Exploring God gave Michael and me a lodestar. Seeking higher ground helped us to relax into the knowledge that if everything is God, and God is perfection, then everything that happens is somehow perfect, no matter how totally fucked it seems at the time.

My parents were both religious high achievers. *Good Catholics*. We never missed Sunday mass in the small weatherboard church that sat white and quaint amidst scattered cow turds on the edge of town.

There was a hierarchy to the seating, every family inhabiting their designated pew, visitors and occasional brethren delegated haphazardly to pews at the back. The God that was proffered for our worship looked like the stern elder of some hippy tribe with a thing for robes and beards – kindly, wrathful, all seeing, all knowing. Confusing matters was God's son, Jesus, and the Holy Spirit. Who exactly to pray to for a new bike? Jesus made God easier to understand, because he had walked among us. It was him in the pictures, his chest a scary wound exposing a bleeding heart. It was his godforsaken body pinned to the cross behind the altar, a graphic reminder of the multitude of human sins for which he had been sacrificed, sins we needed to root out in a never ending atonement for his brutal crucifixion.

I would never complain about being raised a Catholic. *Do unto others, love thy neighbour, turn the other cheek*. The humble, radical goodness of Jesus's life was exemplary and I grew up admonishing myself to emulate his virtues. I was filled with the innocent fervour of Pollyanna; I aspired to be as sinless as the Virgin Mary.

My father's death shook my naive faith in the fairness of life and for a long time all I felt towards God was anger. At school I was required to engage in the rituals but my heart no longer found sustenance there – except in that one eternal moment when the priest is busy turning water into wine and blessing the wafers and the congregation is left to its own thoughts as it mouths the prayers. Every so often I would drift into a realm of stillness and peace, where for a moment the small me sitting in the pew no longer existed.

After my father died, my mother, always a radical, embarked on her own spiritual exploration. She had moved the family to Sydney by then, and the pressures of her new career led her to seek out the stress-release of meditation. Before long, this woman, who not too many years earlier had been arranging lamington drives for the

Country Women's Association, appeared in an Indian sari in our living room, a red dot over her third eye, sacred ash smeared on her forehead in preparation for another evening at the local ashram. She was still a spiritual high achiever, but now worshipped Hindu gods that all seemed to have way too many arms.

'Could you go out the back door?' we would plead, embarrassed that our teenage friends might see this apparition. 'And can you move that picture of the weird Indian guy out of the living room?'

Whatever discomfort we felt about our mother having a guru was countered by her calmer, less driven behaviour. No longer did she bully us to keep a house inhabited by five teenagers tidy. *As if.* So Swami Muktananda's mugshot stayed on the wall, watching benevolently over a messier, more harmonious home life.

As an adult, I left behind the God of my youth. The rational world beckoned and I explored science through my work; other cultures and religions through my travels. I was excited by ideas I could barely understand, grappling with new paradigms in quantum mechanics and particle physics. The discovery of common ground between the worlds of spirituality and science intrigued me, and suddenly the Christian concept of God seemed too small, too *human*, to do justice to these new ideas.

I had long stopped praying to a Christian father figure. When I needed to relieve stress, I followed my mother into meditation. And in tiny moments I rediscovered that place of stillness and peace first found in the church pew. I told myself that I was there to relieve tension, but Eastern ideas about God excited me. It was a revolutionary concept: a universal God that excluded no one.

Oh! But to even use that word, *God*, that catch-all notion for a million different personifications of the divine – Buddha, Allah, the Holy Spirit, Yahweh, Jesus, Mohammed, Shiva, Vishnu, the Absolute,

Unity Consciousness, pure Awareness. It seemed to me that no matter what your faith, the mystics in every tradition and every age talked about God as a force beyond language, beyond space, beyond time. The absolute and universal creative intelligence that is the core, the essence of all life. The unifying, pulsating energy of every thing.

My seeking took me to the understanding that God is the magnificent sunset *and* the slaughter in Rwanda – victim and perpetrator as well as the aid workers who tend the injured and bury the dead. God is the Jew being gassed, the soldier closing the door to the chamber, the steel door, the gas, the cries of the helpless, the silence of the dead. *God is the ship you sail in and the reef that sinks you.* God is the universal energy arising in each moment. God is this here and now. The pause between the breath, the breath itself.

Which means you, me, all of us are a manifestation of divine energy. And yet we all think we are separate individuals. But who we are is not the mind, not our body, our gender, marital status or the jobs we do. Who we are is so much simpler.

We can look for God outside of ourselves, but God is the fabric of our being. As Jesus said, *We are that which we seek.* The Bible points to it, *Be still and know that I am God.* For peace can be found simply by sitting quietly, dropping our dramas and emotions and thoughts long enough to sink into the simple awareness of our true self. Those who have become enlightened describe this state as ultimate peace, bliss itself.

This evolving consciousness was seeded in the East and has been spreading through the West like wildfire. It celebrates the fact that there is no difference between Muslim and Christian, Jew, Buddhist, Hindu or atheist. We are all cut from the same cloth. It does not divide and it does not exclude *anything*. It is an understanding of God that promises a world where science, rationality and religion can coexist within a deep mysticism.

However, there would come a time when no matter which God I believed in, there would be no solace. When I would understand what it felt like to be forsaken by life itself.

Eventually, if our species survives, rationality will embrace all religions everywhere. Rationality, truth and science must be the modern companions of spiritual belief. They cannot be the enemies for, if they are, science will trump religion every time.

Justice Michael Kirby

JOURNAL OCTOBER '94

Nothing exists which is not Shiva
Nothing exists which is not God

Oxford Street was all Shiva, shimmering in its seedy glory. We'd spent a few days dwelling in the spiritual realms, meditating and chanting in an ashram that preferred the top button done up. Prancing along with Michael in my skin-tight black mini, knee-high boots and bare midriff, I was hoping not to run into the flowing-skirts-of-natural-fibres-and-beatific-smiles brigade I'd just spent time with.

We had contemplated the teaching 'Nothing exists which is not Shiva/God'. My spiritual prefect had studied hard. Now the baser side was calling out for attention and we were taking it out for a spin. We wandered down from Taylor Square, both a little stoned, Michael's hand on my arse. Gorgeous gay guys sauntered past, some holding hands, because *it's their street, goddamit.*

I was horny. It seemed like weeks since we'd had sex. Shiva was the passing crowds, Shiva was the garish neons of the souvlaki bar, steaming food behind foggy windows. Shiva was the rubbish on the pavement, Shiva was the itinerant oldfella drunk in the doorway of a closed shop. Shiva was the Pleasure Chest drawing us in, our old haunt where we had conquered our fear of sex shops and browsed like old hands.

We had been downstairs in the booths a couple of times, the first time laughing and fumbling with change – all we managed to do was watch the lascivious movies on show for three minutes per dollar and then creep out feeling guilty and wonderfully sordid.

This time, no sooner than the first dollar was in, Michael had my top off and bra unhooked. He started fondling me, pressing his hard cock against my thigh. I switched through the channels, through the typical range of sex options: two men fucking one woman, one woman licking another's pussy, an S&M scene in a tacky log cabin with a tackier orange bedspread, a man fucking another up the arse, a couple getting ready to do it, mouthing limp dialogue before getting their gear off. Videos with sad-looking porn workers and shocking production values that always offended my film-making sensibilities.

There was something about the tackiness of it all – the bad-quality videos, the booth's chipboard walls rattling when pressed, the sticky globules of masturbatory emissions coating the walls – that both appalled and excited me. That, and Michael's hand lifting my black mini to my waist and probing

51

between my legs, grabbing my arse and lifting me onto the outline of his cock straining against his jeans. I was naked now, except for black boots, a strip of material that once was my mini around my waist and a bra dangling off my shoulders. The screen went black and I fumbled for another dollar. Around us the air vibrated with the groans and noises of sex coming from ten duelling porn movies in the other booths. Ten scenes of Shiva.

Michael crouched down and began to nose around my pubic hair, smelling me. I braced myself, spreading my legs and wedging them against the wall. My crutch moved to meet his tongue as it probed the lips of my pussy, waves of heat fanning out from what had become my epicentre.

I didn't want to come; I wanted to make love with Michael later that night. I wanted to stay in that horny space right on the edge as we teased each other into the rich, deep fullness of the penetrative sex that we did so well. But my God, his tongue – it was like a rod of electric fire searing my clit. His fingers had parted my legs and were insinuating themselves into my fanny, which was, as they say in pornography, *dripping with love juice*, salivating, wanting more. My body strained to push onto his fingers, my clit harder against his mouth. I opened my eyes to the dim light. On the video a man was taking a woman doggy-style as she buried her face into another woman's shaved pubes, which looked uncannily like the arsehole of a plucked chicken. I glanced down. My breasts were exposed like a common slut, my dress hoiked up like a hussy, my legs split as far as I could get them. Michael's face was buried between my thighs, his chin and cheeks shiny with juice as he made the noises of a man possessed. My own groans came between breaths that made me heave as he pushed into me with his tongue. I was only held upright by the wall; I could feel the warm smears of stale semen on my back. Warm smears of Shiva. I was a dirty slut who couldn't contain herself. Something beyond my control had a hold of me and was not going to let go. Shiva maybe. I gave in as I felt the approach of a roaring wave. It swept me up and I became transcendent – the noises of people fucking, sucking, pulling and coming all around me, vibrating from the booths, mingling with my groans and Michael's deep breaths of pleasure. The booth was alone in the universe and I was frozen in time. Michael became a nameless, faceless man, a stranger sucking at my clit, penetrating me with fingers that pushed me up and back against the coin machine, my back arched, my face to the heavens as the great wave of pleasure burst through my body, carrying me away into a timeless, shapeless place of ecstasy with no boundaries, only the white-hot searing pain of rapturous pleasure.

Nothing existed which was not Shiva. For a moment I was not me, not here. Michael was not himself, not here. I had left my body and was travelling light years away, the orgasm ripping my body apart like a tornado through a silken web. I was one with the sordid, exquisite, ecstatic universe and nothing existed that was not God.

Sex touches the heavens only when it simultaneously touches the gutter and the mud.

George Jean Nathan

Safe (Imaginary) Sex

Raunchy sexlife aside, my fantasy life was way more pedestrian. Every so often, usually in bed, a lover had asked me to titillate them with my sexual fantasies. I would stammer and blush, laugh nervously, say *um* a lot. It's not that I'm afraid to traipse the more lewd alleys of my mind. The naked truth, I'm ashamed to reveal, is that my fantasies are usually romantic. I am someone desirable, a beautiful concert pianist or some babe of a neurosurgeon saving kiddies' lives, while the guy is someone fabulous, but not quite as fabulous as me. Plot, structure and character have to be worked over in intricate detail and usually by the time I reach the bit where we are about to have sex, I fall asleep. The complexity of my fantasies is exhausting.

Michael was the first man I came clean with on my lack of a raunchy fantasy life.

'Why do you have to be so desirable in your fantasies?' he asked, perplexed.

'So the man won't leave.'

'You have to create safety before you can have imaginary sex?'

I blushed. 'I suppose so.'

He paused, thinking, then, 'Do you reckon it's got anything to do with your father? I mean, here you were coming into your adolescence and suddenly the man you loved most in the world left you and there was nowhere for all that love to go. So of course you're going to try and create safety in the heart before you can give your body.'

'Yeah, but you know I want to tell you about some filthy, ribald fantasy – like anonymous sex with a football team.'

'That could be good, let's work on that one!'

I could never have invented Michael in my fantasies. He was too kooky, too complicated. Then again I was not some beautiful concert pianist/neurosurgeon. But he loved me anyway.

'Don't stay with me just because it's too hard to leave,' I would say all the way through our relationship, 'just because you don't want to lose me.'

I didn't believe anyone had the right to control anyone else, so I constantly gave him the option to leave. And with the door open, he could relax and together we could sink deeper into one another. But always there was that niggling insecurity – if I was stunningly beautiful, he would never be able to tear himself away.

Crazed Echidna

I am one of millions of women in the world who cannot accept their own beauty. I am disappointed to do this to myself. Just as I am disappointed most days when I look in the mirror. I would like to scramble my programmed perceptions but they are burnt deep. We live in a world where air-brushed, made-up, impossible ideals of beauty stare out at us from bus stops and magazine covers, where endless ads whisper to us of the many ways we don't measure up. This ideal of perfection is hard-wired into our brains in childhood and is with us until we are old and grey and far beyond those indoctrinated ideals of loveliness.

Growing up a tomboy, I attached no judgment to the face that stared back at me from the mirror. It was just the front part of my head, framed by long wavy honey-brown hair that I preferred to tie back so I could get on with my outdoor life.

One day, all that changed. I was on the cusp of adolescence, about to start high school in the city. My mother took me to one of those groovy hair salons with shiny wallpaper that sprung up in the seventies. The hairdresser suggested something called a feather cut and, having no idea what happened in groovy hair salons, I nodded meekly. She reassured me with the words 'David Cassidy has one', and began to hack. With downcast eyes, I watched my long locks fall onto the speckled linoleum floor. After a time she turned me back to the mirror with a flourish. The shock made my cheeks burn and in that moment I became aware of my appearance for the first time in my life. Except I had no idea who that girl in the mirror was. In the trauma of that moment my gaze shifted forever: I looked at myself now as a spectator, a critic. And I hated what I saw. My hair was so thick, a small marsupial could nest there for days on end without being noticed.

Feathered, short and layered, my hair was an electric-shocked pile of chaos on top of my head, spiked out in every direction, nothing like David bloody Cassidy's. An aesthetic disaster. I wanted to burst into tears. Was this how I would look as a woman? I smiled politely at the hair butcher, my eyes pleading with my mother to deliver me from hell. But instead she made comments like, 'It's groovy, darling!'

I caught sight of myself in another mirror a few minutes later, and I could no longer hold back the tears. I was about to face eighty of my new peers looking like a crazed echidna.

From then on, my hair became a kind of battleground, each strand a soldier on a frizzy rampage. My attempts at discipline, with clips, ties and combs, were doomed to defeat.

One night as Michael and I lay together after sex, my hair unruly on the pillow, he took a curl in his fingers and began playing with it. 'Look at it – it's amazing. It curls this way and then it turns back on itself and goes that way and then kinks twice and heads off on a completely new roller-coaster-like thing.'

I laughed, embarrassed at my bad-hair life coming under such scrutiny. 'I always wanted sportscar hair,' I said, pushing my finger through one of the curls he held up. 'Hair that still looks glamorous after the wind has blown through it.'

Michael had sportscar hair, always perfect.

'Are you kidding? People would give anything to have your hair. People pay a fortune to try and fake your kind of hair.'

And so began a slow healing. Michael's delight in my hair, his amazement at its moods, softened my attitude. He gave me the gift of a wooden hairbrush and painted the words 'therapy brush' on its back. He would sit behind me like I was eight years old and he was my mother, and he would brush my hair, saying, 'Now, what did you do at school today?' And I would make up some story about a schoolyard bully, and he would say, 'She's probably just jealous about what beautiful hair you have', as I lost myself in the delicious tingles playing over my scalp. Slowly I began to give my hair its head, coming to accept the way it snaked and sprung like the hair of mad Medusa.

I am fourteen and I look anxiously at my face, searching for signs of metamorphosis. But those eyes don't seem to be getting any wider, those lips any thicker, that skin clearer. I flick through *Dolly* and *Cleo* and a friend's mother's *Vogue* and stare at the spectacular specimens of the female sex. I don't know that much of their beauty is created with make-up and lighting. I think there really are women who look like that and I wonder why I don't see them on the street. I think they must live on another planet.

A therapist once told me that it is often the father who gives his daughter the first sense of her own beauty as she flowers into adolescence, who gives her the first admiring gaze of an adult male. My father died three months after the echidna cut.

My face was no less problematic than my hair. Eyes not deep enough, lashes not long enough, bones not high enough, a snub nose with no authority, lips too thin to carry the full force of the sensuality I felt inside. No one feature too awful, but none spectacular. Failing myself in my ordinariness.

Sometimes I would talk to someone and think, I wish they weren't looking at my face right now. Oh God, what are they seeing? It must be awful for them. Please look somewhere else. This anxiety felt like a wound that would never heal. I covered it with a thin veil of make-up that allowed me to hide my more disappointing aspects.

Sometimes Michael would come straight out and tell me I looked beautiful.

'You can't say that directly to my face,' I would cry. He never argued the point but would sit behind me, cradling me between his legs, and whisper it again quietly as I tried to breathe in the impossible. His own beauty caused me a quiet pain, but within his compassion a quieter healing began to occur.

Working on a documentary once, I went behind the scenes of a magazine cover shoot. A celebrity model noted for her fulsome bustline was being shot for *Elle* by a photographer who was an entertaining cliché of an arrogant wanker. I felt like an anthropologist watching an alien tribe, but I did remember to wear my groovy white vinyl jacket. What interested me most was the level of artifice. The woman I had met the day before was only the canvas. Now she had been painted, she bore almost no resemblance to her other self.

'Stop smiling, Katie honey,' the make-up artist would plead. 'This is not smiley make-up!'

A tiny jersey haltertop had been chosen for the shoot, and it was always going to be a challenge to contain her celebrated ample bosom. I noticed, with the bitchy satisfaction of the less well-endowed, that her breasts were drooping. No matter – they heaved the bosom up by hand, pulled the top tight to keep her in place and twisted the fabric at the back, clamping it with two bloody great metal gaffing clamps. I had never before seen a woman walking down the street with two steel clamps hanging off her back. Oh, but the cleavage! A defiance of both jersey and gravity. The photo was doctored in post-production so her image shimmered and made me weep to look like that, even though I knew that not even the model looked like that.

Don't we deny young women their beauty when we surround them with such impossible ideals? It's a denial that turns ageing into an aesthetic insult.

But still I stand at the counter of the department store, not believing a word of the gibberish the sales assistant is spouting about the restorative, rejuvenating, resurfacing night creme. I give her too much money for it anyway, feeling the shame of the wound that will never be healed as I slink from the store and give the Salvation Army man at the door only a fraction of what I have just spent.

The First Goodbye

It was fourteen sleeps before Christmas and Michael and I had been together for nine months. We borrowed a friend's house at Hawks Nest, a coastal village two hours north of Sydney. I suspected that we had come here to part, although no formal proclamation had been made. We had set each other homework, to write a manifesto of what love meant to each of us.

We took an ecstasy tablet to steel ourselves for whatever was to be done and said. Amidst pillows and candles sat our twelve glasses. As early evening slid into night, I read him my manifesto.

When I was young, my romantic ideal of love was that it would be instant and forever. Like Cinderella, I would be 'his partner'. And although my notions were as shallow as a child's, something about the whole idea of love touched me as being sacred and my desire for union was born.

In fairytales, novels and the heroic liaisons of the classics, love was something that transported people to another place in themselves, a better place. Love was the meeting of two lonely hearts, the merging of two isolated souls, as Cathy's cry of love and despair testified, 'I *am* Heathcliff'.

Over the years, I've investigated love. Love is freedom. With a foundation of honesty and trust, we have discovered it is possible to be both committed and free to explore life and follow those roads less travelled. Love does not choke or suffocate. It is not jealous or unkind. It seeks only to honour. Love needs discipline and commitment as well as mirth and laughter. It should be the bedrock that two people can jump from, secure in at least one thing – we have a witness to our life.

And love changes. Some parts of it die but if we are willing to walk the path, other parts will rise up and live. Sometimes it dies completely, and if we are committed to freedom, we will know when it is right to bury it. But here is my bitter refrain. It is we humans who fail love, with our lies and insecurities and indulgences. We who give up when it all feels too hard.

The trouble with us, Michael, is that we are at such different places in our lives. I remember coming into my sexuality in my late teens and early twenties, feeling like a flower unfurling to meet the sun. Like I had discovered some powerful drug. You've been so recently re-born into your sexuality that you should be given the chance to feel this unfurling.

What happened to me eventually was that each sexual union, without the coming together of heart and spirit, felt shallow, and I began to feel lonely. But I know about desire, and if that's where your heart is, you should follow it. If that's the loudest call to adventure, you should heed its call. Because above all love needs a double will. It needs both people to want to be there. Relationship is too hard if the heart is not in it.

I lull myself to sleep fantasising about having you again when you are ready. I am not the same person as the one you first met and my gratitude for this is endless. But my craving now is for the deep growth that comes through time and commitment.

My fear is that I will not find someone who loves life, freedom, play, discipline and joy with the same force as you do.

Good luck, Michael. May the road rise to meet you.

We sat in silence.

'That's gorgeous,' he said, the way you do on E, 'and it also feels like a letter saying goodbye.'

A hazy pain pierced the drug's goodwill. Somewhere deep inside, I had hoped this letter would be a call to arms.

'Oh my God, I think I have.' I laughed the way you do when something is not all that funny. 'How could I have been so stupid?'

'Vanessa, it's all right, that's just your truth and it's beautiful. I agree with every word. It's just that I'm not there yet. And that breaks my heart because I know if I was up for it, there's no one I would rather do it with.'

The ecstasy was blocking the full force of my despair but the tears still pooled. 'I just wanted you to hear the full gamut of my pathetic idealism. So read me yours.'

Just as it was for you, the idea of love in my youth was all consuming. Love gave meaning to life – regardless of how that love might end. And weren't the endings hard to bear! Dr Zhivago died when about to find his lost love. Songs were full of pain and yearning. Don Quixote loved Dulcinea, who discovered her love for him only as he died.

All this anguish at 'missing' seemed to hint that the greatest loves were tragic. As if somehow love, in its full power, could only be present if the 'gap' was never closed between two people. I've always wanted this to not be so, wanting instead the power and the consummation.

In the living, it seems I've learned much more about what love is not, than what it is. Then again, role models are rare finds indeed. No songs about a 'living love' tear our hearts out. We're not moved to tears by a film about two people who can hold on to love.

John and Yoko stand out in my mind – a couple who didn't die a dull death, who took great chances and who dived deeply into each other's oceans. It's said that he also beat her up more than once and left her for a year with a prostitute of sorts, provided by her.

Perhaps easier to state, then, what love is not.

Love is not togetherness forever.

Love is not always gentle.

Love is not found in one another alone.

Love is different from sacrifice and although they can co-exist, it is a dangerous tension.

Lasting love is not the love I've seen in movies, books or songs. While it has been my great privilege to peek into the world of love on a few occasions, I haven't yet grown large enough to know the action I need to take to allow myself to stay inside that world.

Love, although at times placid, easy and calm, requires at its heart a wild bravery. Wild bravery in relinquishing ego for a clear path to the other and wild bravery in following our own hearts. To set out on the journey and follow our true path, even when it might threaten our partner. A minefield, that one, and yet one I would gladly cross to avoid suffocating in safety. Yet words are easy for me to say.

On the one hand I still feel I would give up everything for my real union, as though it is a holy grail. But a failed marriage is the shipwreck in my soul. Hence this period of re-training, when I am trying to choose myself ahead of all union and avoid becoming stranded once more.

In my current phase, it's as though I carry a kind of darkness around love. So as I look out from this wound, I don't know what it is you will find. But my dear wish for you is this – that all the joy and beauty and greatness I have viewed will, in the presence of this love, in the presence of this lover, find a way to blossom and grow fully. It has been truly a joy and honour to travel this road so far with you.

You have, without knowing, tended gently back to health a dying child. Bringing laughter where there was despair and tears, dancing life back into a timid body. I've taken from you so deeply and strongly. And in the taking, given equally. For the beauty of that and the possibility held within that model, great love and gratitude.

Michael

We sat into the small hours, cooing messages of love – ridiculous, E-fuelled grins plastered to our faces despite what was happening. Then we reached for the other and let our bodies speak the depth of feeling words can only hint at.

Afterwards, dissolved into a limb and torso soup, our eyelids drooping, we couldn't release our grip.

'You've been so constant in your love,' he whispered. 'I can't bear to let you go, even to sleep.'

'It makes no difference to me, because when I dream, you're there.'

Unable to stomach my tragic romantic utterances, I sat up and looked outside. The dawn sun was glowing, a massive eggyolk sizzling over the horizon.

'Aren't you coming to dream?'

'The sun's coming up. I'm working on the symbolism of the moment.'

He raised his head and shouted at the sun, 'Cut the bloody symbolic racket! People are trying to sleep around here.'

'Us breaking up, a new dawn, death of the mystery of night, the rise of new possibilities. I feel like I'm trapped in a New Age calendar. Let's go down and dive in the ocean.'

We whooped along the empty beach, shedding our clothes in a celebration of being alive. The brand new day gleamed, like someone had wiped the sky clean. Sunlight danced across water the blue-green hue of opal. Nature was bragging her perfection.

The surf collided with our bodies, knocking all the joy out into the open, dumping us in our own laughter. 'Let's kiss when it comes,' he shouted and we locked bodies and lips and the wave broke, tearing us brutally apart.

'Deeper!' I yelled, and we dived down to the seabed and held the kiss for as long as we could while the ocean churned above.

He left that afternoon, and that night I climbed into the bath and gave way to hopeless, exhausted weeping, my sobs mingling with peels of laughter coming from a barbecue next door. Howling . . . laughter . . . howling . . . laughter . . . Until I was laughing right through the tears, my heart washed clean, glad that at last I could feel it all.

Perhaps God is a
Little Black Dress

*E*xcept of course we couldn't part. Michael went to Melbourne for a family Christmas and when he returned we were drawn together again. A new joy percolated through me. I was just glad to be with him, here and now, at the height of a Sydney summer. Glad to have some kind of a future, even though he could still only promise an unbearably finite number of here and nows.

Helping a man back into his full sexuality was a tough job but someone had to do it. Much of our relationship took place behind closed doors but occasionally we would push the boundaries of decency and explore a little public brinkmanship.

Walking the Paddington end of Oxford Street on a sunny Saturday afternoon is like stepping into the pages of some hip street magazine – gorgeous babes lolling in summer dresses, sunlight filtering through sheer fabric, the breeze tweaking hemlines. Guys buffed and strutting their stuff in gay pairs or with arms around the babes. The young and the cool of Sydney wandering through the fabulous riot of Paddington market or cruising designer boutiques.

Michael and I strolled the strip feeling languid and horny, riding the erotic currents, rubbing up against each other as we stopped to look in windows and mosied inside on the hunt for a little black dress. Brave, a small, sexy boutique, held potential. I tried on a dress that rode up my arse, the hemline resting somewhere near my waist. I strutted around the shop for Michael, like his personal callgirl. The shop assistants sensed we didn't need assistance and kept out of our way. I draped my arms around his shoulders and he smoothed the fabric down, navigating it sensuously across my body.

'That is so horny, it's dangerous,' he whispered. 'I'm not sure if I could cope with you going out in that.'

Not sure I could cope with *myself* in that dress, I tried on the next in line. It was short, sexy, and the fabric clung less frantically to my skin.

'Bend over,' he said softly.

I strutted around the shop. 'Oh, I think I dropped my coathanger,' I said with mock coquettish surprise. I bent over, pouting my arse upward, feeling the air against my crotch as the dress rode up.

'That's the one,' said Michael.

The world is holy!
The soul is holy!
The skin is holy!
The nose is holy!
The tongue and cock and hand and arsehole holy!
FROM 'HOWL', ALLEN GINSBERG

We went to dinner with friends at the more genteel end of Kings Cross. Walking back along Darlinghurst Road, among throngs of the usual suspects and Saturday-night revellers, I felt slutty and ready for anything. Sex on legs, with the man I loved at my side. Michael kept an arm around me, pulling me close. I was wanton playdough in his hands.

Our car was parked in a narrow, well-lit street lined with apartment blocks and large trees. I was waiting like an old-fashioned girl for him to unlock the door when he grabbed me, pulled me round to the front, laid me back against the bonnet and kissed me. A kiss of unadulterated lust, wholly intoxicating. I was drunk on a few glasses of red, a day of erotic shopping and a love I never wanted to end, and I surrendered to his devouring.

He pulled the straps from my shoulders and let the fabric fall beneath my breasts. I gasped with the thrill of being exposed in public. Gripping me around the waist, he planted his mouth over my nipple and sucked hard. I was gone.

He came up for air, grabbed my arse and lifted me up onto the bonnet. I slipped off my sodden knickers and tossed them away. He pulled me close and began exploring my wet, swollen lips with his fingers, entering me with his middle finger, pushing it to the hilt.

I leapt under his touch. I took his head in my hands, put his ear to my lips. 'God, I want you to fuck me right here on the street,' I whimpered.

'With people maybe looking down from their windows,' he enticed.

'Maybe other people driving by,' I promised.

'You're a horny bitch. I'm going to take out my cock and fuck you right here on the bonnet. I need to be inside you.'

'Yeah, give me that cock.'

My legs were split apart, wrapped around his back. His cock slid easily inside. I was overflowing for want of him. He thrust deeply, pushing me up the bonnet. I had to grip hard with my legs, pulling him inside, frantic. He thrust again, groaning. I heard a noise and looked up. A couple were making their way towards us.

'Stop,' I whispered. He stopped, his face buried in my neck, panting, not too many thrusts away from eruption. Suddenly the street was alive with people. The couple got into their car and the headlights played over us. Caught in the glare we giggled, frozen like shamefaced dogs unable to separate. An elderly group of friends called out plans to each other for Sunday night as they arranged themselves in the back and front of two Range Rovers. They were aware of us but trying not to stare. It was a battle of wills. Moving would mean revealing genitals. Staying suggested we were trapped in our lewd union.

'You slut,' Michael sighed. 'I've got your legs spread and my cock up inside you in front of all these people.'

One by one the cars manoeuvred their way out of the narrow street. I looked up, shocked at just how many windows could be harbouring potential voyeurs. My pussy spasmed. He felt it and let out a groan, grabbing my arse. 'I'm going to fuck you till I come up inside you,' he moaned, pulling my hair back. He planted his lips over mine and his hot tongue probed my mouth, breathing fire. He buried his head into my neck, shoving into me, thrusting, pulling my cunt over his cock, which jerked once, twice, three times as that hot sensation flooded me.

We came back to earth, scrambling to get his now limp squid back inside his jeans, my dress down over my thighs. He was stunned, shocked at how far we had gone. I was thrilled, still swimming in lust. He'd better be in the mood for round two at home.

'That dress,' he muttered, 'that dress – you can only wear it with me, okay?'

A few days later Michael left a note in my study.

V.
Little black dress memories coursing through my veins . . .
I do love to fuck you Vanessa
I do love to love you too
Perhaps God is a little black dress?
M.

JOURNAL MAY '95

Sometimes I watch him sleeping, his face beautiful in repose, eyelids closing off his soul to the world. He lies on his side, curled like a question mark. His feet poking out from the blankets form a full stop. Honey-brown skin stretches over a body that is a playground of contours. His neck is a perfect sweep, the veins run like blue rivers just beneath the skin. I want his eyes to open, to look into my soul so full of love. I want to ask the impossible, ask him to stay. Torn because I also want him to stay asleep so I can drink in his sleeping form.

I want to sit for the longest time until my eyes are sated, my heart satisfied. Scared of getting caught, I position myself so that I can escape if he were to open those eyes. I am an embarrassment even to myself.

Indecent Obsession

The joking motto of our family was 'a Gorman never gives in'. Dad would shout it out as the five of us kids wrestled each other to the floor. Once the victim was pinned, the victor would let a glob of spit hang like a stalactite from the mouth before gravity and vindictiveness saw it drop onto the grimacing face below.

Sibling love was unquestioned; sibling torment a way of life. A sick father and busy mother meant it was not necessarily safe to reveal vulnerability, lest it be used against you.

My parents were strong and capable people and our genes were those of solid, sensible Gaelic stock. Sanity stretched back generations. Gormans were not the sort of people to go mad but to help out when someone else did. Dad subtly made us understand that from our position of comfort and privilege, it was our duty to assist those less fortunate. He would take us with him to mow the lawns of people too poor to own a mower. My mother was a social worker, committed to helping others. As I matured, I couldn't help noting a faint whiff of family superiority at our being so . . . *capable*.

And here was a man inviting – no, demanding – me to reveal my vulnerabilities and weaknesses while he constantly expressed his need for freedom and space. I was caught in the role of hungry lover, forever wanting more.

The nature of my relationship with Michael meant there was no place to hide. I felt exposed as a pathetic, needy creature. One night, as we lay on his bed drinking tea, I tried to explain. 'It's this weird, shameful feeling that I would do *anything* for you – murder someone, rob a convenience store, walk the desert without shoes. It's like I don't want any separation. I want to just . . . *mesh*. Catch any bodily fluids I've missed out on. But I feel ashamed because you need all these boundaries and I'm grovelling beneath your table, hanging out for any scraps thrown my way.'

'I know this seems like a weird response, but there's actually something sexy and beautiful about that. Think of yourself as a brave woman for coming this far.'

When you're in love with someone and they might leave any day, you drink them in as never before. I wanted to soak him up, to inhale him. His touch was riveting, his most mundane chatter significant. Curled about his body at night, I fought sleep just to relish the moment. My body alive to his skin, his breath on my neck like a breeze whispering of far-off places I might never visit.

I was confused because Michael still loved me. Often clung to me when we were together. Found it just as hard to say goodbye. His touch was exquisite, his caress loving. So much poignancy made it all so damned . . . well, poignant. We looked at each other with longing, love and a sad understanding of each other's destiny; we wished the other a smooth passage to unknown destinations.

He left early the next morning and I moved about his apartment cleaning up, loving the illicit thrill of being free to cast my eye over his life. Trying not to pry. Failing miserably.

Life's Longing

When I was about eight years old, I wanted two things. I wanted to know what happens after you die, a yearning so fervent I considered trying to top myself but had no idea how to go about it. Gradually my curiosity subsided. But another urge, primal and intense, took hold. I longed for a baby. I had never felt anything like this, not for toys or dolls or pets. I wanted to be holding and caring for my own child, even though I knew it was impossible at my age. I wasn't sure how I could wait, I wanted it so much. I remember standing in the bedroom, looking at my sister's menagerie of soft toys and thinking, Okay, there is nothing you can do about this for a long time. When you are an adult you can have a baby, so just try to enjoy life till then.

It was a bargain I struck with myself to dull the longing. I was never ambivalent about my desire for children. But I was distracted by life and career. Like my peers, I believed postponement was a viable option.

'Oh my God . . . oh my . . . God . . . oh my God!!!' Michael was having an orgasm that God was in no hurry to end.

'I think he heard you,' I cooed as he writhed. He was panting in ecstatic pain, like he had just won a marathon.

'You have no idea! That felt like all the sperm I've ever produced just erupted. I think that could make you pregnant – no, I'm serious. I think something weird just happened.'

'Well, I'm wearing my diaphragm so it's unlikely.'

'We'll see,' he said, and we did. Three weeks later I found out I had conceived.

Kahlil Gibran's words have been loved to death, but they are still beautiful.

> *Your children are not your children,*
> *they are the sons and the daughters of life's Longing for itself.*

Suddenly, here was life's longing in a jar of urine on my lap as I sat outside the chemist in my car. Here was life's longing turning the white dot on a predictor wand a deep rosy pink. And here was I, swearing at life's longing as I cursed that moment three weeks before, when life's longing was just a longing of the loins before sleep.

A friend's house in Clareville was empty so I took myself off for a few days to think, watching through the gums as the sail boats off Pittwater plied their trade of careless leisure.

Over the phone Michael stated bluntly that he was not ready to become a parent. That the decision lay entirely in my hands and that I would have to accept full responsibility no matter which choice I made. I could hear a pulling away in his voice. A wave of pain swept through me and I understood my options: an abortion or single parenthood. The death of my child versus life as a single mother in a shared apartment with no way to support myself.

I didn't see the beach as I walked, only those two choices sitting uneasily on the horizon. Life with a child meant life without

Michael. But would he leave anyway? Could I cope with poverty? Was this the end of my dream of partnership?

'I'll be feeling nervous with you,' he had said on the phone, 'until you make the decision.'

I covered the handpiece so he wouldn't hear my weeping. How could I balance the scales of my heart – on one side the life of my unborn child, the other heaped with life's practicalities. How could I fit a child into my worklife? My job involved long, irregular hours, getting on planes at short notice, stints filming overseas. I understood that I would have to change my job to accommodate a baby. And I was nowhere near ready to make that happen.

This most massive of life's decisions is shackled to the fiercest of deadlines. I turned thirty-four with no fanfare. *If not now, then when?*

As weeks ticked by, a deep sadness took hold of me. What was wrong with me that I couldn't make a decision to keep my child? What was wrong with men, with Michael? What was wrong with society? Why do we abort tens of thousands of foetuses a year?

'I'm scared you'll hate me whichever decision you make,' said Michael, as we ate fish and chips on Balmoral Pier.

'I could do this in a heartbeat with a partner. I'm so ready to have a child.' I stared out to sea, hoping again for some sudden change of heart in him.

'I just can't do it.' He breathed out with a kind of repressed anger. 'Not in a million years. Not yet anyway.'

My childhood dream, to raise a family within a strong and loving partnership, beat so strongly within me. It was not a white wedding and picket fence kind of dream but it held that same desire for stability and security.

Single motherhood felt like a defeat of everything I held dear. And I knew myself. I wanted to be passionately committed to the life of my child, but my circumstances seemed so diminished that it would be difficult to give that child all the attention, love and security they deserved. Finally, my courage failed me.

After the decision was made, numbness descended. When emotions forced themselves to the surface, I felt a deep anger at the world, which masked a deeper loathing of myself. Intellectually, I would defend a woman's right to choose, defend the need for safe, legal abortion. But on an instinctive, soul level, I understood that what I was about to do was a deep betrayal of both the child and my own desire to mother. I sat in the waiting room of the clinic hating who I had become. Willing myself to leave. Wanting the force of some sudden bravery to rise up and propel me back into the street, to walk past the protesters – an old man and woman waving a foetus in a jar as they urged a different course. I picked up a women's magazine and flicked. 'When Is The Right Time To Have A Baby?' mocked the article headline. I read on, hoping for an epiphany. 'When you've sorted out how you feel about your own parents', the male author suggested. 'When you've come to terms with the emotional baggage of your own childhood.' I laughed. If the world took this man's suggestions to heart, population growth would stop dead in its tracks. The bitter truth for the modern woman is that there is no *good* time.

I am made to wait. A blood test. More waiting. In with the counsellor, who asks questions and I start to cry. She coos sympathetically in what I am sure must be an half-hourly experience for her. She explains the procedure, referring to the foetus as *a collection of cells*. I feel a kind of disgust at this brutal reductionism.

The angel of death calls my name. She is wearing a blue hospital gown over her clothes and tells me it's been a busy day as she leads me upstairs.

Last checks and balances. *You're sure you really want to do this? Empty your bladder in there. Just take off your clothes and slip this on. Bring your bottom towards the end of the table.* I am introduced to the female doctor but I can see she is weary and we make only brief eye contact. I want to tell her to be careful. That I do want to carry a baby to term some day. But I am too ashamed to speak.

I feel the cool steel of the speculum enter, prising me apart, a sting as a needle anaesthetises my cervix and then the pain of violation. The hum of a vacuum machine reverberates around the theatre walls.

A searing revulsion grows inside me – at the violent invasion, at my own betrayal of life's most tender longing as this *collection of cells* is vacuumed from my body. I cry out in distress and the nurse covers my mouth with an oxygen mask and strokes my hair as tears pool onto the pillow.

Adrift in my gassed haze, too late I want it all to stop.

Excavate the reproductive history of many women and you will probably find they have had at least one termination.

Many have had more than one. For some, the decision is clear-cut and holds little drama. Others carry a silent grief for years. In the struggle for safe, legal abortion it seems to me that we have ignored what can be a huge emotional impact. Is it because we have been worried that women's anguish might derail the political process?

I was offered no counselling before the day, and none afterward. I would have to find my own way through the unspoken guilt and sadness; the force of it left me breathless some days. There was shame, too, for the relief I felt in resuming my life unburdened.

Afterwards, the longing for a child became even stronger, but now it had a bitter, silenced edge.

Michael and I had a ceremony at dusk, sitting on the rocks overlooking Gordons Bay, farewelling the soul who had hovered about us, within me. Inviting it to come again someday when the time was right. We were quiet for a while. I sat and held what I imagined to be the child in the palm of my heart, my lament silent.

I failed in that most basic duty of a mother, to protect her young. I put my own needs above yours. I'm sorry. I'm so very sorry I betrayed you.

It came to me that I had betrayed myself and the sorrow would be mine to endure.

An Indian Summer

When I first met Michael, he was in a state of flux, searching for his direction and purpose in life. Pushing to find the truest expression of his deepest self, for the right way to bring himself into the wider world. I admired his courage to be fluid as he experimented with where and how he wanted to live. I understood that his inability to take root was a reaction proportionate to how long he had been stuck in bad jobs and an unhappy marriage. I could be both a companion and an anchor of sorts, but ultimately he wanted to find strength of purpose and love within himself. He was only able to go as far as he did with me because I was able to stand on my own.

'I've never had a truly independent woman who didn't need me to be their father or protector,' he said over a steaming latte one day. 'And it scares me a bit because I think that you could just go at any time. Sometimes I look at you and I see your ease of physical expression and I see men watching your sexual nature being so kind of full, and it makes me insecure and I think, Fuck, you know, fuck it!'

He laughed and I tried to hide the shameful leap of glee dancing in my chest. 'I worry that if you leave, no one will be able to excavate my heart the way you do,' I offered back.

'I used to think that we love the other for something that we can only recognise because it lives in us,' Michael replied. 'But I think now that we are all faulty in some way and it's okay to have those weaknesses and let the other person fulfil a part of you that's lacking.'

Michael's quest to find the truest path for himself involved the courage to let himself be lost and vulnerable – no small task in a society where men are meant to be masters of their destiny. His constant questioning spilled over into our relationship so that each new month it could veer off on new and unexpected tangents. But these openings and closings, partings and reunions gave our relationship a robust quality. As did the simple love of being in the other's company.

Halfway through the last month of winter, summer descended for a sneak preview – long enough to banish our hunched shoulders and pinched faces. In the park, jumpers were torn off and turned into pillows under the dappled shade of the angophora. Children clutched icy-poles. The unseasonal warmth elicited smug comments. *I mean Sydney is mild but this is ridiculous,* we crowed. Michael turned up for an unexpected visit and suggested a swim.

Carved from a rock platform, nestled into the Coogee cliffs and fed by ocean swells, Wylies Baths was one of our year-round haunts. Local leather-backed retirees, *the brown men*, as Michael called them, lounged on chairs listening to John Laws and the fifth at Flemington. On this warm August day, we stretched on the concrete concourse, soaking up the sun before negotiating the rock wall. Waves broke over our legs as we hung onto the silver chain. Steeling ourselves for the frigid assault, we plunged through the foamy surface.

Underwater, Wylies is like a beautiful aquarium and I took a childish pleasure in irritating small shoals of whitebait as I swam. We managed ten laps before our extremities seized up and hot showers beckoned.

Rewarding ourselves afterward with a coffee at Globe, Michael talked of his planned trip to India. 'It's kind of hard to talk about because it's still a way off, but I want to go unattached, as a free man, a free spirit.'

'Of course you do,' I said, relieved to distract myself with my plate of mudcake.

'It's just that I want to be free to meander and explore and not feel as though I have something or someone who's holding me back here.'

I told him about my first trip overseas, when I was eighteen, to Europe and Israel. My sister and I had worked like dogs saving for it, but I fell in love just before we left and spent the whole three months pining for him. Every Mediterranean sunset, every incredible monument – I wished he was with me to see it. I spent the trip seeing everything through a haze of heartache.

'I was there physically but my heart was tethered to another place. So I truly understand.'

'But we have six months till I go away, and I wanted to say that I feel a deep commitment to being with you for that time.'

'Look, it's probably good to have a cut-off point. I can't really go on like this indefinitely, wanting the old committed relationship and to start a family and all that. I have to be free to let myself find that.'

'Of course you do,' he said, and reached for my hand as my tears betrayed me, revealing the pain under my resolve.

The next day on my clifftop walk I stood looking down on

Wylies, and there it was again, the anguish. Going to Wylies, doing anything without Michael, it was not going to be the same. The subtle loneliness that had dogged my adult life would inevitably return and I would be forced to survive with my heart in another's keeping.

Six months later I took Michael to the airport. I stood back from the Air India check-in counter and money exchange window as he did the business and I tried to stop my heart overflowing through my eyes. We found a place to have coffee, sitting pressed together, holding each other's hand. I let myself weep then, pouring out my love with histrionic abandon. I have always felt anxious about any leave-taking and spoke as if I might never see him again. He held me like I was a child and spoke words that soothed my sobbing, and I knew if we never saw each other again we would always be sure of our love. I handed him a small wrapped box to open.

'Condoms!' He laughed.

'Ribbed for your satisfaction.'

'Thank you. For what they mean. Thank you for being free enough to give me this freedom. I have no idea if I'll use them but thank you anyway.'

'You're free for life to take you wherever it takes you,' I said with grandiose magnanimity, my smile a flimsy mask.

We made our way to the gate and hugged quickly. He turned once at the partition and pretended to throw away the box. We laughed silently across our divide and he disappeared through the gate.

In the carpark, as huge jets roared into the smog, I gave way to violent howling, banging the steering wheel and gulping for air. Bereft and filled up with a love that had nowhere to go.

The next night I fell into a desolate void. All the hurt and grief that I had never expressed overtook me. I sat in the hallway of my flat, back against the wall, great sobs tearing at me. At first what burned were the names and faces of those I had loved and lost. Then I was crying for all of us, trapped in our egos, rubbing up against each other as we desperately try to get our needs met. I cried for all our wounds, all our pain. Exhausted, I lay silent, vanquished. As though I had finally surrendered my longing for union and accepted the lonely nature of our separate existence. A deep peace settled over my body and I closed my eyes. The void was still there but I could no longer resist it. I felt myself merge with it, drifting into a place of such stillness, such peace, *such annihilation* that for the first time I felt the true, transcendent union of existence.

JOURNAL FEBRUARY '96

We are all alone. It is an aloneness that can fill us with a desolation so profound that for some, life seems not worth pursuing.

We feel alone, so we search for love to ease the separation, and when we find love, we cling on for dear life, trying to own and control the other. We grab for money or power, feel jealous when our lover smiles at another or sink into a depression when our children leave us for the wide world.

We are all alone, so we overpopulate our fragile planet and then turn on each other in fear and hatred of their otherness.

We are alone, so we search for love and in finding it think, *Thank Christ I've found some love*, not realising that love of another is only the stepping stone to the greater love.

None of us are alone. It is a grand and blinding illusion. Loneliness is a state to accept and then transcend. To understand that all humanity, all nature, all things are one, to understand that separation is impossible – this is to understand the magnificence of God.

Indian Missives

Pushkar

Hey Babe

Looking out over fields with brightly saried women stooping over crops and on the music system . . . ABBA. 'Mamma Mia, here we go again'. Strange world. American woman next to me sending back a pancake because it hasn't enough mushrooms and puppies with broken front legs hopping around waiting to die. The more I see, the more I remember life's a mystery. I'm leaving Pushkar and going back to Delhi.

. . . If nothing else is accomplished on this trip, getting perspective on us is worthwhile. I've been so worried that 'giving in' to relationship meant somehow losing great parts of myself. What's happened with you has been teaching me that it's not the case. Still, I had this notion that I had to prove my independence.

. . . Something is becoming clear. I'm finding that I'm much keener for an ongoing partnership with you than I consciously knew. Maybe if I start to say that, *you'll* back away???? I suppose somewhere I've always felt not ready, as if being 'ready' would mean we would have to change everything – all the freedoms – all the space.

. . . Sometimes I feel like I've got this perverse double nature.

Part wanting security, commitment, money, things, and a part that every now and then looks over disdainfully and pulls the chain, flushing everything away.

We both know how to play the game in the world and both love not to.

But we're getting better at leaving the normal behind and walking our own roads. This is what I love in you too, what is so rare, and whereby springs the rawness of my longing – someone quite similar to me. The whole security/freedom dance we do is as much yours as mine. It doesn't need the extremes any more . . .

Fax: To guest Michael – Room 9
Pushkar Palace

God I've been missing you, Michael. Mourning my best friend. Wondering where you are and what you are doing at any moment. Buying six banaras and then realising you won't be there to eat them. Missing you to whinge to about how hard work is. Missing your gentle heart and love and compassion. Missing your wisdom that listens to a whole lot of surface stuff and then cuts to the real goings on. Missing your laughter and my buddy to work out what needs rebelling against in ourselves and society. Do you see why I love you? I feel closer to you two thousand miles away than I do to anyone in the same city.

Bangalore

Vanessa

Namaste! Caught a plane (extravagant!) down to Bangalore, staying here another 5 days. My heart and mind have finally calmed here after quite an agonising 2–3 week period where I couldn't seem to move out of both love for you and fear of losing you. I'm discovering a quieter love for you, much like you describe having for me sometimes. It's like a certainty about you is creeping in. Not like 'oh you'll certainly be there when I get back', or 'you'll certainly always love me', but a certainty in my love for you that for some reason is making me feel so much safer.

Perhaps truly the only place that certainty can be and breathe and live is in the finding of God within ourselves. When you think about the world, about banks, life insurance, houses, mortgages, political borders – there's an enormous, at times panic-filled scramble through life, looking for solid things to hang on to when all the time we are standing in the illusion . . . Enough, enough . . . This is what India and ashrams do to you. Even a pizza can give rise to an existential thought . . .

Pune

Vanessa

You've been a liberating force in my life the last two years. I want you to come with me in this life, be my partner. It's absolutely impossible for me to leave you now. I've got Vanessa imprints all across my heart and branding on my cock. (I did enjoy the way it got there though!)

Loving the Wrong Person

We're all seeking that special person who is right for us,
But if you've been through enough relationships,
you begin to suspect there's no right person,
just different flavours of wrong. Why is this?
Because you yourself are wrong in some way,
and you seek out partners who are wrong in some
    complementary way.
But it takes a lot of living to grow fully into your
own wrongness. It isn't until you finally run up
against your deepest demons, your unsolvable problems
– the ones that make you truly who are you –
that you're ready to find a life long mate.
Only then do you know what you are looking for.
You're looking for the wrong person.
But not just any wrong person: the right wrong person – someone you
lovingly gaze upon and think,
'This is the problem I want to have.'

ANDREW BOYD

Dying for the Deadline

*H*aving the good fortune to be white, educated and middle class afforded me the good fortune of an interesting career. Even at fifteen, I knew I wanted a job where I would learn about the world, where each day would be different. After university and time as a researcher, my first job as a television producer was with the science and technology program, *Beyond 2000*. For four years, by plane, train, boat and automobile, I travelled the globe, filming stories on every continent and shooting in some of the poorest countries on earth. I remember sitting on a bed in a hostel room in northern Inner Mongolia, my toe tapping the ice puddle on the cement floor as I laughed in amazement at how a girl from a tiny country town in New South Wales had ended up here. Reporter Amanda Keller and I were the first Western women to ever visit.

The legacy of these travels was rich but perhaps most important of all was an understanding of how two thirds of the world live – by Western standards, in dire poverty. Cocooned in our air-conditioned mini bus, crammed with its half-million dollars' worth of video equipment, we travelled chaotic and treacherous roads, through crowded cities, shanty towns and villages. I watched humanity struggle to survive everyday life, passing women walking for miles through searing heat, huge stacks of firewood perched on their head; men pushing bullocks and wooden ploughs through acres of mud; children selling individual straps of chewing gum at dangerous intersections for the smallest pittance.

I never stopped feeling the pain of this struggle for existence, and it cast its shadow over my own good fortune. Into that shadow stole an uneasy guilt. But I also learned to take nothing about my life for granted and I began to live with an immense sense of gratitude.

I loved it when we filmed in villages where the joy and simplicity of communal, traditional life still held sway and grubby children ran free, harassing a scabby assortment of animals. In these places, I was always reminded of how poor our lives in the West can be, how isolated and complicated; how our frantic pace has stolen from us the joy of simply being alive and connected intimately to the earth.

For all that my job was a privilege, some days I felt stripped right down to the bone and would shake under the stress of constantly meeting deadlines. The gift of this high-octane existence was that I had to find ways to cope with stress. I discovered meditation and yoga, which inevitably led to an exploration of alternative spirituality.

While Michael was in India doing just that, I was offered the job of writing and directing a documentary about how the design of women's underwear mirrored the course of emancipation since the eighteenth century; I would track the shift from corsets to underwear-as-outerwear. The production company wanted an intellectual film that could be sold to a highbrow channel in the UK. However, in Australia it was to be screened on a commercial network, and naturally they wanted busty models and plenty of tits and arse. Not only was the shooting and editing schedule punishing, I was being pushed by two masters. The end result was a hybrid film that

I hoped would escape notice. Since much of the budget had been spent on busty models, money was tight and we were given little time to finish the project. For the last two weeks we were locked in a dark edit suite for up to eighteen hours a day. I could barely focus my watery eyes as I drove home at four a.m. through the harbour tunnel. I was a danger to myself and others.

For too many years I had ridden my nervous system too hard and finally I was so exhausted, I felt ready to be put down. Instead, I vowed never to let myself be worked like that again.

Michael arrived back in Australia to a nervous wreck who barely had time to shower, let alone make the languid love of a longed for reunion. We took ourselves off to Byron Bay for a week, to recover and reconnect. I was pleased to see that the forecast was for gale-force winds and torrential rain. We rented a beach shack and I lay down and slept for fourteen hours at a stretch as rain battered the iron roof and the ocean swept the sand dunes of Belongil out to sea.

procreate or perish

Being granted the gift of too many choices can create its own dilemma. As a young woman, I got the message that feminism was all about seizing opportunities, about enjoying choices. I wanted to go to university, forge a career, travel. I thought it my duty to redress the imbalances of a male-dominated world.

It seemed that feminism was telling us we could have it all. To procreate too early would be a cop-out, because the role of caring for children meant the loss of prestige, power and income. Only in my mid-thirties did I begin to hear of women who had left their run too late, who were spending huge amounts of money and emotional energy on IVF.

But it was not only women who were changed by new ideologies. Michael was among the many men of his generation who asserted their right to postpone or avoid having children. 'Why do you want to have a child?' he would ask, genuinely perplexed.

Through many discussions I tried to explain myself rationally, but I always circled back to the mysterious urging of my heart. The gift of bearing a child seemed to me the most wondrous of feats, that my body could create a new skeleton, a new brain, an entirely new personality. I wanted to feel the force of that being flutter and roll, kick and squirm inside me. I wanted to stand, swollen, grotesque and majestic, in the fullness of womanhood.

A childhood spent watching animals give birth had taught me awe. In later years, images of women giving birth became my private pornography. I would steal guiltily into the newsagent's, pick up the pregnancy magazines and retreat down the back like some bloke in a raincoat with a copy of *Hustler*. I would flick through the pages, fascinated and appalled by the sight of women with heads thrown back in agony, vaginas distressed and distended, legs splayed in the helpless and powerful frenzy of pushing forth life.

I wanted it all. I wanted to feel the tug of mouth on breast, the slobbering suck on my face, the feel of down beneath my chin, the weight of a sleeping head on my shoulder. The sheer animal attraction of mother and baby.

I wanted to witness the wonder of an intelligence unfolding, language being learnt, a personality flowering. The innocent hilarity of children. Their gift of being perfectly in the now. The give and take of love and adoration. I wanted to help them grow a healthy heart and send them forth as adults who would add to the store of love in this world. I wanted a noisy, boisterous household of barely contained chaos; the opportunity to whinge about the exhaustion of it all as I lovingly tousled the heads of the culprits.

This need to divide and nurture is written into the DNA of all living things. Yet this longing for a child sat uneasily with my love of adventure. Secretly, each year I had whispered to God, 'Thank you for another year without a child.' For I was under no illusion as to the sheer exhaustion, painful self-sacrifice and plain hard work involved in raising a child. And this reckless part of me thought I still had time. The deadline was closing in with every year, but I thought I still had time.

For Michael, the sheer exhaustion, painful self-sacrifice and plain hard work loomed large as reasons why a child should be indefinitely postponed. Looming largest, though, was the possibility of entrapment. Holed up in one house with one dependent woman and a dependent child. In short, suffocated.

'Look, I'm not saying never ever, Vanessa,' he would assure me, 'just not at this stage of my life.'

'You see, that's the trouble,' I'd say. 'You can say that, because you've got the possibility of plenty more years to pick a stage that suits. I'm running out of years!'

He narrowed his eyes. 'Sometimes I feel that you want commitment in a relationship because you want to have a child, whereas I want commitment to a healthy relationship first and foremost.'

'Yes, yes,' I would say dismissively, 'of course I want that too.'

But when you have always longed for a child, when you see children in your future, when the longing to hold your own baby in your arms becomes a painful ache, the fear of declining fertility seizes you in the very pit of the guts.

I would come home from a trip to the supermarket and rail at Michael. 'How come all the fat, ugly, stupid women who belt their kids around get to have five children hanging off their trolley and I'm not even allowed to have one?' I would cry, knowing how spiteful, how appalling I sounded. It was the kind of extreme prejudice that you only voice to your most trusted intimate. I felt not only a longing but a sureness of my aptitude for the task. Thwarted, my bitterness began to feed on my flesh.

A Rainbow Trajectory

The greatest thing about joining forces with another human being is how it can shift the trajectory of your life in ways you never expected. Michael began talking about moving to the far north coast of New South Wales. He wanted to follow his intuition and take a path into the unknown, something he'd always had the courage to do. With the first mention of a move, both fear and excitement took hold of me. I had always thought that some day I would end up back in the country. Some day when my career was exhausted and all passion spent, I would see out my time in the stillness of nature. But this soon?

Cities and I had a love–hate thing going, although I loved Sydney with a passion, this bejewelled mistress, a wild glittering sapphire. A city who openly celebrates her good fortune, her money and vices, her speed and glamour. A cheeky, funky chick of ethnic diversity and general tolerance. Serene bushland softens her hard edges; her beaches and harbour beckon us into the open, promising that any day might be a holiday if we want to play hooky.

But the city also seemed to me an unnatural place for humans to dwell, hostile even. Crowded in with millions of others, silence is obliterated. The quiet settling of dusk is overtaken by the chaos of rush hour; stars are blotted from the night sky by artificial illumination. We brush against so many strangers that it hurts to look them in the eye and we must shut down in a million small ways just to survive, to endure the grit, the litter, the road rage, but most of all the noise.

But Sydney's waterways never failed to entrance me. Living next to the sea at Coogee meant the wildness of the ocean could soothe the part of me that longed for a more natural world.

The idea of a move grew roots as we began to debate it; then small shoots of trepidation and excitement. It seemed at once a preposterous suggestion and, for two people enthralled by nature, a logical progression.

Still, I wasn't sure if I could leave the streets I knew by heart, the cultural institutions, the nightclubs, bars, theatres and national parks that had become my landscape of work and leisure. A web of family and friends formed a loose network so that I never felt truly alone amongst the crowds. Pulling up roots and relocating seemed so radical. It meant leaving the beautiful old apartment I shared, letting go of a thriving career, moving away from family, friends, everything I held dear. For what? For love. For that was what we were proposing. Just us – living together for the first time, alone in a new place, forging a new life. At last, after three years together, the future with Michael I craved. Nothing else but love would have made me do it.

I tested the idea out on a family that was alarmed and friends who were surprised but supportive, some envious even. I insisted that I wasn't dropping out, just dropping in to a new way of life. Gradually I extricated myself from work and housing commitments. Michael and I spent our summer holiday up on the North Coast, meandering through places that might whisper to us of home.

If we were going to leave the city, we still needed culture, art and music, an intelligent community of like-minded souls. All of this a town called Byron Bay promised, as well as a natural beauty that can take the breath away. Australia's most easterly point on the mainland, it was originally inhabited by the Aboriginal Bundjalung nation and was a meeting place for clans from north and south. Westerners have been trying to make a living there since the 1850s, cutting away at the vast subtropical rainforest and later running beef and dairy cattle on cleared land. Fruit growers and hobby farmers took over a lot of the failed farms. Whaling lasted for nearly a decade from the early 1950s. But it was the counterculture rebels who would give this region its defining character. Over the last thirty years, waves of hippies, surfers, alternative lifestylers, spiritual groups, ferals, retirees, seachangers, artists, filmmakers, IT workers, social security recipients and niche farmers have made it their home. At the same time, tourists, holiday makers and backpackers have threatened to swamp the region, developers turning what used to be a ramshackle town of weatherboard buildings into an overloved tourist mecca, each new mega-development proposal bitterly fought in a desperate battle to stop Byron going the high-rise way of the Gold Coast, only an hour's drive to the north.

Depending on your bent, Byron, or the Rainbow region as it's often called, is to be either celebrated or derided as the epicentre of New Age culture – chakra-infested waters, a tour-stop for all the gurus and masters and healers. It's true that it offers a smorgasbord of body workers, herbalists, yoga teachers, psychics, energy balancers, colonic irrigators, tarot readers, homeopathic, naturopathic, telepathic and occasionally sociopathic individuals plying their gifts to the stressed-out traveller and grateful local.

If you need your chakras aligned by a crystal-healing Bach flower specialist in inner-child sandplay therapy, then Byron's your place. Many people scratch to make a living here but what they have in abundance is quality of life. People are following their bliss, journeying to the source, evolving their consciousness, aligning their posture, reconfiguring attitudes, grounding their bodies, opening their hearts and smoking a little pot.

It is still a meeting place of clans, from the very wealthy to those eking out a permaculture existence on the dole. But all are seeking a place large enough for diversity and small enough to offer the cohesion and support of community.

Now we had found our town, I closed down my Sydney life. I had given up my job, my life was packed into boxes and new tenants were circling my room in the apartment. Michael and I drove up to Byron to look for a house to lease three weeks before we were due to move.

Apprehension vied with excitement. *We're moving in together and it will be fabulous. We'll have a baby and bring up the child together. Sure, there'll be tough times but we'll pull through because we really love each other, and doesn't love conquer everything in the end?*

Apparently not. Michael was already freaking out and planning his escape. Suddenly the word *trial* was being used far too often for my liking. While I stood at a Byron real estate counter, asking about unfurnished houses with a six-month lease, he was over at the holiday counter asking if they had furnished houses we could rent month by month.

It wasn't so much the question of a one- or six-month lease, furnished or unfurnished. The problem lay in the fact that I was so far ahead. I was already settled down and raising a family with him. For every ten minutes in a real estate office, we spent an hour processing our vastly different plans for the future.

'I think I want to leave my stuff in storage and just try it out month by month. If it feels wrong, I need to know I can leave, say, after three months.'

He meant leave me. Anger began to choke me. Then waves of devastation. Then anger again. If he felt this much fear about moving in together, how was he going to feel about having a baby? It was all falling apart.

I fell apart while driving from Brunswick Heads to Byron Bay. It was raining and with my tears adding to the general precipitation, I could no longer see the road.

'Pull over,' said Michael.

I sat and wailed as the traffic swished past. 'How come other people commit all the time? My God, they even get married! Is it me?'

'No, no, it's nothing to do with who you are,' he said, opening and shutting the glovebox in agitation. 'It just suddenly feels so serious, as though all the exploration has gone out of it. I don't know . . . I can feel myself sliding into this sort of panic about getting stuck in some dead place again. Moving in together feels like such a big commitment, because you want a family. It feels like it's no longer just a trial thing.'

'You've chosen your moment here.' I was suddenly wondering what to tell the fifty people due for farewell drinks in Sydney next Friday.

'Look, I'm not talking about leaving. I'm just . . . oh God, I don't know.' He broke down, holding his forehead as tears dripped onto his jeans. 'I just feel so stuck sometimes. To stay here is terrifying, to leave is terrifying. I don't really know what the fuck to do. I'm sorry I'm like this. I'm sorry I'm causing you pain.'

We cried together, holding each other awkwardly over the handbrake and gear stick.

I knew enough about Michael now to understand that if I cleared an exit path, he would probably feel free enough to not walk away. But if he did leave, was I prepared to be up here on my own?

It was a relief to realise that I wanted to make the move anyway. We agreed that we would leave most of our stuff in storage and come up together on a three-month trial.

On the day I left Sydney, the forecast was for showers. Michael and I were driving up in separate cars. The sky oozed grey across the sea and I was glad Sydney was not showing me her glittering best. The rain arrived as a moving curtain across the ocean while I squeezed the last bags into my car, which was packed to the gunnels, sitting low in the water cascading down our street. I began sobbing as I drove up Beach Street.

I sobbed as I circumnavigated Centennial Park and again down William Street as the Coke sign receded in my rear-view mirror. I sobbed on the freeway to Newcastle and in between Taree and Kempsey, Kempsey and Macksville. Crying for all that I was leaving behind and out of fear for all that I was moving towards, including the possible dissolution of my relationship with Michael.

I stopped crying somewhere near the Big Banana at Coffs Harbour (you can't help but laugh). Suddenly I felt exhausted, and at peace. It was a relief to feel the fear and bloody well do it anyway. To jump off the cliff into some alternate, unknown universe. To have all I needed for the next three months packed into my elderly sedan. A thrill went through me as the Big Prawn of Ballina swam into view. I was in *big* country now. I had done it. I rummaged for an old Springsteen tape and Bruce and I belted out the music of the highway and the hopes and the dreams of the dispossessed.

The Life of Byron

We began our new, very tentative life together in a small farm house in the foothills behind Byron Bay. Michael had moved his sales agency with him so at least he had the continuity of work. But he had never lived in the country and found it disconcerting to be working at his desk and see a cow wander past. I found this enchantingly familiar, and each day marvelled at finding myself surrounded by trees and paddocks instead of apartment blocks.

We were in a tender, wary, vulnerable space. Both aware of the 'trial' nature of our arrangement and both coping with the enormous change of the move. I felt a strange schism open inside me. There was peace at finding myself enveloped again in nature but also a deep sense of loss – loss of my old life, compounded by the loss of a certain future.

Leaving Sydney was more than a seachange: I was closing a chapter on my professional life, and the question of how to make a living sat heavily. I felt like a frail creature, tossed by a storm I didn't see coming. A deep grief had resurfaced and I knew enough to find a therapist who could help me through this passage.

Some six years before, when I was about to turn thirty, I had been trying to leave a relationship with an older man that had consumed much of my twenties. 'Tell me about your childhood,' the kind, grey-haired counsellor coaxed the second time we met to work through my confusion.

I began to talk about the utopia of my early years. 'And then when I was twelve my father died,' I said, and wondered which details to give him. But instead of words, something else rose up, a pain that had lain dormant for many years. And with it, my tears. Except they were not gentle, polite sniffles but great embarrassing sobs that made me heave and gasp for breath. I pulled at the air like I was about to suffocate. I was shocked. Where had this grief been living? Emotions I had long thought I had recovered from, that time had healed, had been waiting for a chance to be heard. My kindly therapist sat with my distress with the greatest of ease.

The grief returned again and again and I let myself cry with Michael whenever it arose. Moving to Byron Bay, and the loss of everything that had held me steady in life, brought back the old feeling of drowning in a sea of brutal impermanence.

A compassionate counsellor near Byron was recommended and for an hour a week I lay on her floor and let myself fall apart, regressing to the twelve-year-old girl who had not been helped to cry. Also sobbing for the lifelong dream of family that was slipping through my fingers.

In the not too distant future, when death would knock at my door again, at least I knew one thing: grief is something we bury at our peril. It cannot be placated. Sent underground, it will lie coiled, waiting its turn.

For all our confusion, Michael and I settled into the rhythm of living together with the ease of best friends. But my need to be a reclusive writer clashed with the explorer itching to map new terrain. The explorer could see herself becoming a feral earth mother, but she was held back by the middle-class yuppie who could never come to love a composting toilet. Another handicap was my semi-corporate wardrobe of black and white clothes, many synthetic, marking me as visibly foreign in this land of rainbow-stained hemp cloth and daggy footwear.

I joined a forest blockade and took my video camera to a gold-mine blockade out west, determined to bear digital witness to those risking their lives on the frontline of protest. I merged with the feral throng dancing to drums at the Rainbow Temple that rose five storeys high from the forests of Rosebank. I sampled ganja cake and magic mushrooms and danced barefoot around bonfires. I laughed harder with new friends than I had in years and wanted to know more about almost every person I met. In those early days, this land, these people all seemed to be alive with magic. There was ceremony and singing and dancing, and children everywhere, underfoot and whirling with joy through every gathering.

We joined the naked protest against nudity laws on the beach. Michael assisted at acting workshops and created a program about men for the local radio station. I was trying to keep my life free but within a few months had joined a women's group, a yoga class, a writing circle and a choir, and would stand wistfully perusing the weird and wonderful workshop notices on coffee-shop walls, lamenting the time and money to try it all. We explored the beaches, bush trails and waterholes of hidden valleys. Driving home across green hills bathed in golden light, we concluded that we had landed in paradise.

Seeking community, we had stumbled across a region of like-minded souls – people protesting rampant development, scrambling for limited resources for community projects, arguing about the big questions and experimenting with new paradigms for living.

All the warring parts of myself – the recluse and adventurer, the feral and yuppie, the slut and prefect, the intellect and heart, the spiritual and profane – we could all peacefully coexist in this region populated by the black sheep of the world. While I had been at ease on the farm in my childhood, and had found my niche in the city, this felt like the right home, the perfect home, for who I was now.

Private Country

*E*very relationship is a private country; no one outside that couple truly knows the territory. I find it no less difficult to portray my own relationship with Michael. I can attempt to describe our world but know I can never paint a portrait that will do it full justice. I can never describe all the dark forests and brilliant flowers that grew there.

I look back now and see how the adventure of our new life distracted us for the first months after we moved north. But the upheaval saw us become more fixed – we were clinging to our positions again. I wanted a baby and deeper commitment; Michael wanted to live alone. The fear saw us shoring up our walls.

I hated the precariousness of living on trial. The trepidation was constant. New, though, was the fear of us staying together. I worried that even if he did eventually agree to a baby, he would not be able to surrender to the day-to-day routine, discipline and sacrifice children demand. I worried, too, that I would have a baby and he would leave soon after, condemning me to join the ranks of the single mothers that populated the shire. I feared that if he left, it would take years to find another partner and years to get to know them, by which time it would be too late to start a family. Somewhere in my heart I hardened against him, preparing to let him go if that was our destiny.

'Why can't you rejoice in what you have here and now?' I blurted out one day, exasperated. 'All the great things we have? You're always saying we should live in the present but I feel like a prisoner of your fear of the future and your pain of the past.'

The way he felt a prisoner of mine.

We tried to be kind to each and not lash out. I couldn't help myself at times and would shoot off emotional arrows, only to feel ashamed when he would respond with understanding and love.

We decided on a twelve-glass evening. It was good to sink into the love again after the pain of feeling closed to the other.

'We're on some mysterious road,' he said. 'I'm pulling one way and you're pulling another and the middle ground is a very high place.'

'I know. We are always pulling each other to fearful places.'

'The irony with us is, we've gotten this far by letting things evolve organically. This need to make choices that open my heart is not a passing fancy.'

'The trouble is, I don't know what to do with this desire to have a family. It feels like something I need to plan for.'

'That's okay but I'm not there in my life right now.'

'How do you know that having a family will hold you back from what you want to do? Perhaps it will be the very thing that will make you blossom as a person.'

'And perhaps it won't! Aren't I supposed to *want* to follow a road like that?'

No matter how we circled the issue, the deeper truth was unavoidable: he was not ready. We made love next to the fire, a damn good shag. But still I wanted to cry out, *Surrender! Come with me on this wild meandering of love!*

As the months passed, his fears and my needs shadowed our terrain and slowly I began to grieve the inevitable parting. It was as if

Michael and I had been thrown from our boat and we were out there in the stormy seas, lashed to our separate life rafts, trying to work out a way to get back in – bobbing about, missing one another, connecting, missing again. We didn't want to give up, because it had all been so wonderful, but we were tired of the struggle.

The year was drawing to a close and Michael went south for work. He phoned, and I began to talk about a separation. Through my tears I cried out to him, 'We've been together four years. I'm nearly thirty-seven. How much longer do I have to put my dreams on hold? How much longer do we live your agenda?'

Afterwards, I took myself for a walk along a vast stretch of deserted beach, watching a pair of sea eagles hover, feeling like a great weight had lifted. To my surprise I felt a weird sense of freedom and raised my arms in jubilation. Not because we were separating but because I'd had the courage to make the decision.

We met for Christmas with my family in Sydney, sat on a friend's couch and talked about separating with the same love and respect that we had brought to our coming together. What was strange was that I now felt like the one pulling away, and he was suddenly the one trying to breathe us back to life.

'I think I should leave, Vanessa, but the thought breaks my heart.'

'Oh God, I don't know.' I sighed, wishing there was an easy way. 'I feel like this hopeless fucking romantic sometimes. I want the certainty of true love, the soul mate thing. Someone stable and secure in an unstable world. I feel like it's my destiny to love someone truly. And here I am, loving you as truly and deeply as I've ever loved anyone, and I just feel bereft when you always want to move away from what we have. I want someone who *wants* to be here. I want someone to call home.'

'I know,' he said quietly, pain etched around his eyes.

He talked about a new strategy. Of trying to say *yes* to the other. Trying to give the other what they want in this life.

'You know what I want,' I said.

'I know. All I can really commit to is going forward in honesty and trying to reach that place where I can say yes.'

JOURNAL DECEMBER '97

I had actually started to tell people that Michael and I might be separating, letting the words flow into the air just to see how it feels. Sometimes it sounds like I am stating the inevitable but then another part in me rises up and cries *no*!

I can't bear to let go of his body and his beautiful face, his kindness, his generosity, his emotional and spiritual insights, his laughter and sense of play. The man who listens to me more deeply than anyone. The person who I filter my life's experiences through. Whose outlook on life matches my own, whose path mirrors mine. Who laughs with me at the rapture on a dog's face when it hangs its head from a car window. I realise I am still too hopelessly in love with him to throw away the chance of more life with him and, as he has been intimating, at last a child of our union.

To love is good, too: love being difficult. For one human being to love another: that is perhaps the most difficult of all tasks, the ultimate, the last test and proof, the work for which all other work is but preparation.

Rainer Maria Rilke, from Letters to a Young Poet

My bank balance suggested that my carefree life as the creator of unfinished filmscripts had to be curtailed. I found work two hours' drive north, in Brisbane, as a producer on the ABC-TV documentary series, *Australian Story*. It was and is a beautiful program, full of integrity and helmed by Deb Fleming, one of the best bosses in the business. It tells the personal stories of famous Australians and ordinary people with extraordinary tales. Delving into people's lives was an amazing privilege and crafting each half-hour a creative challenge. In letting go my Sydney career, an opportunity had opened that was richly rewarding, though accompanied by the usual dose of blood, sweat, tears and deadlines.

I made it home most weekends; Michael was also away a lot on business. In our limited time together, we tried not to rock the boat too much, tried to practise the process of saying yes to the other.

With a decent, ongoing income now available, and the *possibility* of Michael agreeing to a baby, the nesting instinct turned every For Sale sign into a future home. House and land prices in the region had started to soar and it was demoralising seeing what I could afford on my budget. Michael was not ready to enter into anything as concrete as owning a home with me, so I was on my own. In a heart-lurching moment of compulsiveness, I made the last bid at the auction of an unfinished wooden house on ten sloping acres.

I thought I was going to throw up as people pumped my hand in congratulation. The final weight of adulthood settled on my shoulders, which were now wedged between my knees in an effort to get the blood back to my head.

The house was just outside a tiny village, Federal, nestled in the hills twenty minutes' drive from Byron Bay. Town life centred around a general store, Pogel's Cafe and Fred the mechanic's workshop.

It was an open-plan house on poles with a verandah that looked out over a beautiful green valley. But the sloping acres unsettled me. I had nurtured a utopic vision – something about the house being nestled *into* the land so the garden was flat and children could safely run around in their pyjamas, the way we used to in the garden at Fairfield.

'So you still miss Fairfield?' Michael asked, as we explored the laneways near the house, and my ambivalence to the ten sloping acres.

'Just the feel of something like it. It's probably the last place I felt completely secure.'

'It's funny how we reach for physical things to reclaim emotional states.'

'I know, I know – the right house or land won't magically bring happiness.'

What it did bring was relief that I had finally found a place to roost, even as the thought of keeping up with mortgage payments terrified me. I began to discover just how much a rambling, unfinished wooden house on ten acres costs to upkeep. But I could imagine raising a child there. Could see them tottering along the verandah and chasing balls down the slope beneath the house.

I had never expected to buy a house alone, but so much of what happens in this life, as I was to discover, is nothing like what we expect.

I could finally feel my dream taking shape. Michael's reluctance was the last obstacle.

Atomic Warfare

It would be unfair to say that my need to have a child was more important than Michael's need not to have a child. The difference was that I had to answer a biological deadline.

I was no longer ambivalent about *when* to have a baby. Instead, I was panicking about leaving it too late. The yearning was a black hole, sucking everything into its vortex – relationship problems, career, financial issues. None of it mattered. Everything was ephemeral when compared to the painful prospect of life without a child.

I was raised with the notion that the highest calling in life is to please others, but I recognised that at least on this issue it was time to fight for what I needed. The fear Michael would leave made me enter into guerrilla warfare.

I announced that I was going off contraception. 'If you would like to use it, go ahead,' I said, 'but I can't sit here desperately wanting a baby and continue to use birth control. It feels like I'm lying to my body.'

'I understand. But I'm not agreeing to have a baby,' said Michael.

Both of us remember the months that followed in ever murkier shades of grey. In his mind he was saying an emphatic 'no', while I read his inability to leave as a reluctant acceptance of my agenda. He was trusting me to tell the truth about my cycle so he could practise withdrawal, while I perceived his failure to use contraception as a tacit agreement. I began taking an intense interest in my vaginal mucus, luring him towards sex when it had the consistency of eggwhite. By the second month, I knew I couldn't keep up my deception and told him what I was doing.

'Okay,' he said, 'so I want you to be straight with me when you're ovulating.'

Michael had described the negotiations around having a baby as a Cold War. His atom bomb was *I'm leaving* and mine was *I'm having a child*. It didn't take long before we realised that whoever dropped the bomb first would win. Deep down I knew we had reached breaking point. He knew he couldn't continue in the relationship and keep putting me off.

It's here that I have to come clean and admit the continuance of guerrilla tactics. It was a Saturday afternoon in May. He was in front of the telly watching his beloved football team lose again, and I was in the toilet getting excited by the eggwhites.

I lured him for a quickie at halftime. I don't remember if we discussed my cycle, but I knew I was lying by omission. The next night we made passionate love by the fire. He left for Germany a few days later.

Appalled at my treachery, I finally sat down and poured my heart out to him in a letter.

June '99

Dear Michael

A letter I need to write right now as I'm in that part of my cycle when all the issues come up. What's been happening is this . . . Basically

I've been lying and manipulating. So much of what has been beautiful between us has been borne of our capacity to speak truthfully. I have gone outside the culture of the relationship and have been withholding the truth. This is why.

I get my period and I despair because probably that month I've tried to lure your sperm towards my ova. The blood comes and both my uterus and my heart cramp up, and then for the next fourteen days till ovulation I'm in this sea of emotion that shifts between grief, rage, powerlessness and frustration. It propels me out of bed in the morning – I'm desperate for the distraction of getting dressed and going to work. And while it jabs at me all day, it doesn't actually burn me if I keep busy. I've been trying to 'feel' it and 'sit with it' but it's not the kind of pain where you can go and do some therapy and have it maybe diminish because you've made a friend of it. It's the opposite. No matter how I befriend it, sit with it, just feel it – IT JUST KEEPS ON GETTING BIGGER AS EACH MONTH PASSES. Each month it gets more violent. (The worry is, I'm sure, a great contraception.)

The experts say that at my age, a woman's fertility is starting to fall off the chart. I'm so scared, Michael. I'm so angry with myself for the abortion. I'm mad at myself for waiting this long to start the process. For giving in for so long on something so important to me. I've loved you so much I haven't wanted to drag you in before you're ready. I've been trying to 'stay with the program' and respect your timeframe but all the violent emotions, all the fear makes me manipulate sex around ovulation. It's been going on from the beginning of the year. Often, though, we are not together when ovulation happens or we don't have sex and then the rest of the month continues with the pain of the first half. So I have weeks of agony. If we have had sex, I get a wild, desperately hopeful euphoria while I wait out the next fourteen days. It must seem to you as though sometimes I am quiet, still. That's because I'm waiting, and in the waiting hope lives, and with the hope the pain subsides. So my life right now is this monthly seesaw. Hating and then loving myself. Hating and loving you. Fear then hope then despair. I'm in purgatory.

I'm hating you because I can't believe you could love me and want to actively contribute to the pain. I'm angry with myself because I can't seem to express the pain in a way that might make you understand *enough* to throw that rope to my drowning heart. I understand your own pain. I try not to judge it; I try to see it and give it space and respect. But here's the truth (from my perspective): your pain and fear over this issue is killing me. If you do happen to get trapped, well, okay, for a little while you are trapped. But it's reversible. You can leave. You can untrap yourself. If I can't have a child now or in the near future, it's not reversible. It's a fact for the rest of my life. And I don't even want to think about the grief of that.

So now I'm just down to begging. I'm pleading with you. I'm lying prostrate before you. I'm on my knees and my hands are clenched. Imagine you're a soldier and I am praying to you to spare my life. I realise I've never really had to do this before. To want something so much – to feel this powerlessness – is a new thing.

But there is some kind of transparency or purity in being so vulnerable. It's against my family programming to beg or plead, but here I am, vulnerable, helpless, pleading and pissed off.

Maybe I've reached the point of needing medical intervention or IVF (even so, there is a 40 per cent chance the pregnancy wouldn't make it). Either way, the truth is that I need to keep trying. Even if it's just so that half the month is bearable for my frightened heart. I need your help. I don't want to keep trying to manipulate you.

So here endeth this plea for my life. (And that is truly what it feels like in this part of the month.) Thanks for listening. Thanks for being the kind of partner I can tell my truth to. I love my life with you. I am full of awe for the journey you have taken me on. I love you so much.

VG

PS And I hate your guts.

Michael never received this letter; I often wish I had found a way to be this clear and unequivocal before the war turned so dirty.

With my period a day overdue, I plunged the magic wand into a jar of urine and held my breath. Two pink lines grew on the blotting paper. I was pregnant.

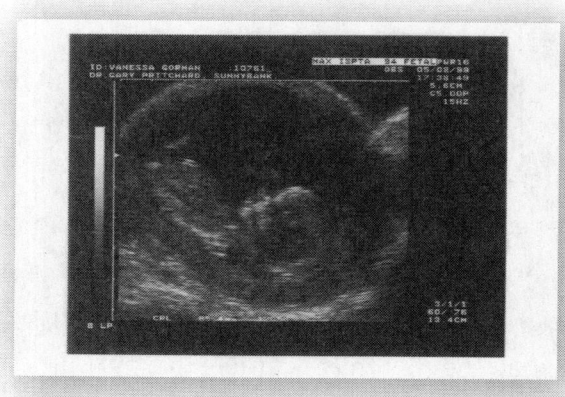

The Thin Pink Line

I didn't think about miscarriage or other mishaps. Such things happened to others, not good Irish Catholic breeding stock like myself. I was pregnant, ergo I was having a baby.

The relief was proportionate to the despair that existed before I fell pregnant. Every cell of my body seemed to let go a collective sigh of relief. The long, slow panic that had risen over years suddenly disappeared clear off my radar. And into the vacuum rose a mad, dancing joy.

All the way up the freeway to work in Brisbane, I kept taking the wand out of my bag and giggling. In the edit suite, sitting behind the editor, Roger, I snuck looks at it, unable to believe the evidence, needing the joyful reminder of what those two pink lines meant. My bliss that day threatened to choke me.

The only thing that was scary about being pregnant was telling Michael. He was still overseas so I had a few weeks to prepare for the moment. When it came, we were lying in bed the morning after he returned, talking vaguely about life as I distractedly tried to recall my neatly rehearsed phrases. But there was, I realised, no easy way to break the news.

'Um, I have something to tell you and I'm not sure how you'll feel about it. Umm . . . I'm pregnant.'

There are hundreds of these scenes in cheesy black-and-white movies. Scenes where our heroine, Doris Day or Elizabeth Taylor, tells her beloved they are expecting a baby. She has set a beautiful table and is immaculately groomed in her tight-waisted frock. She coyly lets him know there will soon be three in the family, and Jimmy Stewart or Cary Grant rises from the table in surprised joy, comically upending something as he rushes to her side and says, 'Are you sure?' And she says, 'Yes', and he says, 'Well, this is wonderful news.' And they laugh and he immediately begins to fuss over her, wanting her to sit down and put her feet up or stop carrying that platter, and it's all an hilarious pantomime of elation. I had always longed for such a moment in my cheesy old soul.

Instead, Michael lay his head back on the pillow and grasped his hair, pulling it like he was scalping himself.

'Oh my God! Oh my God! Oh my God!' was all he could say for a full five minutes. It was not joy. It was not Jimmy Stewart or Cary Grant. For Michael, it was more a schlock horror movie.

'Oh my God! Oh my God! Are you sure? Oh my God, Vanessa!'

I had dropped the bomb first.

part Two

B. UR _454_

M. UR _____

Mothers' Name

GORMAN   B/o
_____

Babys' Name _LAYLA_____

Sex _GIRL_____ Gestation ___

Date of Birth _16 | 2 | 00_____

Birth
Weight _3335_____ Length _S

Obstetrician _____

Paediatrician _____

Life as Art

In 1996, three years before I got pregnant, I began making a film.

I had been working with camera crews for years, lugging around huge Betacam cameras, lighting and sound equipment, monitors and the thousand cables, bits and pieces needed to get sleek, high-quality pictures. During the nineties a new technology emerged, the digital camcorder. Small and relatively cheap, digicams signalled a revolutionary approach to making documentaries.

Intruding into people's lives with a mountain of equipment will always skew reality. With lights blinding them, a huge camera in their face and a microphone dangling about their head, it is almost impossible for a subject to forget they are being filmed, which makes capturing the candid moments of everyday life a challenge. Digicams, however, are unobtrusive and non-threatening, and encourage filmmaking that is personal and intimate.

Perhaps to justify the expense of buying one of the first models on the market, I came up with the idea of making a video diary chronicling my relationship with Michael. Hopefully, I would be able to explore how pregnancy, birth and the first year or two of our child's life affected us.

I started recording our life in the bedroom, bathroom and living room. It was my hobby project, squeezed in around professional

121

commitments. What made the story interesting to me, even though it was making my life hell, was Michael's reluctance to have a baby – conflict being the stuff of story, after all.

'This is not just about a baby any more,' I would complain, tongue in cheek. 'You're also thwarting a creative project!'

Michael refused to be swayed for my art.

I filmed on and off over the next few years, often annoying him in the process. Because no matter how small, a camera changes the dynamic of what is happening in a room. Mostly, even when he felt exposed or irritated, Michael was supportive.

Now that I was pregnant, not only my life but my video-diary documentary was suddenly on track and I stepped up to record the process with gusto. Attempting to be both camera operator and subject was awkward. What I discovered worked best was wasting tape. I would set the camera up at the end of the bath or bed and let it run for the length of the tape, even if we fell asleep. It was set and forget. To turn it off or change the shot would mean changing the dynamic. Little by little we came to ignore the camera's presence, or at least to integrate it into our reality. It was often an uneasy process as I lugged it into my doctor's office and set it up to record my check-ups, feeling narcissistic and self-conscious after a lifetime of being behind the camera. But I reasoned this was a universal story, and secretly I hoped it would become a film about a man who would, though initially reluctant, fall passionately in love with his child and show all baby phobic men that there was nothing to fear.

Except Michael showed no signs of becoming that man. The fact that I was pregnant was more like a prison sentence than something to be celebrated. He watched my swelling like a death-row inmate might watch the gallows being built.

At least we had reached a ceasefire in our constant struggle over *the issue*. Michael had no choice but to surrender to the fact that I had 'won', but a new battle had begun: how to deal with the fact that I had pushed him on to a path he did not want to follow.

But my mind and heart were filled with other matters. From the first, I was alive to the new life inside me. I would grow round and large and then give birth. I would be tending a baby for a year, then guiding a toddler around the furniture. I would be out and about with my preschooler, then helping them settle into kindergarten and school. I would be living with a teenager, then sending them into the world, perhaps to university, a career. I would be watching them evolve through adulthood, and one day I might be holding my grandchild. A deep peace settled over me, even as my heart and mind raced ahead, reconfiguring myself as a parent.

The streets seemed joyfully alive with pregnant women, mothers and babies, fathers and their children, and I rejoiced to be joining their ranks. After so many years of waiting, I wanted to be the best parent I could be. My heart felt like it wore a smile all day, and I revelled in the yelps of excitement when I announced the news to family and friends.

'At last!' they exclaimed. 'At last!'

Supermarkets and greengrocers became my new church, eating well my religion. My body was now a factory, fed by an assembly line of food groups, vitamins and herbal supplements. I exercised and went to yoga. I trotted off monthly to my obstetrician, Phil Steele, for quality control, assuring *him* that all would be well. Mild morning sickness seemed a trophy symptom of a healthy pregnancy and I never thought that things wouldn't turn out well. I look back on myself at that time and think how blissfully unaware I was of the thousand things that can go wrong in this business of bringing new life into the world.

But as quickly as I was flowering, Michael was contracting. His sense of having being coerced caused him to withdraw sexually, just as I began to feel so horny I was eyeing off the doorknobs. He was angry that he had let himself get to this place. He felt he should have left the relationship before it got this far, before I betrayed him. He was dreading the baby coming, describing it once as 'the end of life as we know it'. I had won our baby struggle but now I was losing him.

It came to a head when I was about eight months' pregnant and we were driving home from Sydney. A thick fog hung between us. 'Is there anything you need me to know?' I asked him.

'I find it hard to be present any more. It feels as though you made a decision for both of us, and I can't live with it. I'll be here as a friend but I'll probably be . . . um . . . leaving after the baby is about six months old.'

My stomach lurched and tears ran down my cheeks. Michael leaving was not a new idea but the vulnerability I now lived with changed everything. My strong, independent outer shell had cracked and softened; this was not the time to toughen up. Now was the time to enter fully into this soft, earthy, mysterious rite of passage, with or without him.

JOURNAL 30 DECEMBER 1999

How to tell of all the things pregnancy is? The slow surrender to softness, to a body no longer solely your own. All the joy, all the hurt, all the pain, all the wonder.

I have always feared this: being rejected and dependent

within the vulnerability of pregnancy. And here I am! But also here is the wonder and thrill of creating a new life. The tender pride of being round and soft in a hard-bodied world. The relief, strong as opium, of seeing those two pink lines appear. The cold fear of motherhood passing me by finally thawing, melting the knots in my heart. Watching that fear subside as the baby grows means I can lay down that sorry bundle of desperation at last, at last.

We cheated at the twenty-week ultrasound and found out I'm carrying a girl! Secretly I had hoped!

The joyful expectation – buying buckets and baths, borrowing cots and prams, a hand-me-down array of soft tiny clothes and colourful dresses that I imagine slipping over her chubby body as she grows into a toddler. Bunny rugs stacked under the change table, lined up next to sheets and nappies, the teddy waiting in the cot. Michael has bought her a soft toy. *My first football*.

But mostly what I am preparing is my heart – letting it open and soften as the months progress until I am crying every day just at the beauty of life – Eva Cassidy singing 'Fields Of Gold', the butterfly we freed from the web, the dawn mist in the valley below us. Rubbing my rounded form in the bath and feeling her move a leg, an arm. I am in love with the shape she makes and secretly steal glances at myself in the mirror, both alarmed and proud of this enormous swelling.

Never a midriff girl, I have become a midriff woman – flaunting my rotund form down the main street of Byron, wearing her with the pride of a woman in love. Waiting.

Swimming laps in the pool, I watch the parents with their children and imagine swishing my giggling baby through the water. At the beach the other day I dug a hole in the sand and popped my belly inside, feeling the sun warm the aches in my back. I looked up the beach to where a mother sat with her three-year-old, the little girl straddling her lap, both of them swaying together in a playful rapture, and I sighed and closed my eyes, drifting off to dreams of wrapping my arms around my own little girl. I can hardly wait!

Michael is often very distant. It feels like what I have of him is mostly sullen, defiant and wounded, at a time when I need him more than ever. This level of vulnerability is so new to me that I long to have his strength and company to support this baby into the world. I am trying to relax into the vulnerability anyway. In doing that, a whole new path is opening up.

Somewhere within I am discovering that to struggle only brings more pain. So I'm submitting: to my body changing, to the imminent pain of childbirth, to the possibility of joining the ranks of the single mothers of Byron Bay. Anticipating the changes a baby will bring to life, opening myself to the love I feel for her, accepting that I may lose my best friend and the father of this child. Ultimately, genuflecting to the spiritual lesson that if God is perfection, and God makes up every fibre of this universe, then only perfection can arise from perfection and nothing that's happening is wrong, bad or needing to be changed, even though I am worrying myself to sleep. Phew.

I think the reason I am trying for a natural birth is that it seems like the path of greatest surrender, the path that will teach me the most. I suppose that's the path of parenthood: it teaches you who you are.

Michael has been mired in his own fight between surrender and struggle. Somewhere he understands that being a father will be a powerful experience for him but right now, not having chosen this path, he doesn't feel ready. It hurts to hear that he's mad he let himself be 'trapped'. I had fantasies of us as the happy glowing parents in birth classes, doing all that breath-breath-pant-pant stuff together as his hands lovingly encircle my growing belly.

He's pulled back from talking about leaving, recognising that it's just too much to deal with right now. Some days I feel he is gone for good, others I feel optimistic that he is here for some time yet. Most days I feel a lot of gratitude for the deep friendship we have, which we both feel will last beyond the relationship. So that's a good feeling. At least we can co-parent till we die.

When I think of the abortion I want to weep. There I was, trying to avoid single parenthood, and here I am now, in a relationship that's been going nearly six years, facing it anyway. Fuck it – life sometimes feels like the slow letting go of dreams.

Expectant

I worked at *Australian Story* until my seventh month, swotting up on pregnancy and breastfeeding books in my spare time before retiring for the summer. We employed a woman called Santo to be our *doula*, our birth support person; I suspected Michael might need physical and emotional back-up. She taught us to speak fluent placenta, perineum, amniotic, transition and episiotomy. We were trying for a natural birth but in a hospital setting, to minimise all risk. We toured Lismore Hospital, wrote the birth plan, packed the bags and waited.

I had asked a friend, filmmaker Cathy Henkyl, to film the birth. Part of me was appalled that I was letting myself be filmed in this most private, primal, out of control state. At least, I reasoned, I would have a good home movie. I could decide later whether I would allow this material to be broadcast.

For the first time in my life I had nothing planned. No job, no course, no trip. I understood why the words expectant and pregnant are interchangeable. Everything was on hold. Waiting to enter the void, the unknown. I came to understand something essential about women, the courage they have found to birth their babies. The more you know about childbirth, the scarier it can become, especially if you are trying to do it the natural way. Before the days of epidurals and pain relief, women knew they faced death during labour, might even welcome it after days of agony. It takes courage to face certain pain, and in the months leading up to the birth I felt in awe of all the mothers who had gone before me. I regarded myself as fit and strong, but still I was shit scared. It wasn't so much birth but fear of it that was my initiation into womanhood. Marvelling at women's strength and courage, I also grew brave. Often for a full five minutes at a time.

It was a long hot summer. We planned renovations, walling up a study for Michael and moving the laundry from underneath the house. But as these things do, it dragged on and on. The day the baby was due, there were dropsheets over the furniture as the house filled with the dust of sanded Gyprock, deeply offending my nesting instinct. Michael had been on his own nesting frenzy, cleaning out every cupboard in the house – I think as a way to stay busy and keep his mind off *the end of life as we knew it*. We had reached an unspoken truce, just to be kind to each other and not get into too many heavy conversations. We did laps every morning down in Byron, retired to a cafe for breakfast and quietly read the paper together.

Michael and I were talking around this time about gratitude and how it is a form of love. We lay together in the bath one day, speaking about all the things we were grateful for, and how gratitude can be a way to pay homage to God.

'But the trouble is,' I said, 'sometimes I feel I have so much to be grateful for in my life, I'm scared to admit it.'

'Why would you be scared?'

'Because maybe God will notice me and all the gifts I've been given and think, Geez, she's had it good. I better smote her.'

'A smoting. You'll have a huge smoting.' Michael laughed.

'Exactly. God will smote me down so I *really* understand the nature of gratitude.'

'I don't think it works like that,' said Michael, but he was wrong. I was just days away from an enormous smoting.

The day after Valentine's Day 2000, I was six days overdue and up a ladder painting when strange electric shocks began shooting down my legs. The first serious labour pain hit early evening as I was cooking. I took two steps around the kitchen bench and fell forward onto the floor. Dramatic. Just like in the movies.

I began groaning in the bath but the pain was still manageable. I was in control enough to think about shaving my legs. They had a few days' stubble and I knew they were about to be on public display for many hours. But I was embarrassed to be thinking this, and sent Michael out of the bathroom on an errand. I managed each leg with a contraction in between.

We retired to bed, where I lay resting and moaning at three-minute intervals, Michael trying to stay awake next to me.

'Let's go to the hospital,' I said at around two a.m. 'I may not be able to move if this gets much worse. I think I'll feel safer there.'

Nightmares

There are nightmares you can wake from. Heart-palpitating bad dreams that end when the eyes open. And then there are the nightmares of real life. Sudden ones like car accidents, or those that creep up on you, like the on-set of a life-threatening illness. The nightmares that offer no escape.

Mine crept up on me about twelve hours into labour.

Already I was out of control. Massive waves of pain picked me up every three minutes and surged through my body, so fierce I would vomit from the pain after the worst of them. As the hours passed, I felt life draining from my body, dehydration setting in. Everything I drank came up again at the next purge, acidic Gatorade burning my throat.

I don't know why I didn't 'give in' earlier, why I held out so long without asking for pain relief. I suppose I was trying to hold on to the ideal of a natural birth. I moved from the bed to the shower, standing and sitting there for hours, searing my body with hot water, hollering in full voice at each contraction just to let out the pain. Shitting myself, moaning, panting in full supplication. I was now an animal. Lying on a mattress on the floor, I was too exhausted for thought, riding the agonising roller-coaster as it wrenched my pelvis open. After seventeen hours I was a pathetic

131

creature begging for mercy. If you've been there, you'd know that once you decide you need an epidural, each contraction seems even harder to bear. The anaesthetist was in some operating room and couldn't get there for two hours: the longest two hours of my life. I begged for Michael to find him and bring him here. When the anaesthetist did finally arrive, he was irritated and patronising, but I didn't care. I just wanted him to give me a break from the pain.

The epidural block went in, and I was lost in a fog of exhaustion. I didn't see that the heart rate monitor was showing foetal distress. I imagine that concerned words must have been muttered and someone sent to call my obstretician, because suddenly there was Phil Steele, calling out as he examined me. 'You're nine centimetres dilated, so you're almost there.' Taking off his gloves, his calm, concerned face above mine. 'It's still some time before the baby comes . . . we're seeing deep dips now with every contraction . . . the baby looks like it's in distress . . . the best option is to take you upstairs.'

He didn't mention the word Caesarean but I knew that's what he meant. 'Do it,' I said, my thoughts a mixture of defeat and relief – relief that I had to do no more, that the rest was out of my hands. Crowding in on those thoughts was terror, like an arrow shot straight to the heart. *My baby in distress? Impossible.* Suddenly the room was alive with nurses moving in a fast but very calm way, one shaving me, another leaning over with some form I had to sign, another attaching drips. Everywhere movement.

Michael's worried face hovered above me as Santo called out, 'It'll be all right.' Then I was lying on a trolley, paralysed with epidural and terror. Out in the corridor, other patients made way for us to pass. I couldn't believe I was now an emergency, my baby was now an emergency.

Perhaps God heard that Michael did not want her?

We were in the lifts now and I whispered to him, 'Tell God that you want her.'

He leaned over. 'What?'

'Tell God that you want her.'

I could see the fear and guilt in his eyes.

'I want her to live, Vanessa.'

But I didn't want him to tell *me*, I wanted him to tell God. I think I just wanted him to start praying.

'It'll only be a moment and you'll have your baby with you,' called Santo as I was wheeled into the operating theatre. It seemed crowded with masked faces; some said hello, all of them seemed busy. I was lifted onto the operating table, feeling like a corpse.

Bright lights, the clang of instruments, a backing track of beeping monitors. Then the searing of flesh. Dr Phil calling out his progress. The tug of skin, the dull pulling as she is lifted out, the sucking vacuum as she leaves my body, taking my breath away. A weird grief that she is gone. The loud, choking cry of my baby giving way to the sounds of ventilation and suction.

I strain to hear her. The midwife calls out, 'It's a beautiful baby girl.'

Michael stares at the baby. The clock reads 3.25 p.m. Minutes pass and then the midwife has her wrapped tight and I see her for the first time, her face both familiar and a delightful surprise. But her breath comes in short sharp gasps, the effort creasing her brow. I stroke her face with a quivering finger, wanting her to stay, wanting them to take her and help her breathe. Michael says, 'Hello', in the most tender of tones.

Somewhere above me the young paediatrician hovers. I hear frightening half-sentences. 'Meconium . . . we sucked quite a bit out but there is probably still more . . . see how she's having trouble? . . . have to keep a close watch on her . . .'

I want them to stop talking now and take care of her. To hurry. To rush. 'Do what you have to do', I say, but I want to shout, 'Stop talking and hurry now.'

She is blue by the time she gets to the nursery downstairs and five minutes later her heart stops. They revive her. Her nightmare is underway as tubes are pushed down her throat, electrodes attached, the pain of intense intervention her first experience on this earth.

My nightmare deepens in Recovery when they tell me she is struggling for every breath. The unthinkable. I feel like I am dying. I cannot feel my body from the chest down. She is dying and, still connected, I feel the life draining from my own body. Thinking that if she dies, I want to go too. I don't want to live in a future without her, don't want to face that level of grief.

News comes of the possibility of brain damage. A new wave of despair, *my beautiful healthy baby a vegetable*. The unthinkable. I'd been so looking forward to meeting her mind, downing fish oil capsules to make her brain healthy.

Michael comes to my bedside weeping, traumatised by what they are putting her through. Traumatised that I might blame him for not wanting her passionately, like I did. We weep together. He tells me that a team from Brisbane are flying down by helicopter to retrieve her. The nightmare deepens. My body begins to shiver. Cold pulses of shock. I can't reach her. Strangers are poking things into her, wiring her, no one is holding her. I can feel her primal distress and I cannot move to seek her out.

Life has drained from me, as if my body has gone on ahead and all I need to do is close my eyes and the soul will follow.

'I feel like I'm dying,' I whisper to Cathy, who stands vigil over my bed.

She strokes my forehead, tears streaming down her face.

'I think I'm dying,' I say again, but what I mean is that I am preparing to die if I need to. I recognise I am in a hospital and they will try to keep my body alive. I wonder if I can die by sheer force of will. The thought that *she* might die is like a physical assault. The pain is absurd, monstrous. My heart is drowning. My mind is trying desperately to kick towards the surface, to emerge from this swamp.

'Fight, little girl,' I plead.

Cathy has fetched a nurse who checks my pulse and assures me I'm not dying. She doesn't understand this may not be good news.

They wheel me from Recovery to a hospital room. I hold up my hands to the passing air and inside ask for Jesus and all the saints and all the great beings to come and be with us in this moment, to help her live. The rational part of my brain feels histrionic, self-conscious.

I am parked in a room dim with late-afternoon light and nurses move around the bed clipping and unclipping drips. Someone makes me drink some water. The shaking is uncontrollable now and they pile four layers of blankets over my bed.

I am left alone in the deepening gloom, the last of the sunset spilling eerily through grey tinted windows. I am beyond exhaustion but fear that if I close my eyes, I will pass out. I need to keep vigil. I stare at the wall clock, look away for hours and look back. Only two minutes have passed. The longest hour unfolds as the sunset fades to black.

Michael comes in. He is leaving to drive to Brisbane with a friend, Jeff. I hear the word 'stabilised'. He seems cheerful and optimistic. A weird euphoria begins to grow. Nurses enter and record my vital signs every half-hour. I joke with them. Shock thaws into heat and my sweat drenches the bed.

Another hour passes but I have hope now to keep me company. I am straining to hear the helicopter take off. Waiting for news, trying to stay awake.

About nine p.m., Santo comes in. She is crying. She says, 'She's not so good, sweetheart,' with the downward inflection of bad news, and I know it is worse than that. I plead with the ceiling. Shake my head.

'They want to wheel you around to see her before she leaves for Brisbane.'

I try to think of a question to ask but I can't find the part of my brain that forms sentences. The wait seems to last forever and then a nurse bursts in and rearranges drips to make me portable. She enlists Santo and a friend, Sarah, and suddenly it is like a military operation as I am wheeled from the room and down corridors towards an even wider corridor. The neon ceiling lights pass like a movie cliché.

She is waiting but I cannot see her. She is hidden inside a huge machine, a portable humidicrib, which sits blinking lights and vital signs, flaps pulled over to regulate temperature. The paediatrician from Brisbane, a man with soft, sorry eyes, introduces himself and tells me she is sedated for the journey and they are just about to leave. That it has taken some time to prepare her to travel, that they will airlift her to Brisbane where they will try one last machine, but they don't hold out much hope for her survival. I search his eyes for better news but he keeps the same sorry gaze fixed on me. I plead at him with my eyes because that is all I can do, but somewhere deep inside my brain I am screaming, *You don't understand how precious this baby is, you don't understand how long I have been waiting to meet her, she will be a beautiful being and cherished by many, she will make a difference to the world.*

I want him to know all this so he will try as hard as he can to save her, but telling him would take time and there is hardly any time left to save her. They lift the flaps so I can look at her a last time. The stitches strain to break as I try to lift myself. Someone helps prop me up and there she is, on her side, naked except for a nappy and a little white woollen bonnet. Tubes down her nose and mouth, monitors attached to her chest, no room left for a mother to stroke. Except her forehead. I stroke it but she is not there. Her arm is stretched out, her hand cups the air. I place my finger in her palm, hoping to feel her tiny fingers grip me with the instinct of a newborn, but there is no response. And I know then that she has lost her grip on life.

I look on her, trying to drink her in, torn between wanting it to last forever and wanting her to be rushed to the machine that might be her only chance of life. I whisper goodbye.

I lie down and they cover the humidicrib again. I plead something at the doctor like, *Please try as hard as you can.*

He nods sadly and says, 'We better go now,' and they move away.

I am turned and pushed in the other direction and as she slips away from me a cry rises from the depth of all the grief I've ever known. Santo covers my eyes with her hand and I reach to my mouth to stifle this horrible moan in so public a place.

I am wheeled back to the room and wait to hear the helicopter take off. A nurse gives me a sleeping pill and I am gone. My vigil is over. She is in others' hands now and all that is left to do is surrender to my exhaustion.

My friend Sarah Armstrong wrote this poem the next afternoon.

In That Moment

All that existed in that moment was you and your baby
There were no tubes and wires crossing her tiny body
No massive trolley, equipment humming and blinking
as it breathed for her
No stark hospital corridor, blinding fluorescent white
No specialists standing by in dark blue jumpsuits and backpacks
No grey-haired ambulance men
averting their eyes from your anguish
No nurses, no carers trying to support you
as you lifted your wounded body
to stretch your fingers towards her

In that moment there was just you and Layla,
hand to hand, finger to finger
Mother to daughter
In that moment.

INTERVIEW TRANSCRIPT
Michael's experience after birth

When they took me downstairs to be with her after the birth she was
just doing these huge gulps for breath and someone was pumping
this black bag over her face and she had tubes coming out and I got
a really big shock. That's when reality caught up with naivety because
up until that point I didn't think there was anything really wrong.

They weren't saying, 'Come over here.' I had to push my way in
and I had this awful feeling like it was my fault because I had been

resistant to her coming and I hadn't really connected much to her in the womb. I had been pissed at Vanessa for even being pregnant, so when there was a baby that was in a life-and-death situation, I felt I had caused it. That she was dying through lack of love or something. I thought she was going to die at any breath. I had to barge my way in there and I knelt down beside her and held her hand and I just needed to tell her that I loved her and I wanted her – and that was a big surprise, so I felt like my love could keep her alive then. I wanted to be a pillar of softness next to her so she could get a sense of something human there.

The nurses asked me what her name was and 'Layla' just came out. It was on our shortlist of names and it just seemed to be the one. I just kept telling her I loved her and I wanted her, telling her to live. I just kept repeating it over and over and over.

There was all this love around. The actual people right there working with her were very present and very still and quiet and there was no panic around. I remember thinking, Who are these amazing people? I remember feeling so surprised that I loved her and that I wanted her to live. It was amazing standing over this humidicrib saying, 'I love you. I want you to live,' and meaning it with every ounce of my body. It was like, 'Hmmm, is this me?' The nine months previous I'd been thinking, Bugger off, go somewhere else.

(laughs)

Jeff and I left to drive to Brisbane just after the helicopter people arrived. The Lismore paediatrician said he'd seen cases like this where he had just been to their third birthday and it was probably going to be okay, so when I left I thought it was going to be fine. We stopped for pizza on the way.

We were waiting at the Mater Mothers' Hospital for an hour or so before the helicopter arrived. Then six guys and a big machine with

Layla in it ran in and I thought, My God, it's really an emergency. They wouldn't let me in with her. They said they had to set things up and get her stabilised and to wait. I told Jeff to go back to the hotel and I thought I would hang round with Layla for a while and then go and get some sleep. I was still planning to be there for a week with her.

They took me down to the room. The doctor came out very ashen-faced, looking a bit angry, and I can't remember exactly what he said, more his face, basically intimating that there was very little they could do now, and did I realise this was the case, and I actually didn't realise this was the case at all. But I didn't show the shock. They took me in and showed me Layla, who was all tubed up but very different from how she was in Lismore, very close to death. I tried to get her to hold my finger but there was no life left in her little hand.

They explained that her lungs had popped. When they have to pump the lungs with oxygen, there's a danger of too much pressure going in and the lungs burst, so when that happens they can no longer get oxygen flowing into the lungs, so it was kind of hopeless. So she was just about dead and they asked me if I wanted the tubes taken off so I could hold her. And I had felt all along the pain of my baby not being held, so I said, 'Yes,' and they put her in my arms and I remember holding her and thinking, This is how it feels to be holding a dying person, and I was kind of waiting for a flash or a rush or a jolt in the body. I was waiting for the moment to be delineated and it wasn't. There was no difference between the last moment of life and the first moment of death but I quickly understood that I was holding . . . that Layla had died. I think I just went numb.

The nurses took Layla's body away and suggested that Michael go back to the hotel and get some sleep. They told him they would bathe and clothe her and he could pick her up in the morning. In his shocked state he agreed. But after talking it over with Jeff, thank God he had the presence of mind to ask if he could take her body back to Lismore that night.

There was a whole lot of red tape to get through, a flurry of phone calls, a weird demand that he carry the body in a plastic bag. Then they drove through Michael's second night without sleep to bring Layla home.

Two nurses wake me at four a.m. and I am silently bathed with a facecloth. They are tender and gentle and I understand why people call them angels. I wonder if they know something but I don't ask. I am surrendered to waiting.

At five a.m. Michael opens the door to my room. That he is back tells me that she is dead but I hold my breath and wait. He comes over to me and I read it in his eyes.

'She didn't make it,' he says with soft resignation, and I feel the shock that I knew was coming.

He goes out, and when he opens the door again he is for a moment silhouetted against the light of the corridor. He is holding the body of Layla, a bundle snuggled against his chest, circled by one strong arm. It is the first time I have seen him hold a baby.

He brings her to me and I hold her for the first time, pulling her into me like I will never let her go. Her body in my arms the most natural surprise.

I do not know how to describe that confluence of love and despair.

After a while a nurse wheels in a bath and we undress and bathe her. Cathy has come to film this christening and pads quietly around in the background, crying through the camera's eye-piece.

Michael holds Layla tenderly, like he might a tiny angel with a broken wing. The silence is sacred, just the splash of water as we anoint her, baptising her with bath water. Her body floats on the surface. There are none of the startled thrashings of a newborn.

I can feel a roaring wave in the distance. The wave of grief that I know will pick me up and dump me with animal ferocity. But right now I lie there and watch her still, silent face and know that I am beyond even the place of tears.

LAYLA FRANCES SHAW

*Layla died just before midnight on the night of 16 February 2000,
eight hours after birth. She died from meconium aspiration. Meconium is
the baby's first poo, often released in utero when the baby is in distress.
A sticky tar-like substance, if inhaled it can coat the lungs and make
breathing difficult. Most babies survive this condition.*

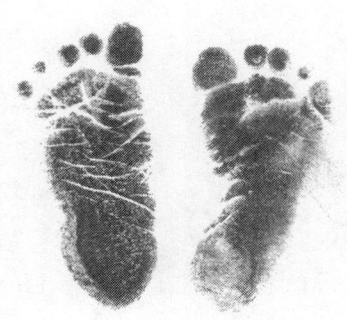

Freefall

An unexpected death, a death 'too soon', is like a portal into an adjoining universe. There are no bearings. You move helplessly on currents of black despair and shock, confused by finding both beauty there and a strange hysteria.

How to describe that next four days in hospital? We were at the centre of a drama we didn't want to witness, let alone play the leading roles.

Dr Phil Steele came to see us that first morning.

'Why, why?'

'We don't know yet.'

'Is there anything we should have done? Could have done?'

'We don't know.'

His face so sorry. Sorry, too, that he had no answers yet. His compassion a calm river of grace.

My mother and sisters arrived a little later, after an all-night vigil in Sydney and rushing to catch the first plane north. I had been hanging on, waiting for them to arrive before I could let go, knowing I would be safe with them beside me. The beautiful, deep, indelible bonds of family – these women that I loved with a passion, their presence unleashing the first great sobbing.

I want them to see her. I unwrap her and show them the

perfection, the chubbiness. So desperately wanting to show her off. So proud of my creation even in her lifelessness.

But the bruises, the cuts around her chest, all her wounds of a battle lost.

'Ness, I fell asleep for an hour this morning before we caught the plane and I dreamt of her,' whispers my sister Alex, her eyes swollen with tears. 'She was there, through the window at the end of the back verandah of Fairfield, speaking to me, bathed in the brightest light, and she was saying, "Look where I am. I am here now", and I knew when I woke up that she must have died but she was in a beautiful place. She looked so beautiful.'

Later I am unhooked from the drips and Alex helps me into the shower. My body feels bruised, exhausted, battered: fragile as a wounded baby bird.

Leah and Richard, two dear friends that have witnessed our emotional upheaval during the pregnancy, arrive in the afternoon. Leah picks up Layla and holds her against her chest. Layla's small, precious feet encased in booties hang beneath Leah's arm, turned out like frog legs, the tenderest sight. Leah begins howling, a full-bodied, no holds barred howl. It feels good to watch her. Imprisoned within my wounded body, unable to scream, it feels like she is doing it for me. Leah, who had never wanted a child, told me later that in that moment she suddenly understood she wanted to be a mother. Layla had begun her work on earth.

The Caesarean added another level of shock but it was a blessing in disguise: I had to stay in hospital for four days to recover, which meant I could spend time with Layla's body. It was warm and soft the day after her death but that night Alex composed her features and took her down to the coldroom where she would be kept overnight. In the morning Alex retrieved her, wrapped her in a bunny rug and brought her to me. I will never forget that moment.

'Ness, she's a little bit cold,' warned Alex, handing me a freezing bundle. Her cheeks hard like iceblocks, her eyes frozen tightly closed.

'Oh my God,' I cried, dissolving again into helpless tears, holding her close, trying to warm her body with my own. Feeling the crack in my heart widen.

Some may wonder why anyone would choose to experience such a thing. Better perhaps to hand the body over to a funeral director and bury the lost one a few days later. But I had learnt through my father's death that to avoid the reality of death was a dangerous and ultimately futile path. Tears were the ventilation of a breaking heart, the only tool I had to aid the seemingly impossible task of healing.

I needed so desperately to nurture Layla in whatever way I could. I needed a chance to be her mother. To be close to her, to see that she had my snub nose and hair exactly the honey-blonde of Michael's. That her ears were tiny like mine, her feet exactly the shape of my mother's, that she had large hands, like her father's. I thought her the most beautiful creature, but each day we felt the lifeforce dissolve, slipping away from her body, preparing us for the inevitable relinquishing.

Mornings are the worst, to come out of sleep and into the terrible reality all over again. Michael climbs into bed and holds me while I sob. From the rooms around me, all day and night comes a chorus of the cries of newborns, a bitter sting to my ears.

Michael's family fly in from Melbourne. Without a thought, his mother Nancy gathers Layla tenderly in her arms and holds her close, her eyes full of tears. Robbed of her second grandchild.

The beauty and the sadness live like the rose and thorn. The dead child seems to strike right to the heart of everyone around us, striking them open, exposing us to the very core of their humanity. A great transference of love occurs until we are covered by a warm blanket of tenderness. Santo tirelessly takes charge of the practical details while our families take care of every physical need. I had always found it difficult to receive; much easier to give to others. Lying there in my wounded state I recognise that the only way to give is to receive. Everybody is so desperately sorry and their way of expressing that is to tend to any whim. My younger sister Rebecca gives me hand and foot massages. My mother makes me laugh, ironing a fresh nightie each day. They fight to bring beautiful food and make us eat. I wonder how people cope without this level of support.

The room fills with the flowers of sympathy. Someone tacks brightly coloured sari material to the walls so I feel like a princess lying in state, my only job to be administered to. Freed from taking care of myself, I hold Layla and cry. And sometimes late at night we all sit and dissolve into hysterical laughter that pulls at my stitches and lifts me into a transcendent state, a weird, heightened reality.

One moment raised high by love, the next plunged back into shock, her loss something I can still barely comprehend.

On Losing a Baby

I am only one in a long line of women who have lost their child at birth. Only twenty years ago, parents who lost a baby to still-birth or neonatal mishap in a Western hospital did not even get to glimpse the child. The body was whisked from the delivery room and parents were advised against seeing their baby, who would be buried in a mass, unmarked grave. Medical authorities believed it was better that way, and parents were told to go home and forget and 'try for another one', as though that baby was replaceable.

In the eighties a new movement began, led by social workers, doctors, parents and healthcare professionals who wanted to give parents the right to spend time with the body of their baby, to hold them, bathe and dress them, take photographs, foot- and hand-prints, locks of hair. These will be the only material trace the parents will have of their child, and will be cherished possessions.

This movement was brought to public awareness in Australia by neonatologist Dr Peter Barr and Deb De Wilde, a midwife and social worker. Support groups sprang up. SANDS, the Stillbirth and Neonatal Death Society, offers support to parents who have experienced any kind of pregnancy loss. The Compassionate Friends, SIDS and Kids, and Bonnie Babes are among other groups that work towards raising awareness of a loss that is sometimes perceived to be 'less than' other deaths, as though 'not knowing' the baby will cushion parents against grief.

By extraordinary coincidence, my sister Alex, a social worker, had been trained only the year before by Deb De Wilde in the sensitive art of obstetric social work, which involves supporting parents who lose a baby before, during or after birth. It was Alex's presence, along with the enlightened professionals around us, that helped make a 'good' experience in the face of a terrible one. Alex quietly snapped rolls of film of Layla, the most precious pictures in my collection.

Parents who have lost a baby are plunged into shock. They don't know what to do, what is allowed, how to arrange a funeral that will be meaningful. There is no right way, no prescription for this experience. Parents need the support and guidance of sensitive professionals who can give them options and a sense of control. They need the compassion of family and friends. And afterwards, the particular understanding that comes from people who have walked the same path.

Ceremony

We walk toward the hospital exit, Layla a newborn bundle snuggled against my chest, making people smile as we pass. Out we go into the obscenely bright sunshine of a February day, into a world that functions as though nothing has happened. We have been released to attend a small family ceremony that afternoon. Alex and Santo have arranged for us to take Layla's body home overnight, a practice not normally allowed. Her body must be released into the care of a funeral home, but a wonderful funeral director, Denise Patten, has agreed to sign the papers so we can take her.

Michael and I return home. I sit alone in the bathroom holding Layla and a blackness descends. Not the dramatic rise and fall of the last few days but a depressing harbinger of the future. Thinking that after everyone has gone home, after the flowers have died and the phone stops ringing, this will be my future, a home without Layla. A slow sinking gloom takes hold of my body, hunching my shoulders, her still form pressed against the aching cavity where once she thrived.

The ceremony began in the golden light of late afternoon in our rearranged living room. Michael exuded a kind of nobility as he spoke of our grief.

'We believe that crying is part of what heals, a sign that you are in pain but also that the pain is dissolving. We both feel strongly that this ceremony is a symbol of letting go, but it's also a new beginning. Life can't go back now to how it was before this happened. So life begins, in a sense, from here. There's a lot of pain and a different way of looking at the world, and I feel hopeful that it actually softens and deepens us. It involves having everything that we are going to have, and not needing to sweep it away. Everybody in this room is affected in their own way. They go on a bit differently, a little deeper, so she is an amazing little person . . .

'I look across to someone that I love, Vanessa, and I see this bottomless place of pain and this deep, deep agony, and I feel like I don't want to back away from that place in you and I don't want anyone to back away from that place. So I chose this poem that I want to read and I mean to offend no one.'

Then he read these lines from 'Feeling Fucked Up', by Etheridge Knight.

Lord she gone done left me done packed / up and split
and I with no way to make her
come back and everywhere the world is bare . . .

Fuck Coltrane and music and clouds drifting in the sky
fuck the sea and trees and the sky and birds
and alligators and all the animals that roam the earth
fuck marx and mao fuck fidel and nkrumah and
democracy and communism fuck smack and pot
and red ripe tomatoes fuck joseph fuck mary fuck
god jesus and all the disciples fuck fanon nixon

151

and malcolm fuck the revolution fuck freedom fuck
the whole muthafucking thing
all I want now is my [baby] back
so my soul can sing

Yeah, I thought when he finished. *Exactly. Fuck the whole muthafucking thing.*

Phil Steele had come and we invited him to speak. He described the circumstances around the labour and birth and the efforts the teams of medicos had made to save her. 'I'd like to share with you as a professional, and here I speak for obstetricians and midwives. We have the privilege of sharing the deepest joy of couples' lives when they welcome a newborn. But for about one in a hundred births, for all manner of reasons, we also share their deepest pain, of losing a newborn child.'

And then he looked at us and spoke straight from the heart. 'What would I say to Michael and Vanessa and to all who grieve her? I would say I'm sorry that I did not help bring your child safely into this world and I'd say I share your grief that your life will never be blessed by the living presence of Layla.'

I'm sorry. The sound of those words sent a great rush of energy through my body, like all the anger and confusion around her death had their first release in the face of his humility, his quiet admission that even in the twenty-first century we still have no absolute control over life and death.

People would later ask me if I had ever contemplated suing the hospital or health professionals involved. And of course it occurred to me, especially when hearing about people receiving ridiculous sums for seemingly inconsequential losses. But I rejected the idea. The culture of blaming others, of seeking retribution through the court, has got out of hand. And technically, everyone did all they could. Ultimately, Layla had the misfortune of being born in a hospital too small to deal with that level of emergency. But there was another reason I did not want to sue – it would not bring her back. And I would always think of Phil Steele's words of heartfelt sorrow, for which I am forever grateful.

My mother read a beautiful letter to her grandchild. Alex read out a letter to me. 'How could I tell you how much sorrow I feel in my heart for you? If I could, I would carry you far, far away to a safe place where the world could not touch you. If I could, I would cry your tears and howl your grief at the moon. If I could, I would turn back time and make everything all right for you. Ness, I love Layla like my own flesh and blood. She was beautiful and gracious and precious beyond words and we will never ever forget her. Ness, I want to tell you that I love you and will do so till the day I die.'

We sang together to finish. 'Swing low, sweet chariot, coming for to carry me home'. And I felt God's hand sweep perilously close, coming for to carry her home.

Still Life

*T*hat night was the stillest I could remember. Not a puff of wind, no frogs, no crickets. Utter silence. Layla lay between us in the bed and when I was sure Michael was asleep, I took her onto my chest and cradled her tightly under my chin. Her body, rock-solid cold that morning, had thawed after the warm bath before her ceremony.

I slept and woke into moonlight, Layla as silent as the night. I began to sing the lullaby we had sung that afternoon. *You kissed my blood and your blood kissed me . . .*

Michael stirred and came up on one elbow. His attention brought me to tears but the movement in and out of tears was not so great and we began to sing together. *Brighter than the brightest star, you are, by far . . .*

We forgot some of the words but sang defiantly on, bruising the silence. Some time after that we drifted off again.

I woke before dawn, emerging from a dream I couldn't hold on to. She was cradled against my chest. I began to stroke her hair and then her face. I loosened the bunny rug and tracked a path down to her neck and shoulders, my breath catching at the softness of the skin beneath her neck. I caressed from her shoulders up to her cheek, around her scalp, curling her hair as I went, then down across her eyes, over her nose, her mouth, down to her chest and back to her shoulder. I stroked obsessively, a desperate Braille reading. Her body was due to be burnt before lunch.

When Alex arrived, we checked her bunny rug for bloodstains. She'd been leaking tiny droplets of blood from her mouth and nose for a couple of days. Alex and I had been tending to her with great discretion, like we would a daughter's first menstruation.

'She's leaked a little blood from her mouth,' she whispered.

We wrapped her in the white muslin with red hearts and joked that the bloodstains would blend in. Alex tucked a tissue in as a bib. 'Keep that there for the drive,' she said conspiratorially, 'and try to keep her head back when you hold her.'

All neatly wrapped now, I cradled her tenderly under my chin, just like she was sleeping. A single teardrop of blood fell from her nose, as if she was trying to tell me that she understood my heart was breaking.

This was my first visit to a crematorium. I remember the day was too sunny, the light too harsh on salty eyes. Rosebushes with plaques lined the drive. Outside the chapel, the grandparents posed for last photos with the bundle.

A sense that we had to get on, as the next group of mourners was due soon. Not wanting to traipse that wretched aisle, but knowing I had to walk forward, Layla in my arms, her tiny white coffin waiting before a red curtain. Sensing that behind the curtains lay cement corridors, stainless-steel trolleys, the oven itself.

The funeral director, Denise, said some words at the lectern. Something about the notion that a rosebud picked will stay perfect forever. And that sometimes a life is lived in a single breath or heartbeat but it is no less precious than one lived for years, and the pain of the loss no less real. Her words were brief. It felt right.

Sitting over her body that last time, our families gathered in a tight circle. Everyone crying now. Anointing her face with my tears, wanting her to take my sorrow through to the other side. Not wanting to ever let her go but knowing it is time. My chest seems to be exploding from within. Michael holds on to me as we place her gently down into that obscene bassinet, making her comfortable, just so, placing a little marble statue in there, and all the tiny paper blessings from everyone, and the single red rosebud on top of her. Kissing her still beautiful, tiny, so still face one last time. Closing that lid and turning the screws. And then finally and literally feeling my heart actually break, the surprise of that. I had thought it a figure of speech, but there it was.

Singing 'Swing Low Sweet Chariot'. Wanting to sing it loud. Really wanting God to hear it and swing low for her, to carry her to a good home. Singing badly but loud. Not caring. And then Michael presses the button and the belt moves and with our families in full voice we sing her through to the other side.

The weird relief that the hardest job of all is over. And then the numbness.

As we drove slowly away from the crematorium, we passed a woman with a baby in a pram. I looked away and there coming down the hill on the other side of the road was another woman, pushing a small girl in a wheelchair. The girl was bent over, twisted, suggesting she had some kind of brain damage. I could have shared either woman's destiny.

Ordered to bed for the next few days, I opened the plastic bag that had been sent from the hospital, what I came to call the *dead baby showbag*. Literature from SANDS gave me the cold comfort that I was not alone in this journey. But still it snapped my head back in shock – that instead of a baby in the bed, I had a showbag full of pamphlets and booklets with titles like 'Your Baby Has Died'.

'I thought this only happened in the Middle Ages,' I cried to my girlfriend Ruth, 'only when the baby had something terribly wrong with it.'

Inside, I was crying the universal lament, *why me, why me?* My need simple and hopeless. Wanting it to be different. Wanting her back.

Two days after we cremated her body, I woke to find the front of my cotton nightie drenched. At first I couldn't work out where all this moisture had come from. I genuinely didn't know. And when it dawned on me, I felt a kind of alarmed embarrassment.

I had loved watching my breasts evolve during pregnancy, swelling from 12B into magnificent 14C's, giving me the first cleavage of my life. I had longed to feel her mouth on me, my love flowing into her body.

In hospital I'd endured cold cabbage leaves stuffed down my tightly bound bra, trailing the aroma of garbage rotting behind a Chinese takeaway. People brought sage tea and homeopathic remedies and the flow was stemmed. Now it was back and I rang the district nurse, who suggested in polite words that I should 'milk' myself.

I stood naked at the bathroom mirror, stared at all that useless stomach flab and the angry scar of Layla's entry into the world. I squeezed each breast toward the nipple, marvelling at the sight of sticky fluid weeping from my flesh, split between triumph and despair. Mourning her.

A week later, we held a ceremony at home for our community of friends. I still felt a raw nakedness that made it hard to be the focus of all those faces, raw with their own compassion. Cathy had edited footage of Layla to music, so we could make her real for others. The tender sorrow of our friends encircled us as poems were read and we sang together. I felt such enormous gratitude to belong to this open-hearted tribe that understood grief and welcomed it as an inevitable passage of life. All during that time, and for many months afterwards, we felt sympathetic arms reaching out to hold us, friends offering help in a hundred ways, so that finally I understood the true meaning of community and the healing it offers.

I can speak of my empty arms and aching breasts, my sadness of a future without her in it, but I also grieved so terribly for Layla losing her chance to experience life. That she would never feel the comfort of being held skin to skin, never know the two-year-old's exhilaration in jumping from a couch onto a pile of cushions. Never sit in the warm spring sunshine and make daisy chains, feel her legs accelerate down a grassy embankment. The laughter of being tickled, the taste of chocolate, the wind in her face when riding a bicycle, spooning with a lover. The million experiences of a lifetime stolen from her; her only taste of life outside the womb saw her helpless in the face of what must have felt like torture.

I would wake sometimes at four a.m. and wander the house, opening doors, knowing I would not find a miracle but still compelled to search. Questioning the fading stars and dawn glow for her whereabouts. Ending up before her urn of ashes with the bitterest disappointment etched on my heart.

Michael and I began a sexual relationship again, soon after Layla's death. Which was surprising, because it had been a while since we'd had sex.

In the last half of my pregnancy I began to embody those old English words, fulsome, mettlesome. I felt all woman. Unfortunately, Michael was closed down, feeling betrayed. It was not until Layla was struggling for breath that his heart opened in love for her. After she died, his heart expanded even more as the wave of love from friends and family washed over us. And as his heart rekindled, his sexuality seemed to find fire as well.

As I lay wounded in bed, tended to by my mother and younger sister, he began to stay up late and surf the porn sites of cyberspace. Our Internet bookmarks became a study in hilarious juxtaposition - nastyandrudesexacts.com sat uneasily above babymemorial.org.

He would come to bed and hold me while I cried and I would feel his erection grow rock hard against my thigh. I would lie there, four layers of my abdomen sewn together just above the shaved strip of pubic hair, my heart broken in two for the loss of Layla. And I would feel my passion for him start to rise. It was part passion and part desperate need to feel someone close. We would whisper earnest truths about our love, reassuring each other of survival through the storm.

And because it was too soon after birth for him to penetrate me, he slid a pillow beneath me, spread my legs and kissed me so gently, like he was licking dewdrops off the edge of a palm frond. A confusing thrill of lust shot through my veins and I shook my head in disgust that I could enter into an act like this so soon after her death. But I lay there and let the wave rise, too exhausted by grief to do anything but surrender to desire.

As the wave rose, an image of the green-and-silver of the operating theatre flashed through my head, and the stiffness of Layla's body when she came back from the coolroom that second day. It was as if the scar above my pubic bone was a line separating a disembodied pleasure zone from the tortures of my mind.

After this many years, his tongue was skilled and so the orgasm rose and Michael let out a low rumble, responding to my confused passion. I was worried I might tear the stitches and somehow render myself infertile forever but still the pleasure grew and I moaned and thought, What kind of slut would allow herself this pleasure when her baby daughter is only recently dead? And still Michael's tongue worked on me until the wave overtook thought.

Ecstatic shivers of sexual ecstasy washed over me, unleashing the sobs that rose from every cell, vibrations that pulsed right through the soul. I made wild noises, sobs of pain borne on the wings of bodily delight. And with this, a wave of utter shame.

Michael embraced the mystery of this as he came up to embrace me, cradling me to his chest like a crumpled parcel of fragile, damaged goods, unperturbed by the unnameable.

JOURNAL MARCH 2000

Grief is another country. A land of wandering aliens, shocked to find themselves there. Disorientated, disillusioned, without a passport.

The days pass like I am on some roller-coaster ride of shock, rage, fear, despair, sorrow and beauty. I couldn't leave the house for weeks and then with a deep breath I let Michael drive me down to Byron. We pivot that first roundabout and there is life again. Shops open, people wandering the street, buskers playing. Life moving, turning, churning – the way it always has. But my head was cocked sideways, trying to make out the familiar territory in such a strange place.

I am trapped in a no-man's-land. I feel a kind of panic rise at the thought of joining a world where I no longer belong. Michael shepherds me tenderly from shop to shop. I am dreading meeting someone I know and yet I scan the crowd for some familiar face who might understand why I am screaming on the inside.

The world seems full of pregnant women, babies in prams. I look at every pregnant woman and I wonder if her baby might die and I wonder if she knows it could die. I want her to know. I want to squeeze her arm and tell her to be careful. But the horrible truth is, in some dark part of my heart I also want to hear of other babies dying so I am not alone with this grief. I want to run down the street screaming, 'I lost my baby, I lost my baby.' I want to grasp everyone by the hand and impress upon them that I am living my worst nightmare, that I am in pain. I want them to know the depths of my disappointment and the murky waters of my fear. Yet I cannot meet a single person's eye.

Instead of running down the street, I walk normally to the post office. A mother wrenches her toddler's arm to keep him in the queue. I hate her. I hate my life.

The Labyrinth

I didn't know how to be in the world any more. Restlessly pacing the house, I didn't even know how to be in my own skin. In the future I had planned and dreamed of, there was a baby centre stage.

I felt both harder and softer. Death at birth had robbed me of an innocence, had hardened my naivety. The softening was around this wound that was now my heart. I could regress easily into an uncomfortable helplessness and life could bring me to tears four or five times a day. Sometimes I would save them up and wait for Michael to come home.

'Did you have a good day?' I would ask as he put down his bags, not really caring about his day.

'Yeah, it was fine. How are you?'

'Oh, you know . . . do you have time for a cry?'

He would lead me to the bedroom and, safe in his arms, I would dissolve into torrents, crying out my wretched thoughts and *what ifs*, crying for the one, impossible way I wanted life to be different. I needed his presence so desperately. I needed just one person to walk with me through the labyrinth.

Television, newspapers and books were an impenetrable jungle, the chatter of an irrelevant world. When I did turn on the news

one night, I saw a story about the war in Bosnia. A man was leading a camera crew through a forest, showing the place where he
had found his oldest son slaughtered, and where his second son
lay dead, and where his two daughters also died. And here his wife
had lain dead, her corpse covering the body of his three-year-old
son who died later in hospital. My mouth dropped open in horror, my whole body throbbed with him in his anguish. I turned off
the television, full of anger at the terrible ways humans can destroy
each other. Flailed by my own grief, the pain of the world hit me in
the gut and left me breathless with futile rage. I knew my grief was
nothing compared to what some must endure.

JOURNAL APRIL 2000

It's funny, the way some people won't mention a recent death
because they don't want to remind you, upset you more. As if
you had forgotten . . .

In any conversation I am waiting, furled, surreptitiously
searching for the opening to speak that which sits most
urgently in my thoughts. To hear her name out loud. For her
to be real to them, just for a moment.

I experienced my first encounter last week with the
elephant in the corner.

Michael took me to visit a couple from Adelaide who
were up in Byron on holidays. They were old friends from his
previous life. Lovely, decent people, 2.5 five kids exactly, two
on the ground, one at 20 weeks' gestation.

It was only two months and ten days since our daughter
had died but for an hour and a half we talked about
everything but. Mostly we talked about their kids, who ran

around underfoot. Their son's speech therapy, her pregnancy, the father's golf lessons. I kept up a pretty credible line of banter and occasionally slumped in my chair. Only Michael, hypervigilant to my needs, noticed it and leaned over and cupped my thigh. It was not until we were about to get into our car that the wife grabbed my elbow and in a low tone, like it was a dirty secret, mentioned that she was sorry to hear we had lost our baby. Afterwards we stopped at the fruit store and as I stacked carrots into my hand, the tears came.

The next day, on our walk around the lighthouse track, I began to feel angry and stewed as we walked in silence through the rainforest. *How dare they sit there and talk about their kids for an hour and never once mention our daughter. How dare they think their son's speech therapy and fucking golf lessons were more important to talk about than Layla's death not two months before. How dare they. How dare they.* It was strangely satisfying to sink into this rage. *How dare they.* A delicious thrill of indignation coursed through my veins.

It was good for about twenty minutes but we were on the main beach of Byron by now and the ocean expanded me, so I blurted out my monologue to Michael.

'I've got an idea,' he said, and led me out to the water's edge, across a sandbar, away from people. And he said, 'You just vomit it all out, just scream it out for five minutes or however long you need, right?'

'Okay,' he said. 'I'll go first.' He began flailing the air and swearing out all the churnings of his mind. It was great, if a little scary to watch. In that state, any hidden thought could have revealed itself.

I was itching for my turn. I began with the *how dare yous*

about the Adelaide friends, chastising them with venom, *How dare you!* I punched the air, swung my arms violently, lost sight of the horizon and let my eyes fall back into my sockets. Staring up into the sky, I opened my throat and let go a banshee wail and in that state the truth of my anger came flying out and I screamed, 'I'm so fucking mad at God and the universe for letting this happen. I'm so fucking mad, I wanted her so much. I'm so fucking angry I can hardly speak sometimes. It's so fucking unfair it's happened to me. I would have been a fucking fantastic mother, those fucking parents who abuse their children, how fucking dare they, some people don't deserve to have children, she would have been loved, she would have been so loved.'

And underneath that, the source of all the rage. I cried out to the ocean, 'I want her back, I want her back, I just want her back.' Sobbing now with the exhaustion of it all.

Michael pulled me to his chest. Another chance to grieve. That's the magnificence of Michael. He just lets me grieve.

Searching for Signs

Deep grief rips open the heart, rips us open to new understanding. There is agony in grief but what people don't talk about is the ecstasy. A terrible loss is often met with a great outpouring of love from people and in that love a deep connection is made. We are suddenly connected to the terrible, eternal impermanence of all things but also more deeply connected to that other eternal force, God.

Quite soon after Layla died, I went for a walk one afternoon down a lane near my house. I asked that force of nature that I call God to give me some sort of sign that this had happened for a reason. I think what I really wanted to know was 'is there a God'.

I wanted a sign so obvious as to knock me off my feet, like a wild bird landing on my shoulder and singing to me. As I walked, I cried out in hope and hopelessness, begging for omens. In that state of intense looking and desperate longing I began to see the beauty of what was around me, the afternoon light dancing on the edge of silver gumleaves, the hundred shades of green in the trees, the grass; I could hear the exquisite delicacy of the currawong's call. And from this broken-open state I began to cry for the extraordinary beauty of it all.

Layla, God, who knows who had given me the sign I was looking for. God is this. Here. Now. Majestic in its cruel, fleeting beauty.

In the months after Layla's death I felt this strange euphoria more than once. It was alarming at first, hard to let in. Exalted, in the middle of the worst grief of my life? I can't describe it. I could barely even comprehend it. But one hour my sobs would be ripping at my heart and the next I would choke on this exaltation rising through my body.

JOURNAL LATE APRIL 2000

Sometimes I feel like I'm being summoned into mystery. Called by some profound secret of existence. All around us is a lullaby sung by the earth, as simple as a sonata played by rain against the roof on a Sunday morning. The mystery is everywhere, common as an everyday gesture of goodwill, as indefinable as spirit.

It is there when we listen to a musical lament from a faraway land, watch the majesty of clouds boiling against a cobalt blue sky, breathe in the peace of a sleeping child, examine a fluorescent beetle, admire the dew chandelier of an elaborate web. It is there when you run your fingers through the coat of a purring cat.

These are moments when life asks us to stop and wonder, nothing more. All we have to do is turn towards it, stop thinking and just be.

Initiation is easy. Music, art and literature are an invitation into the mystery. 'Art is concentrated nature', wrote Balzac, but nothing matches nature. Initiation is there in the explosion of wave against rock, a walk through forest, the metamorphosis of a moth.

Standing in awe, I reconnect to the peace of existence in a silent prayer of rapture.

167

JOURNAL 7 MAY 2000

Today Michael and I ate breakfast in a cafe in Byron. Seated at an outside table was a collection of women I know, with their small babies. I couldn't say hello. I made us move tables so we weren't near them, but stared from a distance and hid my tears behind the menu before Michael gathered me against his shoulder. They were so carefree, some holding their third child. I fumed at the injustice, my sobbing muted, not wanting to be seen in my distress.

There is a subtle distinction in what I need – the gaze of compassion rather than the glance of pity. Even though I feel like a victim, I don't want to be known as that. Even as I pity myself, I don't want to be pitied by others.

Re-entering life, I am greeted once more as a normal person. People approach me head-on now. It is a double-edged sword. I still need their mercy but shy from showing them the grief I feel, for fear of their pity. I don't want to be the sad woman in the cafe, crying because I don't have a baby. Yet that is exactly what I am.

I used to think that I was a flawed but essentially good person. I didn't know that my heart could hold such a maelstrom – wanting other babies to die, wanting death and destruction to befall others. Small slights send me into a rage that leaves me shaking with fury.

Tears are my only weapon, the only way to air my heart. Crying and speaking out the grief are helping me battle these deeper enemies, despair and hate. Strange how the depth of your love can take you to such a dark place. Maybe if people understood that the tears of grief are just a melancholy celebration of love, the world might be a softer place for us all. What I know is that I have to keep my heart *engaged*, even though it means feeling this wretched stew of emotion.

Layla, you are my muse right now. I sit here at the computer with your photo spotlit by the desk lamp and glance at you perhaps a hundred times a day, trying to *read* you. I search your face for the five-year-old, the teenager, the young woman. But in your newborn mask, all I can see is the face of the cherub. I had wanted to see your mouth wide open, smeared in an ecstasy of mash, your eyes dancing with the surprise of it. It is intensely futile, but like an alcoholic reaching for another drink, I fantasise that you are here and we are dancing as mother and child. But I know the hangover of reality waits just beyond intoxication.

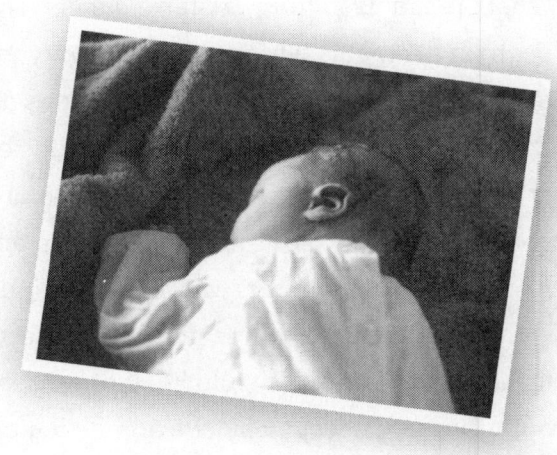

A Long Gentle Hug

My friend Wendy's teenage son, Tristan, is believed to have committed suicide, although his body has never been found. Not long after, she lost her partner, Eric, to illness. She emailed me about her own experience of grief. I had written to her about the hopelessness of wanting Layla's death to be different.

From: Wendy Norman
To: Vanessa Gorman
Subject: grief

Dear Vanessa

What I recognised from Tristan's disappearance and from Eric's death is . . . that it's important NOT to try and get over it, but to embrace the experience . . . this includes desiring it to be different! Somehow in embracing that desire in myself, not making it right or wrong, or expecting myself to be able to handle it, get over it, or get on with my life . . . as most people advise . . . but simply relaxing into what I was really experiencing and just being fully with that – it makes all the difference! We've been given so many ideas about HOW we should be, that we rarely get to be gentle with ourselves and accept what we are feeling and not move from that.

What I've discovered with grief is that the only way through it is to let everything be as it is. In other words, to feel it fully, to notice everything around it, including my resistance to things being the way they are! What I realised was that death isn't something you try to get over. I no longer feel I have to put what I shared with Eric behind me, rather I include him as though he is still present . . . because in a sense he is and always will be part of 'my life'. The same applies to Tristan . . . They are.

If anything, grief tore me open to such an extent that I had to surrender to what is! And this is part of the secret – embrace everything, then there is no longer a struggle with life . . . as things come and go, a deep surrender and relaxation arises . . . let life take you! Allow yourself to be held by life! That's where the gentleness comes in, the reassurance that whatever you are experiencing, it is okay.

At school I speak about the importance of being willing to be totally present in whatever is occurring, not trapped in our heads. I also feel that grief taught me to look deeper than the emotion, to realise that emotion was connected to thought . . . and thoughts are just thoughts . . . they are not who we are . . . who we are is *aware* of thoughts, aware of emotion . . . I began to rest in that gap of stillness, to feel with my body, feel everything around me . . . the beauty of the mountains, the warmth of the sun. I listen to sound fully, with my body, my whole being, not my mind. What I discovered is that there is a joy of being that isn't reliant on anything, just the sheer joy of being!

Acknowledge everything you hoped for in this baby, don't judge any of it! And allow whatever wants to be there to be expressed fully, but more as something felt in the body, rather than a story running in your mind . . . nothing is stupid . . . it's just how it is . . . so don't push anything away!

So let yourself be held . . . I'm sending you a long gentle hug.
Much love
Wendy

JOURNAL 23 MAY 2000

There comes a point in grief when death becomes part of
life, when you no longer have the power to shock yourself by
remembering. I stand at the fridge to get the milk out and I think
of Layla, that she is dead, and I pull the milk from the door and
pour it into my tea. No pause. I program the exercise bike at the
gym and start pedalling and remember she is dead and keep
pedalling. The thought no longer snaps my head back in shock
the way it used to. Often, the thought passes through me without
that familiar short, sharp stab of pain. It just is. She is dead.

If I mention her in passing to someone, I can now sound
vaguely normal and matter-of-fact. The psychologists might
say something like 'it has been integrated into your life', even
though I can still become a slobbering mess three times a day.

Today Michael and I were at a cafe and Steve waved at us
as he crossed the road. He veered off course to come and look
at our baby. He walked up to us craning his head, expecting to
see a capsule or pram.

'Where's your baby?' he asked. I peered into his face to see
if it was a bad joke or if he really didn't know. He really didn't
know.

'Didn't you hear?' I said, warning him with my expression.
'She died . . . She died eight hours after birth.'

'Oh my God, I didn't hear. I didn't . . .' his voice trails off.
'I'm so sorry, I didn't know, I didn't hear . . . Jesus.'

'You've probably been a bit out of the loop in Sydney,' I said, absolving him.

'Yeah, I've been going down every week for two days, it's tiring.'

'Sorry to ruin your morning,' I said, immediately feeling presumptuous.

'No, no, you haven't, I mean, I just feel . . . you know, *sorry* for you guys.'

He was moving away, recognising that he could make a quick escape but if he stayed for much longer, he would have to get into the story and that might take a while. He hesitated only long enough for me to see his panic. 'Take care of yourselves,' he said, shuffling off.

I don't pass judgment. We are far enough out of the shock and into the healing to deal with any reaction anyone throws at us. But driving home I was quiet and Michael put his hand on my thigh and stroked it firmly down to the knee and asked if I was troubled.

'What should have happened,' I said, 'is that Steve should have walked up and there should have been a pram there with a chubby-cheeked little girl asleep in it and he should have said, "A boy or a girl?" And we would have said, "It's a girl, Layla Frances." And he would have said, "Wow, look at those cheeks, she looks healthy." And I would have said, "Yeah, she's like her mother, she likes her food." And he would have said, "How are you coping? Is she a good sleeper?" And we would have said, "She's settled down a bit now, only waking once or twice. It was a bit hard going the last couple of months." And you might have laughed and given him a male-to-male conspiratorial wink and said, "Sleep's a bit of a distant memory at the moment . . . so is sex." And we all would have laughed and he would have taken another glance at her and said the usual "beautiful baby and cute as anything and lucky she didn't get your nose, Michael", and we would have laughed again and talked a little of his life and parted soon after that.'

'But that didn't happen,' said Michael quietly, still holding my knee.

'But that didn't happen,' I echoed, and turned my face in defeat to the passing view.

There was a maze in my head that could keep me trapped forever. *What if I had tried not to be so brave in labour? What if I had been braver? What if we had induced a week before? What if the helicopter had arrived earlier? What if I had gone to a city hospital? What if . . . ?*

I am driving the ridge of Coolamon Scenic Drive on a sunny day but the radio brings news of floods, an eighty-year-old man swept to his death from a causeway. I imagine the scene. Water levels rising with his fear. Suddenly it is me on the causeway, my child strapped into the back seat as floodwaters surge around the car. *Wind the windows up or down?* I undo my seatbelt and dive into the back seat as water pours into the car. With one hand I unbuckle my child, with the other I roll down the window. The car is almost underwater. *Should I cover her mouth and nose?* Almost frantic but trying to stay focused as I slither through the window and kick toward the surface. *Shoes off. I should have taken my shoes off.* Trying desperately to hold my child as the water swirls around us. *Swim with the current.* I am flailing toward the embankment, shoulders aching.

When I come to, I am holding the wheel so tight, my knuckles are white. I call out, 'Stop it,' and turn up the radio, grateful to be distracted by the latest violence in Israel.

So many nights I wake from dreams of mishap and emergency, my confused mind grasping at strategies to save my child from death and destruction. Strategies that could not save her. That will never save her.

'Losing Layla'

All of us, I believe, harbour inner voices that whisper to us throughout our lives. Some speak with a nobility that we are proud of. Others make us cringe with their strident demands or shameful thoughts. I sometimes feel uneasy with the filmmaker/ writer part of myself, the dispassionate observer who can on occasion embody the cool detachment of a sociopath.

As Cathy filmed on the first day of Layla's death, it occurred to me fleetingly that the documentary had gone awry. But I was glad she was there to record the moment – I dimly understood that these images would become our memories of Layla's brief physical time on earth.

Over the next few days, there was another observer, watching my demise without emotion. This sociopath – or to be kinder to myself, what Eastern mystics call the witness – whispered to me that the documentary had taken a 'dramatic' turn.

In the depths of shock and anguish, I set up my digicam in hospital once or twice and let it roll. I feel ashamed to admit this. It felt bizarre to record not another's darkest hour, but my own – as though I kept filming while the napalmed Vietnamese girl ran down the road, except I was both photographer and napalmed girl. Witness to my own demise.

I had spoken to Dasha Ross, the ABC's commissioning editor of documentaries, about my original idea for the video diary. After Layla died, I sat down and wrote Dasha a letter and sent her a copy of the footage Cathy had put together for Layla's ceremony. She rang back a few days later. Watching it had made her cry. 'Put together a proposal quickly,' she said. 'I think we can find some funding.'

Only six weeks after losing Layla, I found myself standing on a rainy street in Byron, handing a courier the proposal package and crying bitter tears. Only six weeks old and I was sending my baby into the arms of strangers who would talk about above- and below-the-line costs when they talked of her existence. I imagined a time when the film would be delivered to the offices of some magazine and someone would shout, 'Who wants to review the dead baby film?' The journos would groan and someone would put up their hand and Layla's life would be flung onto a desk, packaged in its hard vinyl coffin, fodder for a few column inches.

But I also knew that what I had was evidence of a loss not usually seen or acknowledged in society, a death seen as *less significant* than other deaths. In the months after Layla's loss, all I wanted to read were the stories of other people who had lost a baby. Trying to make sense of my loss, hungry to know I was not alone, I searched for clues that would show me how to survive. If a film like the one I was proposing had existed, I would have walked over hot coals to watch it. I wanted to share my story so that other parents who had lost a baby could say to family and friends, *There, that's what it's like, that's how much it hurts*. The social activist in me wanted to show what had helped us, so that friends and family of bereaved parents would know what is useful, what is ultimately healing.

But I was worried about the audience's reaction to the camera's intrusion into this most private and sacred of events, death. I would

177

never have invited the camera in if I had known what was to come. Cathy was meant to film a joyous event, but she found herself filming something very different. If she had been part of a TV crew, it would have felt wrong to have her there. But she was a close friend, padding quietly about the room with her small camera.

The process of making such a personal film was strange. I stood outside myself as witness to my own suffering, caught in the schism between subject and director.

Four months after Layla's death we were back at Lismore Hospital with a Betacam and Mini-Jib, creating a dramatic reconstruction of Layla's struggle for life. This struggle, thank God, was the only part of the ordeal that Cathy had not been allowed to film.

Of course we didn't push tubes down the throat of the healthy little stand-in, Chelsea. Or cut a hole in her chest to drain her lungs. The nurses pretended to do things with cardiac monitors and tried to keep her dummy out of shot. I stood in a corner and cried and then came over to direct. I felt distraught but my witness took control so I could get through the shoot.

I re-lived some part of the loss of Layla every day as I logged rushes, wrote the script and sat for a couple of months in an edit suite. Editor Harriet Clutterbuck and I had an edit-suite rule that we could cry at any time, and we did, often.

The vision and sound mixes were spectacularly schizophrenic experiences. Sitting there looking at a frame of my daughter's dead body on screen, my heart thumped sickeningly, but the witness carried on the discussion about cropping the shot or upping a sound effect.

I worried that in the process of making the film, I would have to watch our story too many times and become immune.

It did get to the stage where I recalled what happened only as I watched it onscreen. It was too hard to go inside myself and remember what it felt like to inhabit my broken body and shredded heart. It was easier to watch it on a monitor and experience it as if I were a stranger, from a distance. But I found myself weeping through the final sound mix, glad that I was not immune. The gestation of this 'second baby' took nine months to the day of Layla's death. We called the documentary *Losing Layla*.

Lulu

In the early days of my pregnancy, before the news was out, I got a phone call from a girlfriend in Sydney. Michele and I had been friends since we were thirteen years old and had been through all the ups and downs of relationships and the struggle to find ourselves in a situation where we could even think about having a family. She had fallen in love with Simon and they were planning to marry, but she was worried that she had left the baby-making thing too late. In an earlier call she'd told me of visiting a specialist who talked about how women's fertility starts to drop after thirty-five, and how it falls over a cliff in the late thirties. We worried together. But now she had news.

'I'm pregnant,' she joyfully announced. I screamed down the phone, 'Oh my God, so am I!' We screamed together, laughed, talking over the top of one another, ecstatic. At her wedding a few months later, we posed with our six-month bumps. We both knew we were having girls and we planned their lives together, imposing a lifelong friendship on them, whether they liked it or not. Lulu was born by Caesarean three weeks before Layla. Michele's own joy was marred by terrible sadness when she heard my news.

Three months after Layla's death, I travelled to Sydney to see them. Gathering her gorgeous daughter in my arms was so very bittersweet – Lulu, who would no longer have Layla to grow up with.

'I tell her about her guardian angel, Layla,' said Michele.

I wept at Lulu's aliveness.

We sat on the couch and talked about our birth experiences. I showed Michele the photos of Layla and we cried together. She talked of Lulu's first three months, and it dawned on me that it would always be like this: I would only have one story to tell about Layla. Her birth and death. Other parents would have a new story every week.

Driving home through dark, wet streets, I had to pull over. Peak hour in the rain was no place for an overwrought woman pleading with God behind a steering wheel.

JOURNAL JUNE 2000

Feeling the grief start to lessen creates yet another form of grief.

A colleague calls and leaves a message that he is coming to film at Rosebank and would love to catch up. I haven't spoken to him since the death of Layla. I call back and, without saying hello, launch my old self down the phone line. 'Didn't anyone tell you that only gun runners and drug smugglers live at Rosebank?'

He laughs but there is also surprise in his voice – at meeting my old self when he had probably steeled himself for the broken model.

Still desperate for sympathy, I assume the tone of the broken model. 'Good to hear your voice,' I say more quietly.

He asks how I am.

'Up and down,' I say. 'Up and down.'

'Right,' he says, hesitant.

My answer is standard nowadays. It's a shorthand that people seem to understand and not question further, unless they're interested. Up and down. Up and down.

Sometimes the grief is monstrous and at other times it is a dull loneliness and despair that deadens the heart. A blunt-edged knife.

There's that thing we always hear about, how the Eskimos have fifty words for snow. I wish I had fifty words to describe the myriad emotions that churn away inside. From fierce hatred to overwhelming love, from raging envy to dark depression, from hopeless despair to manic optimism.

Up and down.

But in the 'up' is the weirdness of normality. The lack of passion. The guilt that perhaps a cold heart is forgetting too soon. The sympathy that is slowly sapped from the face of another as they see my old self return. Missing is the intense dance of pain borne of love, and therefore the love itself is missing. All the downs to being up. My old self is not my old self. No one makes the journey to the edge and back without being scathed.

I am up. A sunny winter morning in Byron Bay. Twenty laps in the freezing public pool, breakfast at Fresh, an hour to kill while Michael sees a buyer.

I am feeling up nowadays because I have a mission, my documentary about her life and death. She is my business for the next nine months, my income. We have opened a production account called 'Losing Layla', which makes me gag when I look at those words on a cheque. Those two words still have the power to shock me when placed together. I am applying for an ABN number to tell my daughter's story. I joke that soon I'll be merchandising Layla T-shirts.

I am up. Last night Michele and Simon asked me to be the godmother of Lulu.

I am up and browsing the jewellery shop for Lulu's christening gift, negotiating with the unemployed part of myself over what I can afford. I think, If Layla had survived, I would have spent thousands in her life, and suddenly my 'up' crumbles and I am staring numbly into a display case, begging her death not to be so.

But at least the thought of her makes my heart pulsate.

At least when I am crying I can still feel her close.

Nowadays, it's up and down.

JOURNAL JULY 2000

It is still so hard to be in the world. I wonder sometimes when I will emerge from this parallel universe. At social gatherings I feel like some kind of human black hole, a dark vortex sucking energy in, needy, with not much to offer.

My girlfriend Virginia's fortieth birthday dinner is in Sydney, at Amanda's house. I fortify myself with two glasses of champagne too quickly and then a glass of red wine with dinner, so I can enter the fray. Serve volley, serve volley, keeping up with the banter, and then suddenly I can't play any more. The wine has gone straight to my heart and a great sadness engulfs me. I sit and hide beneath my hair and I know if someone looks, they will see my face has fallen. I get up and go into the kitchen, looking for something I might need, *yes, yes, a glass of water*, calculating how long I can loiter. In the family room I stare at the photos of Amanda's boys from babyhood on: skiing holidays, feeding animals, school portraits.

I slip into the bedroom where Cath's newborn is sleeping, trying not to look at him for too long. Quietly I dial Michael's number, desperate to reach out to my lifeline, but all I get is his message. I call out to him, 'I don't know where I belong, there's nowhere to turn, you are the only real thing in my life.' I find myself almost begging down the phone. 'I love you. And I love that you are real and tender and beautiful.'

I feel tipsy and ashamed of needing him so much when some of my oldest friends sit outside at the table. Friends who understand, who have been so good to me through this. But the need for Michael is the need to feel the direct linking of my soul to his, a desperate yearning to be understood in the passion of this sadness. I put down the phone and hold my head in my hands, leaning over, careful to let the tears fall onto the floor rather than letting them run down my cheeks and leave track marks.

Cath comes in to check on her son. 'I know it must be hard,' she says tenderly.

'Yes, it's hard,' I say, 'but there's nothing to be done.'

The dinner passes and sometimes I can swim along the surface and sometimes I drown but I have sobered up enough to accept that anecdotes and funny stories are on the menu tonight and this hopeless intensity will have to wait for the solace of release.

Approaching the Bereaved

It's almost a cliché to say that in the West, we don't do dying, death or grief all that well. Maybe it's because I live in the progressive community of Byron Bay, but I think society has made great strides in the last few decades. Still, it is often hard to know how to reach out and offer comfort, even if we have experienced death. It is hard to know which word, which gesture might bring solace.

After this year I know the sad truth at last: there is nothing anyone can say or do to take away the pain. This is why another's grief can make us reel back in terror and cross the street rather than look them in the eye. But I know for sure another, greater truth – we must still try to reach out, no matter how clumsy our attempt. It is a frightening concept: *There is nothing we can do but we have to do it anyway*.

There are no words that heal, but not to hear any words is worse. The terrible loneliness of grief makes us desperate for anything anyone has to offer. We want to feel hands reaching out, even if they manage to hold us steady only for a fleeting moment. We are blind and struck dumb when grief hits and we need to feel the voice and touch of others in that dark cave, no matter how fleeting.

I understand the brutal truth. To other people, my loss is an abstraction, as their deepest losses are to me. If we have experienced our own loss, we can feel others' more deeply. But that's as best we can do.

I could always feel the difference between people who have experienced deep grief and those who have not. While the experienced don't know my place, they know *the* place. And mostly they are not afraid to go there with you. *Thank God*, we cry when we meet them. *Thank God they have known loss as well*, we selfishly cry.

In my community, the experience of compassionate connection was overwhelming. But occasionally I struck people who hid behind a spiritual complacency. Tongue-tied in the face of my plight, they would forget to offer any kind of simple 'sorry', but would instead nod knowingly and offer a spiritual diagnosis. *These things happen for a deeper reason, she's in a better place now, this must be her karmic destiny, it's only her body that has died, you are never given more than you can bear, God's plan is bigger than we can ever know, she didn't need to be on this earth plane, everything happens for a reason.*

On good days I would nod meekly, glad to get any tidbit of acknowledgment, knowing dimly that maybe some of it was true. On bad days I would want to lunge forward and grab them by the neck and shake them into the world of my pain and cry out, *Just say that you're sorry. Just tell me that a child dying before its parents is a devastation to the natural order.* It is surprisingly rare to get a pure, unadulterated 'sorry'. It can be said or gestured in a hundred different ways, but it's all that is needed.

The death of a baby can bring particularly hurtful comments. *At least you know you can get pregnant. You can always have another one.* Sometimes people would look at me, wide-eyed and panicked, almost shouting, *There's nothing I can say, there's nothing I can say, what can I say?* I would nod and mutter back, *Yes, what is there to say?* But what I am greedy for is a flicker of their own pain.

Aah! But let me show you another side. What we got in this community was something beyond sorry – what we got was love. People spoke their sorrow for us in the most beautiful gestures, the kindest, most unexpected deeds. Michael and I were picked up on this wave of love that rolled onward and onward all year. And I was hungry for it. I exhausted myself trying to receive it all, so rapacious I almost got emotional gout.

Then there were the letters and the cards. Glorious white and pastel missives. Don't hesitate – no matter how busy you are, take the time to write. A little or a lot. It doesn't matter. If you feel like you don't know the person well enough, write anyway. I loved the letters that flooded in. Handwritten balms amidst the bills. People's loving tendrils reaching out: *I have heard, I am aware of your pain, I am trying to soothe you*. I would devour their words greedily and reach hungrily for the next message. A grieving person has a voracious appetite for hand-addressed mail.

And yet and yet and yet. Still nothing takes away the pain. Finally, we must walk alone.

So this is where my understanding sits for now. In the face of grief, the only responses that matter are love and sorrow. Not advice or esoteric wisdom or avoidance. Sounds simple, but watch me stumble and fall when next I am the one trying to offer comfort.

I think to meet another fully in grief, we have to let our own hearts break just a little. I love these words of the American novelist Alice Walker:

> We're used to thinking of broken-heartedness as a position we
> don't want to be in – we want to live our whole lives without having
> our hearts broken but to do that would be truly sad because we
> would never grow. A broken heart is what leads to an open heart.

It's a process of having our hearts broken and seeing that we don't die – something in us dies but we don't – and then we continue. That's the bravery of human nature.

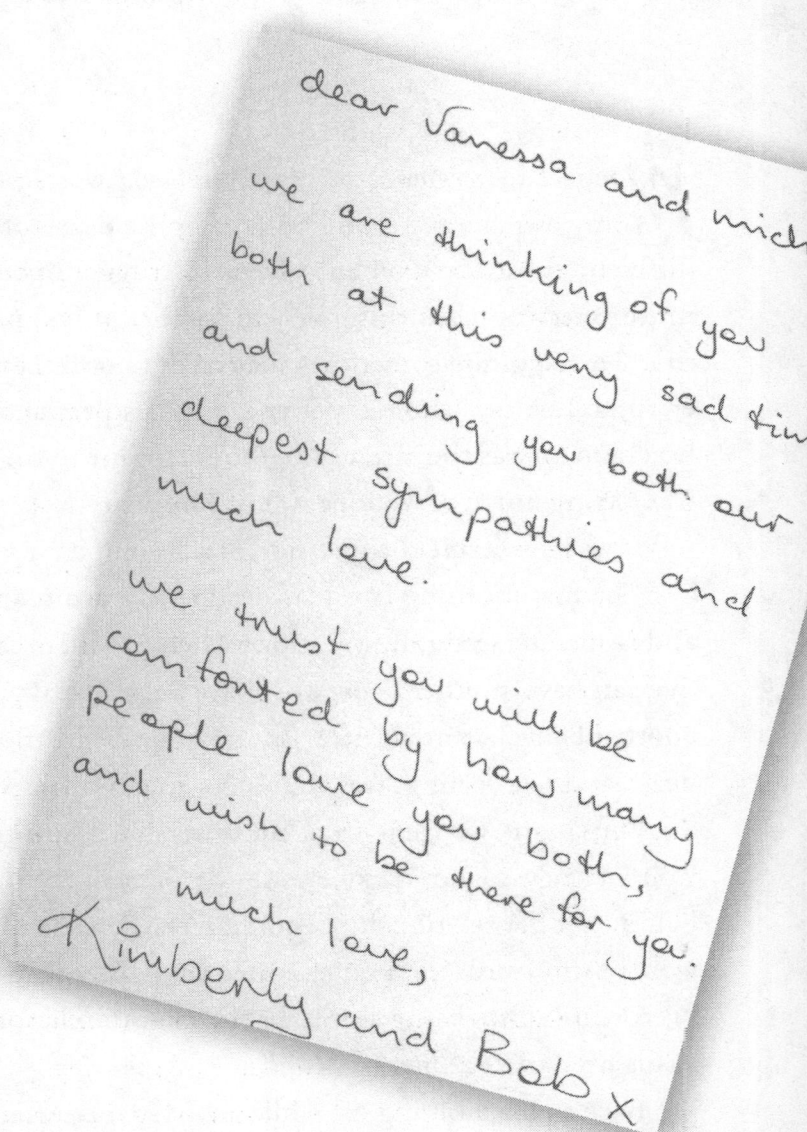

dear Vanessa and nich
we are thinking of you
both at this very sad tim
and sending you both our
deepest sympathies and
much love.
we trust you will be
comforted by how many
people love you both,
and wish to be there for you.
much love,
Kimberly and Bob x

The Big Question

Michael's experience of life after Layla was so different from my own, as any man's path after the death of a baby will be different from the woman's. Layla's struggle opened in him an unexpected love; but this love was so brief, it was hard to hold on to it. He felt guilty sometimes that he did not feel enough, feel sad enough. But the whole experience had also expanded him somehow, and he was the safest of harbours for me to turn to. Perhaps I was feeling much of what he was too numb to feel.

It was inevitable the question of a second baby would arise.

The first morning Layla lay dead in our arms, amidst the tears and desperate, searching questions, Michael held me and whispered, 'We can have another baby, we'll have another baby.' I didn't want another baby. I wanted Layla. But now it was five months since her death and new feelings were bubbling to the surface.

One night we went to a talk given by a spiritual teacher. A woman got up and spoke about the pain of feeling half in and half out of her relationship. I could feel Michael resonating to her words. Afterwards, in a quiet coffee shop, he began talking about his torture at not being able to be fully in our relationship, because of his need to be alone.

Back home, holding me while I sobbed, he softened his stance.

He felt that he had violated his role as my heart's protector. We talked later about him taking some time out to be alone. The big me could see that he would never be present in the relationship while he was thinking he should be somewhere else. The big me wanted him to be happy and fulfilled, no matter what. The small me felt devastated at the possibility of losing him forever.

Michael was no less conflicted. Wanting me to be a mother, knowing I could not be with him without trying again. But another part of him was anguished – he knew he did not want this for himself.

'Get the sperm,' urged many of my girlfriends. My friend Ruth was one of the more pragmatic. During one visit, she planted her feet on the table and lounged back in the late-afternoon sun. 'Women fall pregnant all the time. It's the most natural thing in the world,' she said. She was on a roll, holding a pretend baby, gazing lovingly into its imaginary face. 'Why are you two talking about this endlessly? Re-hashing, psychoanalysing, pre-empting. Just fall pregnant. Take control for both of you, have another baby!'

Ruth wasn't so much urging me to deceive my partner as urging me on the path of procreation. And so I began to tote up the dates in my diary, noting ovulation and calculating conception possibilities. But as soon as I began the process, I realised I would have to tell Michael my plan. We had come too far in honesty for me to jump ship now.

It was around this time that Michael suggested I see a psychic. She had a good reputation, whatever that means in such an esoteric line of work.

'Will I have another baby?' was my obvious question.

She tuned in to whatever it is psychics tune in to. 'You will.

You'll have a son,' she said. 'There's an image of you walking down the street holding a little boy, blond hair and blue eyes. You look very happy and he's a very happy and healthy little thing.'

When I wanted to know other things, all she could talk about was this child. And what an extraordinary life his would be.

It was money well spent, even if none of it was true. I floated from her house cradling the news, hope beating in my chest, a lightness to my step for at least four days afterwards. The only unease, a veiled suggestion that perhaps Michael was not the father.

JOURNAL JULY 2000

A death. A rebirth? Perhaps a new future begins from here?

Michael is about to go overseas on business for a month so we rented a beach house at Belongil for the weekend. On Friday night we set up the living room for an ecstasy trip, pulling the couches together to make a boat filled with cushions and doonas. Lining up the glasses.

We blessed the space and paid homage to the pictures of the great beings on the makeshift altar and also to Layla. And then we began. Talking for fourteen hours straight. Right through the night as the moon rose majestically over the Pacific Ocean outside our door, and into the dawn as the sun rose and followed the moon's trajectory.

Debriefing on the whole journey of the pregnancy and the birth and losing Layla. For the first time Michael really saw the gifts she had brought into his life. How in one sense she was liberating him. We marvelled at the ways she had been an angel in both our lives. He told me again about his time with her when she was alive and carrying her body home and all the multiple confusing layers of things he was feeling then. I loved sitting with his tears instead of the other way round.

Michael needed to take some time out and we were trying to reconfigure our relationship. As friends? Lovers? We didn't know. We talked about how often we had been in this place of unknowing – him wanting to leave, me wanting more. We suddenly realised that this place was somewhere we had always been scared of, always wanted to pathologise.

Michael talked about his desire for independence. It gets criticised so often as being the juvenile part of himself, but it is actually a higher calling to expand more fully into his own heart.

'I want to be free of this fear of suffocation. Part of what Layla has taught me is about respecting my own path, respecting my essential nature. I just need for once to make my needs more important than someone else's and I don't know if it's permanent or just a stage I have to pass through.'

'Your need to do this has been my nemesis from day one. There is nothing I can do but give you my blessing.'

And then he said, 'I'll give you another baby anyway, because I love you and it's what you most want in the world.'

There we were, back on the couch together on that very first night. Him wanting to explore life in freedom, me wanting children. And here we are seven years later, trying to give each other exactly that.

We talked about how the year had changed us, apologised for all the ways we had hurt one another or hidden and not told the truth. And we spoke again of all the things we loved about the other. Ecstasy was originally used as a relationship-guidance tool. When used safely, it can be such an expansive experience. At the risk of getting my head blown off, I would recommend the pure stuff to couples to sample as a once-a-year form of relationship maintenance.

We didn't stop talking till nine the next morning and then only to move into the bedroom. I was ovulating and we were going to try to conceive. When we lay down, we began breathing together and looking into each other's eyes and his fear started to rise.

'Oh my God, what am I doing?' he said, his breathing shallow. 'This thing I've been terrified of for years – this thing that just caused me nine months of agony – how could I be contemplating it again!'

I was certain I wanted to do it, even though at that point it meant walking into probable single motherhood.

The waves of fear rose and fell and I didn't know how to open him, or release him into the act, and finally I said, 'Do it because you love me', and he recognised then that he loved me enough to do it.

Oh! To be making love knowing that we could be making a baby – it was so sublime, and so immensely erotic. I surrendered to him as he pushed inside me, whispering, 'I'm going to give you a baby. I'm impregnating you with my sperm', and it was just so horny hearing those words that I orgasmed uncontrollably and then he started to come and exploded inside me – a triumph of love over fear. Once the deed was done we made passionate love twice more that day.

That night we started talking about a way that he could stay. A way that he could have freedom and we could still have connection and a deep commitment to each other. All of us have wounds and they are going to make it hard for two people to love each other. We acknowledged that those wounds were the source of our longings and that to love each other was to try to give what the other longed for.

Later in bed I unleashed my adoring sex slave, worshipping his body with mine, climbing over him, telling him how much I desired him, was powerless in the face of him. He demanded his slave put her nipple in his mouth and then ordered her to rub her wet pussy over the smooth knob of his cock. All I cared about was obeying his commands. I whispered in his ear that I loved him to the ends of the earth, that I wanted no other but him. I rose up and plunged down until I could see him reaching the point where he could stand the rapture no longer. He grabbed the arse of his sex slave and pulled me deeply over his penis, using me for his pleasure as I submitted, feeling all his love and pain explode deep in my solar plexus.

He left for Germany a few days later and since then my body has been pulsating open. I want to conceive so much. And I can't think of a better place for a new soul to enter than into the middle of the joy, chaos and surrender of that beautiful weekend.

Postcard for Michael

That last photograph when I was happy
laughing from behind my sunnies.
We'd been forty hours without sleep
marooned on our couch boat
in a sea of love and ecstasy.

That last photograph
framed by the sand and the sea of a deserted Belongil

and then you left across that sea,
rang to say I was on your mind
I was in your heart
and that you would come back to me.

That last photograph when I was happy
and all the world seemed made of potential.
I laughed into the lens
not knowing that two weeks later I would start to bleed
and all hope would seem lost
except the thought that you would come back to me . . .

JOURNAL 20 AUGUST 2000

Bit of a relapse. Michael is still away and the house has been lonely. Dena, my yoga teacher, is expecting her baby soon. She had a blessing ceremony down at the Pass and asked me to lead it. A lovely gesture from her and I enjoyed that part, but it was so hard to be there. Little children ran everywhere. I sat on the rugs designated for the childless people while the mothers and babies sat on rugs in the shade and swapped tips and experiences. I left early and charged up to the lighthouse, trying to outrun my emotions. Trying to make my pain feel insignificant before the expanse of the ocean.

For a few weeks I was delusional with hope that I was pregnant. When my period came, I felt all hope was lost. 'Trust, trust, trust the universe,' I said to myself as I scurried to the cafe toilet to stem the flow of blood. It will be another two months before we can even try again.

When I got home a beautiful pigeon had flown into a

window and lay dead on the verandah. The world felt like a cruel place. I buried the pigeon late afternoon and looked up to see the most exquisite rainbow gracing the valley. Life takes and life gives.

Last night I went to a party. It's been months since I could manage a party. I went alone, arriving late, telling myself I only needed to stay for a few minutes if that was all I could manage. But the strangest thing happened. As I walked into the house, I felt utterly sure of my attractiveness. I felt like a beautiful woman with a beautiful body and I understood that what gave me this beauty was my heart. It felt so open, so transparent, and in this lay a fragility that was also a strength. I actually felt *powerful*.

I knew if I wanted to attract a man, I could. In fact one did sidle up with the line, 'A woman like you surely has a man in her life?'

'Yes,' I said, but let myself flirt with him anyway, sure that I could control the situation. I managed two hours there and came home alone, longing for Michael's return.

A Love Letter

My Dear M

I've had a note, written on a small green sticky, buried in the mess around the phone for a few weeks now. I'd scrawled some questions you asked me over the phone from Melbourne, after the beautiful weekend at Belongil.

You asked me to think about how I could be as big in love as I can be. What do I need? What works for me about my relationship with you? I've been looking at the note, contemplating the questions, gearing up for some logical and well thought out answers.

But as I sit down to write, I recognise that my deepest notion of love is not in the realm of logic. If I was to attempt the well thought out answer, I would end up with a shopping list of what works and what doesn't and we would be back at the negotiating table.

In a sense, up till now our love has been conditional. You can only love me if I promise not to hold you down and 'trap' you in a situation where you feel suffocated. I can only love you if you give me what I so desperately crave, another baby.

The thought of the baby makes you feel trapped, and the thought of having a baby with someone who might leave soon after makes me feel afraid.

These are our particular fears but every couple has their own that make it harder to love each other deeper.

That weekend at Belongil, we surrendered to the other and loosened the conditions.

'I'll give you a baby because I love you,' you said.

'And I'll accept it, knowing you might have to go,' I replied, and we lay down and let our fear expand into love.

But suppose we both aimed for the truly unconditional? A love that is beyond marriage vows, beyond our fears? So that all we try to do is love each other minute to minute, day to day. A love that cares only for your happiness, so that you might care only for mine. A love as unconditional and free as the force of nature we call God.

Having spouted those lofty words, I have to admit my own failure, moment to moment, to live up to these ideals. I think why I long for a child is to feel the expansion of my unconditional love, to get in some practice, if you like.

At least if we were to attempt the impossible, we could trust that our love would bring us closer to an enlightened state. That it could contain everything we need. That we are both just consciousness loving itself and our day-to-day lives are arising perfectly in every moment.

I just want to love you.

That will make me as big in love as I can be.

See you soon, honey,

V

JOURNAL 25 AUGUST 2000

I feel so mad tonight. So abandoned. I'm not sure what I'm doing in this relationship. Tonight I feel like a sad creature being thrown scraps. I have a man who may not want to live with me any more but will throw me the scrap that, if he leaves, he'll come and visit from time to time. Who doesn't want to have children but will throw me the scrap of his sperm. But who wants to talk about how we will arrange custody if he ends up living with a new lover.

And I feel like I'm so desperate, I'm prepared to eat these scraps off the floor when they are thrown at my feet.

I feel like I am trying to love Michael as honestly, and without artifice, as I know how. Trying to give him what he wants as generously as I know how. But constantly my love for him and my open heart feel like they get boarded up by his fear.

Dear Michael

I want to scream at you sometimes, like right now, and say, DIDN'T LAYLA'S DEATH TEACH YOU ANYTHING? All through the pregnancy you wallowed in the fear of 'what if? what if?' and you missed the love she could bring until she was gasping for breath and near death. None of what you were afraid of happened. What happened instead was birth and death, the only two sure things we will ever know. Let Layla teach you that none of us know the future and what you fear most probably won't happen, but something else sure as hell will. You say you believe that our destiny is not in our control, but you are talking like you can legislate for the future. You can try but you're just pissing into the wind and giving the gods a good laugh.

Sure, let's have the conversation about access and custody but ultimately all you can do if you decide to proceed is trust who you know me to be. If you feel like you can't trust me or, more importantly, if you don't want to love me, then get the hell out of my life and leave me to my unfolding destiny.

You asked me what I want and I wrote in that letter that I just want to love you. But the truth is, I want more than that. I want you to love me too. I want to know if you still want to try.

If we are going to have another baby together, I want to know if I should prepare for instant single motherhood, or if you are prepared at least to enter into the journey of parenting that child together. Because if you aren't, it would be difficult for you to form an attachment to the baby. The child would be a stranger to you and perhaps a nuisance to look after.

And if all you can promise to be is the sperm donor, then so be it. But the conversation about access and custody will be different then, because it will be predicated on the fact that the child will hardly know you.

So if you want to talk about the future like this, we could get down to the nitty gritty, and by all means let's go for it, if that's what your mind and body need. But stop letting your fear strangle your love for me. Neither of us can know the fucking future. All I want to know is if you think you can keep trying to love me.

If the answer is no, then perhaps it's better that we proceed no further.

Vanessa

Weakness

*Y*ou're much too nice,' my mother often tells me, but what she means is that I'm too weak.

Too often I put aside my needs to take care of others. I turn into a Pollyanna, doggedly anxious to earn people's good opinion. I work hard at making myself lovable, full and rounded, funny and interesting, but expending all that energy can be exhausting. I bend over backwards to please. I don't state my truth, so as not to offend. I spend an inordinate amount of energy thinking about others and their wellbeing. I often drown in my river of empathy.

I wonder about the source of this anxiety. I have enough self-esteem, I know I am loved, but there's this small dog peeing on my inner carpet and I feel powerless to control it. Caring for others or being friendly are not faults – it's just that I don't always like my motives. Still, I try to relax and understand this part of myself without judging it too harshly. But sometimes, after I have been walked over again, I wish I could change. I wish I could be free of this need.

Perhaps my motive for including the last letter is about proving that I had reached a point where I refused to be walked over. That I could stand up for myself. That I am no wimp after all.

Perhaps I was playing a game of brinkmanship. If it was a game, the stakes were high and history was not on my side. My journal from that time records no reaction to this letter, and my memory also lets me down.

All I can recall is my own desperation to have another baby, and Michael's pain in wanting to give me one while also respecting this calling to be alone. All I know is that we had reached the brink. In the leap that had to be made, one of us would land safely and one of us would fall.

The Sword of Damocles

*E*arly September 2000, eight months after Layla died. We took a break from editing the documentary and I flew to Sydney to bask in the city's Olympics mayhem and glory. Michael picked me up from the airport on my return and we drove to the Urban Cafe in Bangalow for lunch. I could tell something in him had shifted, that he had something to tell me. I might even have been aware that the sword I had lived under for seven years was about to drop.

'It feels like you've got something you want to talk about,' I said, feeling tentative.

'I do,' he replied, 'but let's not talk about it now.'

We ate our lunch and spoke of life since we had seen each other last and decided to go on the lighthouse walk at Byron for some Sunday-afternoon exercise. I wondered what he wanted to talk about but thought we would curl up with a cup of tea when we got home and do it face-to-face.

Why did he choose to tell me there on the beach, three minutes into the walk? Perhaps he could not face me head-on, but found comfort in facing the horizon. Or perhaps he was scared I'd create a scene and thought I was less likely to do that on a crowded beach.

I had never created a scene in my life, but now I wish I had given vent to the wave that dumped me that day.

I wish I had let myself drop to my knees and grab handfuls of sand and throw them at his face and pile it on top of my head and rub it into my scalp – some manifestation of the animal pain that surged through me when he said those words, 'Vanessa, I need to go and live by myself. I think it's permanent. I'm not coming back.'

I wanted to flail and spit and scream blue murder at the ocean and God and him and not give a damn about curious onlookers. But instead I politely kept on walking and dry-retched on the surge of anger and sadness that rushed up from my guts.

I remember that the crowd around us was at leisure, swimming in the aquamarine sea, paddling yellow kayaks out to deeper waters, the gaily coloured sails of catamarans flapping like a mad flag convention. Hang-gliders circled lazily overhead.

I walked past them all as the shock of finally losing Michael pierced me, re-opening all the wounds of losing Layla.

I had begun the walk with only the usual background noise of grief that accompanied my life at that time. I finished it with the hopeless despair of a childless, suddenly single woman five months shy of her fortieth birthday.

And I hate . . .

I am pounding the boardwalk. Salt spray diffuses the brilliant glare of the sun as I round the broad sweep of Byron Bay.

AUSTRALIA'S MOST EASTERLY POINT brags the sign.

Long white breakers roll in, carrying black dots of surfers and fleeting grey fins of the family of dolphins that cruise this strip. Past the orange granite cliffs, up and down stone stairs. Breath, footfall, breath, pounding footfall. Skin brushing against salt-encrusted coastal scrub. The words of a song playing in my head are caught in a groove: *And I hate. And I hate. And I hate* . . .

AUSTRALIA'S MOST EASTERLY VENOMOUS THOUGHTS.

I want death and destruction to befall others. I want to spit words into the faces of health professionals. I want those I love to be restored to me. I want my life back. I want peace from this torment. I remember a line from Solzenitsyn, 'The line of good and evil runs right through the human heart.'

I find it hard to understand this darkness. I thought I had a good heart.

I push on towards the lighthouse, legs burning, head down, ignoring the stream of tourists taking in the majesty of the bay. I slice the air with toxic thoughts. A man absentmindedly holds the hand of his daughter as they navigate the stairs. She is two years old or so, and wears a frown. She pulls away from her father, declaring: 'No hold hand!' I laugh at her determined innocence but there is a bitter aftertaste. Why is he lucky enough to have a daughter?

I leave the path and enter the bush, the brilliance of the sun muted by the wild foliage of palms and acacias. Bush turkeys forage, lizards crackle across the forest floor.

Finally I stop, exhausted by my bitterness. I take a moment to listen for other walkers . . . and then I scream. I scream again. I want to root out this terrible pain, this acid.

I cry out until I am hoarse and my chest hurts. Then I sit and take my head in my hands. Wailing. Feeling all the pain under the hate. All the dismal grief of this place of loss. Wanting her back. Wanting him back. Wanting it all to be different.

My life has gone so wrong. I am lost as the sun disappears behind the trees and the shadows of another long evening descend.

In the time after Michael left, I remember nights pacing the house like a madwoman, grief, anger and hopelessness at war in every cell of my body. I knew enough to open my mouth and let the inhuman sounds of distress out into the night air. My tiny, fragile family was all gone and I shook with the adrenaline rush of feeling too much, too often.

I hated telling people. I hated that they would judge Michael even as I needed their sympathy. I understood that his leaving looked like an atrocious thing for one person to do to another. But I also understood his need to finally go and do this thing he had been longing to do. To live alone, unburdened. Truth be told, the angry part of my heart thought it a shallow move. But I had to understand that his desire was as deep and true as my need to have another child.

The weeks before he left, he held me many times as I cried. We talked a lot, bitter and sweet words. Sometimes I lashed out at him and he mostly absorbed it and didn't argue back, understanding the source of my anger. Besides, he was tortured with guilt. I tried not to make it worse.

We were leaving each other in a strange place. Still loving each other deeply, still with an enormous amount of respect for the other. But in the end, it was that old chestnut, timing, that undid us. When two people fall in love and are at a similar stage in their life, wanting to move in a similar direction, everything seems to click. Michael and I fell in love but the timing was against us from the beginning. Simple as that really. But so complicated.

We were halfway through editing the documentary about losing Layla when he announced he was leaving. I turned up to work on Monday, made the announcement to Harriet and Cathy and tried to concentrate on the task, watching my story stony-faced, enduring each day until I could go home and take off the flimsy mask I wore to keep it all together.

Dear Michael

I came around tonight to meet my nemesis. Crunching up your gravel path in the night, reeling from a glass of wine and the late hour. Groping for switches, everything unfamiliar. Only the second time I have been to your new place, your brick, tile and laminex cave.

I wanted to come tonight, while you are away, for maybe five or six reasons, some I can't even explain. But mostly to see you here. And I find that you are indeed here and not at our home any more. That this place, sparse, impermanent, is now your home. It feels perfect that it is cavelike.

I come to meet the ghost of you, knowing this place is too young for ghosts. You've been rearranging since my first visit. All your stuff, so familiar to me but so strange in this new configuration. I look carefully around, noting the detail. Still covering all the bases with five gurus on the altar, the Polaroid of you with Layla. You would cringe to see me eyeing off the walls of your cave. I know I am infringing on your privacy with my prying eyes. Noting, too, you have left some dishes unwashed in the sink.

I wanted to come and meet my Waterloo, your other lover, this longing to be alone. The jealous part of me glad it is not more beautiful than our home, in fact has all the charm of a public toilet. But I know your heart is here.

So I've come to sniff about your cave and tell it that it has won, and let you go a little bit more. No, I let you go. Or perhaps being here confirms that I have no choice. So I've come to say goodbye. For some reason it feels easier to say it formally here, where there is only the ghost of you. The ghost of us is too present at home.

There are a million things to say but we've probably said them all, so I will just wish you well on your journey. Release you to your own destiny – free of the responsibility of being my partner. I welcome in our new relationship, however it may evolve, and hope our love and respect for one another continues to deepen and nurture us, as it has this last seven years.

Thank you for teaching me how to love well and for showing me how I could love better, both myself and others. Thank you for opening up my heart and for giving me Layla and helping me survive when she left. I will always love you and I feel happy to know that you will always love me. I will mourn you in the way you and Layla have taught me. And I will continue to hope that one day I will thank you for delivering me to my destiny. I leave feeling happy I loved you well and I thank you for leaving me so gently. I will myself to stop now, it is late. Enough.

Au revoir, mon ami.

Vanessa

PS. I did the dishes

JOURNAL OCTOBER 2000

People still ask me how I'm doing. Not as often as they once did but often enough to make me grateful they haven't forgotten. 'Up and down,' I say, still using my shorthand for the roller-coaster.

But now this double whammy. The two most precious things in my life, both gone. Stella asked how I was and I found myself telling her I was on the edge of what feels bearable. When the waves of grief break over me, that is the shore I wash up on – the rocky edge of what feels bearable.

But sometimes I have been washed up and over the rocks and on to a tiny patch of shimmering sand. It's like I have no fear any more of emotional pain. I just surrender to it or sob with a friend down the phone or lie on my bed and let the pain wrack my body. And I know from the experience of the last eight months that if I let myself do this, in time, maybe fifteen minutes later, maybe four hours later, I will cycle back into the light. So I surrender to my sorrow with great trust, and twice now, in the depth of my despair, with tears streaming down my face and my voice almost broken, I have felt my heart start to resonate with joy.

In these moments I feel almost exultant in my pain, as though it is taking me to the deepest part of myself and setting me free.

I understand it is my love that has taken me to this place of despair and my love that will guide me back into the light.

Layla's gifts have been extraordinary and this is perhaps her greatest.

Grief is a wound that needs attention in order to heal. To work through and complete grief means to face our feelings openly and honestly, to express and release our feelings fully and to tolerate and accept our feelings for however long it takes for the wound to heal. We fear that once acknowledged, grief will bowl us over. The truth is that grief experienced does dissolve. Grief unexpressed is grief that lasts indefinitely.

Judy Tatelbaum, The Courage to Grieve

Every so often through this time, someone would gently suggest that perhaps what I needed was a course of antidepressants. I rejected the idea, knowing that grief and depression are different beasts, although the first can often lead to the second. I knew the source of my grief, and the fact that sometimes I could still feel joy and laugh until I cried was a sign that this was not depression. I sensed a wisdom emerging through the emotion and to anaesthetise myself was to reject it.

I knew I had to sit with and learn to endure my emotional distress.

And it was during the worst of it, when the violence of my sobbing left thought impossible, that I would be carried upwards on the wave of emotion that felt like the pure energy of existence.

I didn't know about it then, but there is a Buddhist practice of welcoming this pulsing energy. When we feel strong emotion, what comes with it usually is fear: fear of losing control, of not being able to stop feeling. Fear of the past, the future. During meditation, by coming back to the simplicity of the breath, we can practise letting go of all the *stories* around the emotion, all the words, thoughts and pictures that come with it. You lean into the emotions and the fear, open the heart and just sit with this restless, painful energy. A transformation can occur when we move toward, not away from our emotional distress.

Another Buddhist practice, Tonglen meditation, instructs us to let the story go and breathe in not just our grief or anger or loneliness but the pain of others who are feeling exactly the same thing at that moment. Instead of stewing in our personal woes, we breathe it in for all, we discover empathy in the wish that all should be free of suffering. And then we breathe out love, we fill the air with compassion, with the wish that all may relax and experience the euphoric essence of the true self.

Another practice involves calming the mind until we are ready to cease judging, to cease viewing the world with fear or desire. Instead, we can begin to see everything as being part of the awakened energy of the universe – an energy that encompasses suffering and darkness. There is pain in our hearts, pain in the world, but it is not some terrible mistake. It is simply a natural part of the energy of life.

Westerners have taken different approaches to dealing with grief. Dr Elisabeth Kübler-Ross's work with the dying, for example, saw her develop a theory about the emotions people experience on being diagnosed with a terminal illness. She believed that if we are granted enough time, we shift from denial to rage, 'bargaining' to depression, until finally we are able to accept with some measure of peace that we cannot escape death.

Many grief counsellors have used this model in their work with people recovering from loss, but the theory has been updated. Australian counsellor and author Mal McKissock talks about a grieving process that doesn't follow stages but is more akin to Chaos Theory, with each individual's path being unique. This idea makes perfect sense to me, given how many factors shape our grief – our age, our relationship with the person we've lost, the way they died, our experience of the funeral, the level of support we receive from friends, family and community.

There is no 'right' timeframe for the resolution of grief. No map to follow. There is only the individual's struggle to move forward in a world that looks different. Only when we recognise that impermanence and loss are at the heart of life – only when we embrace this truth – can we begin to live life more fully.

Cinderella Unshod

For as long as I had dreamed, I had imagined a future that held a long-term, stable and loving relationship. Mr Good Man and I would raise three or so healthy, boisterous children. Work, play and daily life would revolve around that solid core.

With Michael gone and Layla dead, the approach of my fortieth birthday felt like a milestone that marked not what had been achieved but what had been lost.

Not that all hope was lost. It wasn't that I thought I would never love again, never know happiness again. The fear that I would never have another child filled my days with gnawing unease; what was staring me in the face was the reality that my long cherished dream had slowly and stealthily slipped through my fingers. The thought nagged around the edges of my consciousness, but I still could not look at it head-on.

Until one day when I stood outside the newsagent's in Byron Bay. I had stopped to buy a newspaper but a scene on the opposite footpath arrested my attention. An ordinary scene. A mother and father loading their two children and baby into a shiny new Subaru stationwagon.

I stood transfixed. I was meant to be that woman climbing into the Subaru, with my nice husband and my healthy brood. Not the childless, partnerless woman on the other side of the street.

Having a family was a simple dream, achieved by millions. But somehow fate and I had fucked it all up. Standing there, watching that family drive away, I understood I had to let go of that dream, finally and forever. A sickening lurch inside bent me over and I began to cry quietly behind my sunglasses. I had missed the boat.

Over the next few weeks I cast about for people to blame, muttering dark thoughts about feminism, about the men's movement, *why didn't my mother warn me?* As I sat with the pain, I grieved not only the loss of the dream but the loss of the optimism that had fuelled my voyage. Feeling, too, the loss of youth as forty approached.

Dimly I began to understand the way forward. I might perhaps find someone to love, but if not, it was time to embrace the possibility of having a child on my own. It was either fit one in soon or not at all. It would be me and that child – we would be a family. But it was not the picture I had been raised on and had nurtured inside my heart. *The Subaru family*.

Why should we call
these accidental furrows roads?
Everyone who moves on, walks
like Jesus on the sea.

You walking, your footsteps ARE
the road, and nothing else;
there is no road, walker,
you make the road by walking.
By walking you make the road,
and when you look backward,

you see the path that you
never will step on again.
Walker there is no road
only wind trails in the sea.

FROM PROVERBS AND TINY SONGS, ANTONIO MACHADO

JOURNAL EARLY DECEMBER 2000

Quick Sunday-night write.

God, I've been thinking this lately so I better write it down. It feels like I am admitting something distasteful. In this last year after Layla's death, I have a sense of stepping into some larger part of myself. It feels illegal even to write it. Big-noting. But I have come to inhabit my own wisdom. To give way to honesty more often, cry more deeply and laugh harder and louder. To dance, as they suggest, like no one is watching, but admit to myself that I love it when they are. To relax into whatever beauty and grace are mine.

So many years carrying the terror of abandonment. Now I am officially abandoned! And I have grown bigger, not smaller because of it. I have come to know myself more deeply and thus the pain of all humanity more deeply. Surrendering to the pain has made me stronger, in a weird way more *accomplished*.

Like a New Age student swotting at the mirror, I accept and love that I am compassionate, capable, funny and a bit odd. And that I can be controlling and bossy and needy. But I accept how much I love others and how much they love me. I thank you, Layla, for your gift of loving myself more fully.

(And I would still rather you were here.)

Ignore all of the above.

God, I've been feeling so wretched lately. So angry and out of kilter. I want to kill people. That man in the van who was driving too fast and nearly collected me around the corner. I wished that his testicles would contract so violently, he would have to pull over and writhe in agony until he promised God that he would slow down from now on.

I held it all together until the film was finished and since then it's like these rolling waves of anger threaten to swamp me. The littlest of things, the most well-meaning act, the most innocuous comment, sends me on a path of venomous thoughts. I was at my sister's house in Sydney and read a Christmas letter from some friends living in New York, the type of letter sent to lots of people, full of chatty news about their year. How it had been wonderful for them all, what the kids were up to, holidays enjoyed, strides made in their careers. And I wanted to puke with anger.

'Go and get fucked,' I said, throwing the letter down on the pile. Is this me? Where did this bitch come from? Everybody else's lives seem so on-track while mine is swirling down some plughole and I hate who I have become.

I used to believe that common experience united us. Now when I look at a crowd, instead of a mass of people, all I sense is separateness. More than six billion people in the world. Born alone, dying alone. Alone in their pain and angst. I feel such an odd sadness about this. I still feel besieged by the world. So deflated by life's unfair slap. So sorry for myself. I hate this state of victimhood.

My life is such a mess, bills unpaid, tax undone, everything

I haven't coped with all year coming back to haunt me. I am dreading Christmas this year. Life is so overwhelming that if someone stole my wallet, it would feel like the end of the world. Having survived these huge losses, the tiniest thing seems to bring me undone. God is a long way away.

Death Denying

*I*n the early days after Layla's death, when my mother was staying with us and holding the fort, she muttered something about a book she was trying to find. After visiting a friend who belonged to the same meditation group, she came home and brandished it in triumph. 'I've been trying to find it all week and there it was on Sue's shelf!'

She placed it with a flourish on my lap. *Does Death Really Exist?* by Swami Muktananda.

I looked at it in disgust. 'Does death really exist?' I shouted. 'I've been holding death all week. We just burnt her dead body. Yes, death fucking well exists.' I flung the book against the wall. My mother, chastened, fetched it and quickly left the room, murmuring, 'Too soon, too soon.' She was only trying to bring me solace, but it *was* too soon, too soon.

I knew the theory, that death is a continuum of life, a mirror in which the entire meaning of life is revealed. That it is only the body that dies; the true self is revealed in death as a vast nature that is ageless and unchanging. This self does not die but dissolves back into the endless energy of the universe. Death is in fact a liberation of the true self.

I also knew that my emotion and fear were only a function of

my ego. But I could not find peace. I wanted to experience acceptance but I could not. Misery has a way of blocking not just the road
ahead but acceptance of what is here and now.

I knew I should be surrendering to 'what is', and I tried and
sometimes succeeded for short moments. But mostly I railed
against 'what is', losing myself in the torment of 'what could have
been', 'what should be'. I knew these were hopeless and destructive
thoughts but my record was scratched, the needle jammed right
where the rapper cries *fuck*.

I couldn't stop myself worrying about the future, even though I
knew I couldn't control it. I was unable to sit in the present moment
without feeling an uneasy restlessness that propelled me to the
fridge or some other distraction that might take away the pain.

I began to feel envy for those who believed in a 'personal God',
the fatherlike figure who watches over you and protects you, hears
your prayers; the being who might deliver you from pain if you
prayed hard enough.

'I can't seem to find a God who cares,' I lamented to Michael on
one of his visits. It was a warm summer evening on the verandah,
and we talked above a soundtrack of crickets and frogs.

'The spiritual force that I believe in feels like such a big, imper-
sonal force of nature. Monstrous, you know? It's random, cruel and
beautiful but not there cradling me in my darkest hours. It's useless
to cry out or ask to be spared, to be given what I need.'

'I know what you mean, like there's no one listening, no one
with their eye on you or your pain,' said Michael.

'Exactly. There is only nature rising and falling, the way nature
always rises and falls, and me a little ant crawling around in circles
wondering where to turn. It feels useless to even ask for help.'

'I think maybe just forget that notion of God for now,' Michael suggested. 'I really believe there are loving presences in spirit form who are there to guide us or help us. Layla even. Just sit and put your hand up and ask them for help when you need it.'

And so I would sit and invoke the spirit of my daughter, and it was her presence that allowed me to stay vulnerable within the sorrow, that was opening me to a greater compassion for others. The pain forced me to look for that still place beneath the suffering. It would become a guiding ray to my understanding the true nature of this mysterious existence – that God dwells within us, as close as our own heartbeat.

A few days later, Michael sent me some thoughts.

A Meditation for the Broken-hearted

Heartbreak. What does it mean, this pain? What is it really but broken attachment? Something longed for that never arrives or that is held closely but then lost. Another in the endless stream of broken attachments that follow us in this realm, some small, some as large as life itself.

We reach out small tendrils, looking for the sun. Twisting over each other . . . hoping. It seems such a miracle to feel the light sometimes. A new love, money unexpected, recognition . . . Light has many forms. In a world so wounded, it can be an overwhelming relief to find it, to point our leaves to the sun and drink and pray and feel that 'God' must love us somehow. Until, of course, change and loss come again.

If it is big enough, all the darkness in our mind and heart covers us and then we are only the dying leaf. God must have withdrawn his omnipresent grace. We are only this myriad of broken attachments to things and people, with a God that leaves us alone in an endless stream of losses. What is this world where no one gets out alive?

How can a dying leaf really know it is part of the vine? And if the whole vine were to die, how could it know it is part of the earth and sky?

The mystery is that we are changing forms in one changeless reality. In our heartache, are we crying for what is lost or quaking in fear at the glimpse into that enormous emptiness that at once annihilates and binds us?

Does it sound too much, this death and disappearing? This constant loss and change? If it doesn't, are we really awake? For nothing here is certain. And yet if we lie shaking in the deathbed of change, isn't it like endlessly weeping for the ocean each time the tide recedes?

Deepening the Wonder

Death is a favour to us,
But our scales have lost their balance.

The impermanence of the body
Should give us great clarity,
Deepening the wonder in our sense and eyes

Of this mysterious existence we share
And are surely just travelling through.

If I were in the Tavern tonight,
Hafiz would call for drinks

And as the Master poured, I would be reminded
That all I know of life and myself is that

We are just a midair flight of golden wine
Between His Pitcher and His Cup.

If I were in the Tavern tonight,
I would buy freely for everyone in this world

Because our marriage with the Cruel Beauty
Of time and space cannot endure very long.

Death is a favour to us,
But our minds have lost their balance.

The miraculous existence and impermanence of Form
Always make the Illumined Ones
Laugh and sing.

HAFIZ

Four Oh!

et me help you turn forty,' said a male friend when I talked of my dread. He was an alternative medical practitioner whose long marriage had ended, leaving him free to play the considerable field of single women in Byron. A true eccentric, he was also a man at ease with the emotions around death and grieving and had held me many times as I talked and cried through my distress.

He lived on top of a mountain, next to a waterfall, in a simple wood and glass house, one wall formed by an outcrop of rock.

It was the eve of my birthday, and at dusk we sat on his flat roof and meditated together. After a while we talked about aspects of death and the surrender inherent in the milestones of ageing.

His stone courtyard overlooked a dramatic gorge. In one corner, hewn into the rock, was a steamroom and an outdoor bath sat beneath a huge flame tree. An open fire roared in a rock alcove. It was a magical, mysterious place. Even though I lived only thirty minutes' drive away, I felt a million miles from anywhere. We disrobed and sat panting in the steamroom, the heat beginning to melt my anxiety away. Pink and sweaty, we plunged into the waterfall pool together, letting out a banshee wail of shock and exhilaration as the freezing water scoured our skin. 'Now for my birthday gift,' he said, pushing me under the warm outdoor shower.

Inside the house, soft music played as I climbed onto his massage table and settled into a nest of warm towels. He gave me a massage that until my dying day I will remember. Slick with scented oils, his hands plied every knot of tension away. No area was out of bounds. After a time he began massaging me with his naked torso, the feel of muscle and skin bearing down on me a delicious weight, his breath as intense as my moans.

We ate dinner by the outdoor fire before climbing into the courtyard bath. We lay on a bed of river rocks, limbs entwined, staring through the branches overhead at the vast night sky bragging galaxies of stars. Talked of life and just listened to the silence.

'It's nearly midnight,' he said later. 'Time for some champagne.'

'Oh my God, I don't think I could drink more than a sip.' I was sated already.

But he emerged from the house with a bottle and shook it as though we were on a grand prix dais. The cork exploded, followed by an eruption of champagne, which he poured over my head, almost the entire bottle. I let out a wild scream as it ran down my face, the freezing effervescence stinging my eyes, gurgling over my tongue, bubbles popping against my skin.

'I declare you forty!' he laughed.

'I've reached the apex! I'm on the downward slide!' I yelled down the valley. 'I think for tonight we should declare forty the new twenty,' I announced.

'Here, here!' He poured the dregs into a glass and handed it to me.

Somehow, lying in a warm bath under the night sky, covered in champagne, middle age did not seem so traumatic after all.

Layla's Anniversary

When a person you have loved has died, you have endless memories to mourn. When that person is a baby, you are mourning someone you never had a chance to know.

All year I had sensed Layla's spirit close by, inside me, around me. I sat with her picture next to my desk and I would talk to her in my head. Often when I was writing, I felt like I was channelling her. In my work on the film, I was convinced by a very private experience that I was simply doing her bidding. Always I was trying to know her more deeply. Sometimes, when I tuned into her after a night spent working, expecting some profound message, all I would hear is, *It's late! Go to bed!*

Standing at her altar one night, I pondered my motives for making the film. I blew out the candle, turned to go, and she spoke up inside me, telling me it was all right for the project to meet all my needs, that it could provide everything I longed for, no matter how base those motives seemed. She felt to me the essence of compassion, a spirit vast and old and wise. Which was strange, because what I was missing was a baby girl.

The first anniversary of her birth and death was only a few weeks after my birthday. I was in turmoil, knowing I would be re-living raw pain. Someone said to me that often the anticipation is worse than the day itself, and this was so for me.

On 16 February 2001, Michael and I gathered a circle of close friends for a ceremony at home. We had already scattered some of Layla's ashes into the air and ocean off the point at Byron, and today we wanted to put some of her ashes into earth. A dear friend had given us a bodhi tree for Layla, the tree that Buddha had sat beneath as he became enlightened. We planted it in a beautiful ceramic pot and asked each person to place soil and ashes there, to talk about what her death had meant for them.

The documentary was due to air in two weeks and I spoke about how we were now sending her spirit off into the wider world, on a pilgrimage we hoped would be healing and enlightening for many.

Now, my brain has always leaned toward the rational, the provable. Esoteric experiences happen to others, not me. I am not someone in touch with 'the other side', wherever that may be. But then came an experience that language cannot fully convey, a happening delicate and sacred. We began to chant together around the circle, sound vibrations softening the air. Slowly the room became suffused with energy and I felt the distinct presence of what I can only call angels. With tears streaming down my face, I understood they had come to take her. My sobbing made breathing difficult but every cell of my body was alive to the sensation of her spirit actually lifting from within me and ascending into the company of these great beings, moving into the vastness of a wider sphere. I knew in my heart that she was being set free to do the work she had come to do, that her realm was now the infinite. And I suddenly understood that her presence within me over that year had been the source of those strange, magical moments of exaltation.

But still that day I would have given all the world to feel her soft hair grazing my chin as we blew out the candle on her first birthday cake.

Do Not Stand at my Grave and Weep

Do not stand at my grave and weep,
I am not there, I do not sleep.
I am a thousand winds that blow.
I am the diamond glints on snow.
I am the sunlight and ripened grain.
I am the gentle autumn rain
When you awake in the morning's hush.
I am the swift, uplifting rush
Of quiet birds circling in flight.
I am the soft stars that shine at night.
Do not stand at my grave and cry.
I am not there, I did not die!

MARY FRYE

Making Meaning

We have all heard stories of the many ways people commemorate someone lost to them: setting up a foundation to raise money for research into the cancer that killed their wife, lobbying for laws to be changed, cycling the continent to raise awareness of the disease that claimed their child.

The death of someone close can bring many of us deeper into life. For the gift of that, we want to honour not only their life but what they have shown us through their death. Only when I was in grief myself did I fully understand this need to make meaning from loss. I needed to express the way grief had changed me.

We cannot control fate; we can only control how we respond to it. Opening myself to the gifts of Layla's death was one way to make it bearable and to honour all that she had bestowed on me.

Making meaning does not have to involve some grand act. I made a documentary because that's what I knew how to do. Making meaning can be a private affair, a small gesture, like planting a tree or gluing things into a scrapbook. One guy who emailed me about losing a child had built a house as a memorial. 'It's a guy thing,' he said. For others, it could be the tiniest gesture, like feeding a stray dog in honour of the one they've lost.

Creating the film was sometimes the only reason to get up in the morning. I was operating with the missionary zeal of the freshly bereaved. Working both helped me grieve and distracted me from grief.

Michael was very brave in allowing himself to be seen warts and all through the pregnancy and aftermath. But if people described me as brave, I would blush and stammer that this was not the case. Making the film wasn't about bravery – it was about something far more complicated.

What viewers could see was my anguish. I allowed myself to be shown in labour, naked, sweating and vomiting, my face crinkled with grief (the film was a terrible affront to my insecurity about my looks). What I was ashamed to admit, though, was the part of myself that wanted all the world to feel sorry for me because I still felt so sorry for myself. The film was part social document and part primal scream. Mostly I was just a pathetically proud mother who wanted everybody to meet this baby that I was in love with, to make her real to a world that would never know her.

The week before the film aired, I came close to the experience of a nervous breakdown. By four o'clock every afternoon my hands were shaking and my heart felt like it was leaping through the wall of my chest.

Michael and I did a round of interviews for newspapers and radio, explaining our purpose in making the film. The reviews were positive. Still, I felt like I was physically sending Layla's body into the collective arms of a nation that might recoil in horror and say *too much, too much*. I wanted people to see the reality but I feared they would be revolted by the sight of her corpse being bathed and cradled. Put off by a woman in the throes of unbridled grief.

On 1 March 2001, we watched the film go to air on the ABC. We were at my mother's house in Sydney, with family and friends there to lend support. I held on to Mum's hand and wept through the length of it, noting all its flaws, all too aware that strangers were witnessing Layla's life. As the credits rolled I felt drained to exhaustion but had to pick myself up and join the online forum. With Michael to one side and Alex to the other, I could barely focus on the computer to read the responses flooding in.

Ten, twenty, a hundred, a thousand. We couldn't keep up. We would try to answer one and a hundred more would flood in. People were amazed and startled, thanking us for this glimpse into death and grief. People who had lost their own baby were grateful to us for bringing this experience out into the open.

But the greatest response was from parents who had not lost a child, telling us how they had just gone into the bedroom of their sleeping baby or child and picked them up and hugged them. Thanking us for reminding them of the blessing of their child's life. Over the next two hours, a quarter of a million messages were posted. The ABC rang us to say their system was starting to melt down under the volume of traffic.

There were a few detractors. One teenage boy enraged the forum by asking what kind of weirdos would drag a dead baby round for four days? People jumped on him and told him to shut up and get off. All us weirdos could do was laugh with relief that a revolted teenager was the worst of it.

I felt so proud of Layla over the next days, weeks and months as emails and letters flooded in, thanking us for the documentary and telling us how it affected them. One woman shared in a letter how watching the film had been part of the reason she decided not to commit suicide as she battled postnatal depression.

When I thought of all the ways Layla had changed us, and what she had done in a wider sense with the documentary, I couldn't help feeling that her eight hours of traumatic life were like her time on the cross, her journey of sacrifice so that others could more fully appreciate the gift of their own children. That through her death, Michael and I, and thousands of strangers, could more fully live.

The pride, the pain and the ambivalence around that feeling will stay with me forever.

Part Three

NYONE who has loved well and lost will feel chords of their own stored pain and grief ly struck should they watch to-nt's Australian Story, Regarding phael.

n an unusual move, one of the BC program's own production am, Vanessa Gorman, tells her ory. It is about the death of her aby, Layla, shortly after birth 2½ ears ago, the slow rebuilding of her ife and the recent joyous birth of son Raphael.

Gorman has been responsible for some of the program's most ac-claimed stories, including A Ma for All Seasons with Wayn Bennett, Raising the Rafters wit Pat Rafter's family and Happy Garry with Garry McDonald.

A program aired about two ye called Losing Layla — was a

A Meeting

'Come for dinner,' said Ruth, 'just come and have a bit of food and a laugh.'

'I can't. I'm not good company.'

'It's fine, bring whatever mood you're in.'

'I'm just a pathetic basket case at the moment.'

Ruth's warm Jewish nature couldn't bear the thought of a friend in need while a place sat spare at her table. And she had a house-guest she wanted me to meet. She and her husband had just come back from India and James had minded their home while they were away. They had returned to find the living room filled with candles and incense, an Indian feast on the stove.

'Would you like to stay longer?' she'd enquired.

And so he stayed. She had been telling me of their musical nights, her daughter twirling to James's mandolin, singing, laugh-ing and playing the guitar till all hours of the morning. It sounded wonderful but the thought of all that joy left me defeated.

'I just can't,' I said again.

'Come at seven and you can be gone by nine. I'm worried about you schlepping round that house by yourself night after night. Just come. You don't even have to enjoy yourself.'

Ruth could convince a starving dog to drop a juicy bone, and

I could tell she wasn't going to give up. 'Okay, I'll come,' I said, knowing I was going to ring back later and cancel.

She could hear the lack of commitment in my voice. 'Really, really, you can leave early. It will be good for you. You can't mope around at home by yourself forever.'

I was defeated. 'I'll come, but I'm leaving early.'

'Just for two hours,' she said.

James was standing in the kitchen stirring a pot when I arrived. He was tall, fortysomething, darkish to greying. Weathered in a roguish, handsome way. Eyes the blue of summer sky, intensified by dark lashes. I could barely look at him for fear he would look back at me. I didn't want to be looked at. I had not dated anyone new in more than seven years, and being free to follow an attraction left me confused and ambivalent. I didn't know if I had the courage.

After dinner we sat around the outside table and talked about Eastern mysticism. I liked James, sensing a kinship in our exploration of the spiritual. Ruth began joking about how we could hire out James for whatever a person was needing: music, lovemaking, spiritual guidance, betting tips, lawn mowing. The conversation became more and more hilarious until I had to lay down on the bench seat so the laughter would stop hurting. I was surprised at my openness.

At four in the morning I got up to leave. 'Nice meeting you,' I said to James, and stepped forward to deliver a brief kiss on the cheek and a demure, A-frame hug.

He folded me gently against his body and held me there. I tensed and then relaxed as he pressed against my back with his hands. I let my breathing fall into line with his, our chests rising and falling together in a soothing rhythm, the world of separation starting to dissolve. He let out a deep rumbling noise that vibrated from his chest into mine, a kind of mantra without words, a sound that reached deep down into the emptiness.

Reluctantly, I pulled myself away. I drifted home, intrigued. The laughter and communion had left me sated. A reminder of the impermanence of sadness, if only for a night.

JOURNAL MARCH 2001

Ruth and I have dubbed it the summer of love.

I think I've been trying to root out Michael from where he lives in my body. Literally. But when I look into the eyes of the other man, I look into the void. Where am I? Where is he? I look and only see the pain of my isolation. Searching for contact that is impossible to find in any meeting so young. Sometimes when I looked into Michael's eyes, it felt like I could see all of the universe, and myself, floating there, cocooned in love.

Once I am alone again, I come back to myself and my pain. Sometimes Michael is there at the other end of the phone and we cry together and tell each other of our travails. He has slept with someone else as well. We both feel jealousy and sadness. Once or twice we fell into bed together, vowing not to let it happen again.

The prefect in me feels very ashamed, as though I have been trying to fill the gaps in my life with strange *penii*. (If that's not the plural, it should be.) Shoring up my crumbling walls with a pathetic grab for love and acknowledgment. Wanting to be seen, still not wanting to be looked at.

Spent an afternoon last week with Michele, Simon and

Lulu, who are up here on holiday. Lulu is thirteen months, my touchstone – doe eyes, absolutely gorgeous, gurgling, pulling herself up on the furniture. I came home to a dark and empty house and grabbed Layla's urn and sat on the living-room step, rocking back and forth with her ash and bone shards, the unbearable heaviness of being pushing forth ugly noises from my throat. I feel a constant low- to high-level anxiety in my life. I have very little tolerance, very low reserves. Anger is never far from the surface but its sharpest thrusts are reserved for when I berate the weakness that has led me to this place.

I went for a walk before Christmas with Alex, my free therapist. We strolled the leafy streets of Northbridge while her labrador hunted for homeopathic dashes of stale dog pee.

'You know, Ness, after something like this, it can be about a five-year cycle before your life feels like it's back to normal.'

'Five years.' I shuddered.

'It may take that long,' she said, and we walked on in silence.

The Song of the Reed

A few months after we met, James and I began a tentative relationship, the hesitation a reflection of his light tread upon the earth and my disorientation. He arrived in my life with only a sarong, his flute and the twelfth-century poetry of Rumi and Hafiz, padding about the house with the grace of a gazelle.

A musician, a romantic, spiritual fugitive from the conventional world. Interested in finding peace and staying there. Sometimes shy, sometimes gregarious. Reverently irreverent. Accustomed to being looked at but somehow also made uncomfortable by attention. Used to being wanted and accepted, adored even, in the way good-looking people are. But wary of it all. A loner. A gypsy.

His family had moved often during his childhood and adolescence, because of his father's work as a journalist and army officer. That peripatetic existence continued into the wild days of his twenties, when he worked as an actor and at survival jobs, with time off to travel Asia. Good times, drugs, depression, women. An existential longing that sent him on the quest to find understanding, that made him question everything. *What is love? Why do people suffer and treat each other the way they do? Why is this world divided against itself? What is our reality?*

All the questions of a divine discontent.

Seeking answers, he left for India, planning to stay two months. He arrived home three years later, after meeting a teacher who put to rest his questions. He had been following the teachings ever since, downsizing his life so that he now owned just a handful of possessions, with no intention of acquiring more.

Acting gave way to a passion for ritual theatre, and he began narrating profound and beautiful mystical texts at festivals and concerts. Last weekend he went to the football, the races, and performed with his Persian group, Khidir, at a sacred music concert. With a voice like warm honey, he recited the poetry of Rumi and Hafiz, the words woven through classical Middle Eastern music, a performance that brought many in the audience to stillness and tears.

A dashing figure, he seduced me with his grace and his touch, yet wanted nothing more than what I could surrender and offered nothing more than his presence in that moment. While making love, we could surrender everything to each other, but in our lives we could not. Having a child was not on his horizon. He had no interest in the world of regular jobs and routines. And I knew, from painful experience, not to take someone on a path they had no longing for.

'Why do you want so much to have another child?' he asked once.

My answer was simpler now. 'It's a unique relationship of love that I want to experience.'

Our weekends embraced the gentle anarchy of pleasure – walks in the bush, on the beach, a coffee, passionate love in the afternoon.

At our best, our lovemaking was like an explosion, an exquisite dance of union and resistance, our breathing synchronised in an instinctual, tantric flow. A leaving of planet earth for a wild, noisy rapture that could conquer the void.

We would lie there for hours afterwards, resting in each other's arms, at peace. Into the dying light one day, he began to recite the words of Rumi. We lay on the living-room floor, our bodies pressed together as I listened to the words resonate through his chest.

Listen to the song of the reed
How it wails with the pain of separation.

'Ever since I was taken from my reed bed
My woeful song has caused men and women to weep.
I seek out those whose hearts are torn by separation
For only they understand the pain of this longing.
Whoever is taken away from his homeland
Yearns for the day he will return.
In every gathering, among those who are happy or sad,
I cry with the same lament.
Everyone hears according to his own understanding,
None has searched for the secrets within me.
My secret is found in my lament –
But an eye or ear without any light cannot know it . . .'

The sound of the reed comes from fire, not wind –
What use is one's life without this fire?
It is the fire of love that brings music to the reed.
It is the ferment of love that gives taste to the wine.
The song of the reed soothes the pain of lost love.
Its melody sweeps the veils from the heart.
Can there be a poison so bitter or a sugar so sweet
As the song of the reed?
To hear the song of the reed,
everything you have ever known must be left behind.

My soul was reed thin, adrift, the words echoing my own separation from all that I knew. My breath caught in my throat as he spoke, his voice falling as peacefully as water. Eight-hundred-year-old words speaking of the wretched beauty that pain can open us to. *My secret is found in my lament* . . . I felt my heart constrict then literally burst open.

After a lifetime of hard work, and a year of frantic effort on the film – after all the exhaustion of grief – James was an angel sent to help me rest. He would get up and play the flute, naked in the twilight, the mournful notes of his Turkish *nay* filling the air. I would rise dizzily and stumble to the bathroom, drugged from lovemaking, the world dreamy and undefined.

Early evening would drift into night and we would sit outside on the couch, watching the stars in a state of ease. We talked about everything – spirituality, the nature of consciousness, Shakespeare, the performance of the Brisbane Lions, the pros and cons of therapy, me an advocate, he a sceptic.

'You see, I think some people really need therapy when they're facing emotional upheavals they can't sort out by themselves,' I would argue.

'Some people do need therapy, but it's not the emotions that are the problem,' he would counter. 'It's the story that goes along with it. Our lives are not that important. People get too identified with the story and forget who they are underneath that.'

'But most people aren't even aware of who they really are, so they might as well get help to sort through the confusion and heal the pain.'

'Yes, but if they were able to just sit in the meditative presence of awareness, all that would be healed anyway. It all just naturally drops away and they can take a rest from this dysfunctional world.

242

It's the easiest way to be, but I'm not saying it's easy.'

'That's a relief to hear.'

'Big game tomorrow, Ness. The Lions play Port Adelaide.'

'Do you think you're too identified with your team winning?'

'Definitely,' he said in mock seriousness, and burst out laughing.

James offered nothing but himself in the present, and even then, he was hard to locate. He was comfortable in esoteric realms; I wanted to unveil his personality. But if I was wanting him to unpack his heart, I wasn't in a position to do anything much with it.

Then he would go, or I would have to go back to work, and in the days afterwards I would crash and burn. Coming down from our time together, I would fall into the loneliness again, knowing that James was not the one who could save me. In fact, there was no one who could save me from the pain of having to face myself and my fucked-up life again.

I'd been thinking about the faces of grief and how we cope or don't cope. The way I coped? I got out of it, on joints and James and rest and passionate sex, my version of hitting the bottle. But the summer was over and now I needed to face the winter.

He had helped me to glimpse peace again. To find joy and solace, if only in small, quiet moments. But children were not part of his reality. Feeling weak, I asked him to help me separate. I needed to give myself the possibility of having a baby with a partner. I needed to look life square in the face again.

JOURNAL APRIL 2001

I have come to Suva to teach women from non-government organisations how to make documentary television. Passing the crumbling apartment buildings and shanties on the way from the airport, I marvel again at my Western good fortune to be born into a life of comfort and relative ease. Which makes the depression I am feeling even stranger, overlaid as it is by First World guilt.

The work is important, strengthening the media as an arm of democracy, and I am pushing my students to do their best. I usually enjoy teaching but every day is a trial, my mantra, 'This day will end, this day will end.' It's like I am outside of my life and I can't find a way back in. Like I am sleepwalking through a bad dream, the isolation exaggerated by being so far from home. I feel rootless and bereft. I belong nowhere. I should be in my house tending Layla instead of walking through this isolated parallel existence. I just want to go home and yet there is nothing and no one there for me.

A few days later . . .

I have travelled to some dangerous countries in my life but I didn't expect Fiji to deliver the worst.

I went out to dinner with a journalist from AusAID. A soft rain drizzled as we walked home along the main road. We were just outside his hotel when the footpath narrowed and he walked ahead of me, towards two burly Fijian guys coming our way.

I knew when they walked on either side of him. Because normally they would have both stepped off the narrow kerb to let us pass. I smelt the danger in the moist air. They wore blue shorts and white T-shirts, dirty grey tennis shoes. A strange uniform for robbers. They broke into a sprint as one lunged towards me. I grabbed at my bag hanging round my neck. He slammed me into the pavement. It was finally happening to me. I was getting mugged. I clung on, not wanting to lose my identity, money, credit cards.

I understood the inevitability of the loss. But I held on and let out an unholy scream of terror and outrage. A scream so inhuman that even as I made it, I felt embarrassed. I was down on the pavement, soaked, being strangled by the force of his grip on my bag, and I knew I had to let go. That they would hit or kick me hard if I kept up my struggle. I let go my grip and felt the violent tug as the bag was ripped from my neck. Turning to watch them tear off over the road and disappear into the shadows of an old church, I knew the worst was past. I lay wet and shaking on the cold pavement. My umbrella was inside out a few feet away. My hip bone was beginning to throb, grazes on my leg starting to sting. Over the next half-hour, as we informed the hotel security, as the adrenaline wore off, I felt the soreness and bruising settle in. Gradually the shaking subsided and I began to laugh too loudly, with that near hysteria of the survivor.

A couple of frustrating, comical hours at the police station followed, with an officer who had a timeshare apartment on the Gold Coast and wondered whether I'd like to join him there soon.

Back at the hotel I sat down on the bed and gave way to ugly sobbing, adrift in misery. It was too late and too expensive to call anyone. Another forced surrender to a life I didn't even want to be leading.

JOURNAL APRIL 2001

I sat in my chair in the big metal bird and for hours watched the endless expanse of the Pacific Ocean shimmer beneath us. My face was ghostly in the window, tears reflected against white-capped waves thousands of feet below.

They say adversity makes you stronger, a better person. Maybe. Maybe not. A thousand quotes in a thousand New Age books all point to the pain and joy of metamorphosis. I've bought the odd book but often don't get past the first chapter. These personal catastrophes certainly change you forever, but as for joy . . . ?

I can't seem to reconcile my old self with the new. I grieve for Layla and Michael and the optimistic, trusting person I was. Finding in her place just someone in pain. A shell, with a big hole in my chest.

Coming through Sydney, I attended an old friend's fortieth birthday party. All night on a large screen an endless procession of family photos was projected. He and his wife and their three kids, growing from babies to children before our eyes, clutched at picnics and on the beach and on the deck of a yacht. A happy stream of images that tortured me as I moved amongst the crowd of nice married couples. I asked after their children, heard their condolences about Layla, and felt again that queasy shock at missing the boat.

I recognise that I have had an amazing life. I have travelled to some extraordinary places and moved through the landscape of my wildest dreams. I have met many inspiring people; known the power and pleasure of creative and meaningful work. I have danced in wild abandon and cried and laughed at life from the deepest place. But in my most desolate moments, it all feels meaningless. I have failed to do that which was most sacred to me, what I longed for at the deepest level. It feels ridiculous that at forty, I am attempting to start a family from scratch.

Reconciliation

There had always been the hope of reconciliation with Michael, if his bolt for freedom didn't work out. A suggestion, too, that he might be a sperm donor if no alternative presented itself.

We'd had no contact for two months, on his insistence. Some days I cried out to him and wanted to pick up the phone. But I kept away.

'The time away has been good for me,' he said, when we finally caught up.

I snorted, 'I'm glad it was good for you.' I tried to stop myself scowling.

'I needed to do it,' he said, ignoring my barb. 'I can't be the one to hold you up. I can't get sucked back into that place, because if I do, I'll be doing it to save you, not because I want to be there. I miss you, I love you, but I feel like I am heading in the right direction, being by myself.' He looked at me, cocking his head the way he does when issuing a challenge. 'I'm not coming back.'

It was matter-of-fact. A bald statement that sat heavily between us. I gave almost nothing away, but a thrill of painful energy surged through my body and I took a deep breath. This was it then. The final full stop.

I had guessed it was coming. But hearing it was something

different again. His words settled into the deepest place of my heart. Somehow I was a little sad I did not feel more.

'Don't think I don't find it hard. Don't think I don't miss you and think about you. You are what I hate to give up. I just know I can't give you what you need right now.' His hands formed a prayer as he continued. 'I need you to save yourself. I can't save you. I need to ask you a favour.' He pressed his hands to his forehead. When he drew them away, he had tears in his eyes. 'If I could ask you for one gift. Please take care of yourself. Find happiness. Do whatever it takes.'

I began to cry. That *he* cared enough to cry. That I had to find happiness without him. And all I wanted to tell him was something he didn't want to hear. 'I miss you,' I cried out.

I heard him suck in his breath. 'I know, I miss you too. Shit, I've felt lonely. I still have sexual fantasies about you. I worry about you, that's all. Fuck, I worry.'

'I'll try to take care of myself. I am taking care of myself,' I lied. 'Okay, I am *trying* to take care of myself.'

'Good. Because now it's time to choose life, it's time to do whatever it takes to move into happiness. It's time to take my photos down, it's time to move Layla's altar from the centre of the house. Time to get your train back on track and moving towards whatever it is you want. I'll be here just for practical help.'

'How are you feeling about the sperm donation thing?'

He hesitated. 'Look . . . I hate saying this, but definitely not, Vanessa. I know myself. I know how I will get sucked back into it all. I couldn't even think about it for two or three years. But I'll be your number one uncle.'

I got up to change the CD, partly to hide my distress. 'You shouldn't promise that,' I said bitterly. 'You shouldn't promise anything around children, because that's one place you never keep your promises.'

'Sorry, but I don't want to be seen as the uncommitted, flaky male just because I didn't want to have children. I was very committed to finding a love that worked for us. In a sense you left the relationship first. You left your commitment to me, to follow your own need to have a child.'

'Wanting to have children with you was also an expression of how much I loved you.'

'Yes, but not wanting children was not a reflection of my not loving you!'

Our spats had always been shortlived, both of us more interested in finding a deeper understanding than playing some fault or blame game. Eventually eight glasses sat between us. Without a hint of a damn good shag.

'You know you taught me the freedom of honesty,' I said, feeling nostalgic.

'And you taught me that love doesn't have to always mean suffocation.'

'I guess we just did the best we knew at the time, and it was brilliant and faulty. Our dreams cancelled each other out.'

'Maybe I'll miss out on a few things,' he said, 'but when they finally put me in my coffin, at least I can say I followed my questions as truly as I knew how.'

'When they finally put you in your coffin, you won't be able to talk.'

'Pedant.'

We laughed, came to rest in the other's gaze and raised a glass to the future.

JOURNAL 10 JUNE 2001

Cathy and Jeff, the producers of my film, asked me to come to South Africa to work on their documentary, *The Man Who Stole my Mother's Face*. Again, all I can feel is immense gratitude for the peace of Australia when I come to a place like this. Johannesburg is a city at war with itself, the whites and the Afrikaners and the blacks all jostling for a piece of the new Africa.

The disparity of wealth is enormous. We are staying with Jeff's cousin in a wealthy part of town. This ordinary suburban street, like so many, has boom gates manned by armed guards letting people in and out. The houses all have massive walls topped with spikes or barbed wire, electrified fences, fierce guard dogs, alarms, electric gates – and still no one feels safe. Car hijackings are common, and muggings, rapes and attacks are everyday occurrences. Everywhere we go, people give us the drill in case our car is hijacked: *get out of the car, leave your belongings, don't look them in the eye, don't resist.*

There are four million blacks living around the city, in shanty towns and tiny boxes. They are dispossessed and have very little opportunity and they look over to the rich whites and think, Why not get a piece of whatever I can? I watch them anxiously from the warmth and comfort of the car as they hawk everything and anything at the traffic lights. There is a black woman we pass every day near the city, her time spent on a busy traffic island selling newspapers. She does it all with a toddler at her side and I want to weep for that child. We pooled some money and gave it to her, hoping it might give the child some relief from days trapped on a square foot of concrete in the stench of traffic smog. The sheer grind of everyday life for the poor is overwhelming.

We are here researching and doing preliminary filming for Cathy's film about the sexual assault of her mother twelve years ago, an unsolved crime. But it will also be about the extraordinarily high incidence of sexual assault against women and children in South Africa.

My skin is so thin at the moment that hearing about these cases is a kind of torture. I recognise that my own suffering is inconsequential in this wider context but I feel their pain so keenly and can find no safe place to lay it down.

It is sixteen months since Layla died and in a sense it feels like all the fuss has now died down and everybody else has moved on and I am left here with the grief. I suppose now I just have to make a decision to move on with my life. To move forward rather than sink. But where to move on to?

I feel so lonely for that one other in my life. I want to pour out my heart to someone but there is no one to pour it out to. I have so much love to give and no one special to give it to. It's like this blank page is my closest friend.

We are spending two days in Cape Town at the end of the trip and then it's back to the Byron hills, where people don't even lock their houses.

Postcard for Layla, from Table Mountain

I sit perched on a cairn on this sculptured, magnificent mountain towering above this strange city (strange to me at least). And all alone I call out your name in anguish, yelling it three times across the heath and rocks, desperate to hear the echo. And sob deep wracking cries unashamedly into the cool crisp sunshiny air, but still careful to glance about for other walkers. And I wonder if the dead travel with us?

If your spirit can hear me at home, can you also hear me thousands of miles away? And what sort of mystery is this? It feels as though I am the only one that mourns you, although many others care. I carried the rage up the tough trek of the gorge, fuelled by the injustice of it all. The sobs freed by the hard work of the body now, but they never will be spent. They never will be over, I realise, for all the days of my life. Just one tiny speck of time in the aeons these rock formations have weathered, like silent sentinels observing the city forming beneath it, watching the ships wrecked on its cape. Witnessing the atrocities of Robben Island as Nelson was condemned to hard labour and his country struggled towards freedom. There is nothing for it but to cry and then eventually to stop crying because the sun is getting lower. I add a stone in your name to this cairn and move on over the mountain in the direction of that Cape of Good Hope.

It was on that trip, on that mountain, that I made the decision to have a child alone. If someone had told me in my twenties that I would be forty, childless, partnerless and planning to be a single mother, I would have laughed.

I flew home newly resolute, although still weighed down by a melancholy cargo of thwarted dreams.

New Horizons

*F*unny how it happens – when you stop grasping, things fall gently into your empty lap. I returned from South Africa to find James still wanting to pursue a relationship. More than that, in my absence he had realised that he could give me a child. That it was something he wanted to do, for my healing.

'It's what you said about the parent–child bond being a unique relationship of love,' he said. 'Something about that struck me. It suddenly made me think, Yes, that's the best reason I've heard to do it. I don't know whether I'll even enjoy the experience but I can see this is something you really need to do.'

So there it was, a man offering me this most precious of opportunities. The simple *yes* I had been longing for. And there was I, frozen in a new ambivalence.

I had come to love being in his presence, experiencing peace and silence together, the amiable chatter of everyday life, unravelling the messages of the mystics. The explosive force and tenderest moments of our lovemaking. However, what we were asking of each other now was a new level of commitment. Was I ready to open my heart to another? To trust and throw myself back into the fray? Dimly I understood that perhaps it was too soon to enter that territory again – in short, I had serious baggage. I was still in the process of letting go of Michael, not ready to absorb fully all that James was offering. I didn't want to burden him with my grief.

I found it difficult to express all this; the way James and I communicated was different to how Michael and I had talked. Often I had trouble opening myself so James could see all that was in my heart. Often I found it hard to read all that was in his. But his was a roguish mysticism. He had a refined sensibility that could give way to cruder musings, an ethereal grace that could morph into earthiness. A sense of humour that could see through it all. All this buoyed me.

I fell in love with both the mystic and the precious tender soul beneath the man the world saw. And he was patient, so slowly, slowly it began to happen. Our coming together was as subtle as life – confusing, beautiful and everything in between.

Ultimately, there was a simplicity to our love, an honest, uncomplicated enjoyment of each other that promised a kind of relief.

And so we set our shoulders to the task of conception.

JOURNAL SEPTEMBER 2001

I'm on the treadmill, caught up in the perennial human search for something outside of ourselves, something to save us from misery and despair – someone's love, another child. Perhaps winning the lottery?

I am coming to understand that nothing will save me except myself. That I have to go deep inside and find the place of silence where nothing is touched by external events, where painful emotions can rise and fall but not permeate the peace.

I think I am scared to sit and meditate, because it means sitting with my grief and to do that makes me agitated.

My mind can feel like such a sewer – with all its anger and resentments, all its sadness over those I have lost. The frustration of wanting it to be different. Who would want to give all this its own special time when it seeps through the cracks of everyday life anyway?

I feel like a broken record. I miss Layla. I just miss her. I want to have something novel and interesting to say to people about the grief but there is nothing new to say except that I miss her and people seem no longer interested in hearing it. I want someone to ask me about all the ways I miss her. So I can tell them I miss her body meshing with mine. Her babbling and tottering form around the house. Her surprise and delight as the world unfurls around her. Her sleeping face in the rear-view mirror as I drive home, her flattened curls and red cheeks after sleep. She would be nineteen months old now. Finding her noises, her words, her song, her separate identity. I just want someone to let me talk, not about how I am, but about her. But she is invisible and I have nothing new and interesting to say about grief. So I stay silent.

Grieving parents are more alike than people think.
They have at least one thing in common: they have to
make Herculean efforts to hold a normal, banal, bouncy
conversation. They can think of only one thing, the moment
when they might introduce a sentence about their child.
Thirteen years have passed and I still cannot last half a day
without evoking my daughters.
Genevieve Jurgenson, The Disappearance

September 11

Other people's celebrations can be tough, their happiness casting my own anguish into starker contrast.

It was nineteen months since Layla had died. I'd had a day wandering the house, persecuting the walls with the victim's lament, 'Why me, why did this happen to me?' Leah called to say a friend of hers was having a spiritual initiation that night and there would be food and dancing and laughter, and why didn't I come along? Since another night by myself was not a happy thought, I put on make-up to hide my tear-stained cheeks and joined her.

I hid down the back of the hall as the initiates were inducted into a local spiritual group, ecstatically going through their paces as I sat numb and wretched. I disliked them as they hugged each other with rapturous tears, their world as expanded as mine was contracted. After people left the hall for dinner, Leah held me in her arms. I sobbed, blotching the stupid make-up, feeling the sheer desolation of missing Layla so much.

We talked over dinner, shared a joint and then the music began.

'Are you up to it?' asked Leah.

My misery was spent for the day and the joint had prised open my heart. We took to the dancefloor and immediately I felt the joy surge through me, the euphoria of the music rushing through every meridian as I moved to embrace the rhythm.

Such a relief to feel myself suddenly in the flow of life again. I raised my arms and danced, offering up all my sadness and all my misery. And with that feeling of joy and pain came a deeper awakening to the obvious, ultimate truth – that I am not alone. That the whole planet is filled with people in pain, in grief, in despair. That this is the nature of being human and alive – pain is part of the universal flow just as joy is, and who was I to be exempt from suffering? Who was I to be outraged that it had happened to me? Instead of 'Why me?', I asked, 'Why not me? Why the hell not me?' A surrender that at last felt like a liberation.

For the next two hours I threw my body around with the wild, creative dancers of Byron Bay and celebrated the flow of life with the trancey, dubby, doofy beats of freedom.

I was home after midnight to hear my brother's urgent voice on the answering machine: 'Turn on the television.' It was morning in America and planes were plunging into skyscrapers. Flicking from one news report to the other, I sat open mouthed with shock as people on fire fell from windows, great towers of glass collapsed and survivors staggered out of dust clouds that devoured half the city.

These haunting, terrifying images were seared into the collective memory of the world in the days to follow. The analysts talked of terrorism, al-Qaeda and Osama, but like most people, all I could think about was the pain, the waves of shock and grief sweeping through the hearts of the thousands left behind after this most violent and public execution. People queued in the streets of Manhattan, looking for a place to pin their 'missing' notices, weeping as they held up pictures of the lost. I sat on the step in my living room and cried for them all, all the children and lovers and families and friends catapulted into this country of grief. Knowing something of what they would face in the days and months ahead – the disbelief, the hate, the terror at life's capacity to destroy, the desolation of missing that one so dearly loved.

I wanted them to be spared the terrible pain of deep grief, the way I had wanted to be spared. I tried to breathe in their pain and breathe out love but too often my breath would catch in my throat with the horror.

After four days of blanket coverage, I turned off the television, exhausted. I sat and prayed for these strangers, sending love and courage as they began the long road back to wholeness. The house settled into an eerie silence in a world that seemed changed forever.

JOURNAL SEPTEMBER 2001

None of us know the day our life will change forever. This is the exhilaration and terror of life, knowing that as sure as there will be a day when we find love, there will be the day we lose it. The day when life beckons but death delivers. The day when our life turns 180 degrees and heads off in some direction we never expected.

To love deeply is to expose ourselves to the possibility of profound loss. The deeper we love, the deeper we grieve. But this is life's challenge: to open ourselves wide and embrace everything life hurls at us. To smile at our destiny. As Joseph Campbell said, 'There is no meaning in life. We have to find the meaning.'

It takes courage to stay open, courage to take those tiny

steps forward, those occasional great leaps of faith and trust. The hardest question to face when the world is dark is this – do we close down or open up to all that life sends us?

JOURNAL OCTOBER 2001

And life resumes. Except I have a secret.

I have been back working on *Australian Story* for a few months. It has been so strange to return to my old job as though nothing has happened. Looking normal, making jokes, wearing my old self but feeling the chasm yawn just below the surface.

I am down in Sydney now, starting a story on Gary McDonald. My period is four days late so I stop on the way home from filming and buy a pregnancy test and then wee on it in the romantic surrounds of the ABC toilet. It's positive. I start to laugh, yelps of disbelief that catch in the throat. And then I spend the entire weekend crying, missing Layla in such an unbearable way. All I can remember is the sheer joy when I found out I was pregnant with her. The innocence.

Now I know too well that being pregnant does not necessarily end with a new life. I have read too much. I am a walking encyclopaedia of what can go wrong. Blighted ovum, unexplained miscarriage, incompetent cervix, placental malfunction, cord strangulation, Trisonomy 18, Down's syndrome, stillbirth, neonatal mishap – the entire sorry landscape of fertility loss is branded on the part of my brain marked 'fear' .

Still, the last few days I have been walking around with a quiet, joyful hope starting to fill me. I told my sister Rebecca, just to make it real, but I am holding my breath. It will be a long forty weeks.

JOURNAL NOVEMBER 2001

I was nervous about telling James, our relationship still so new. I think he got a shock. Agreeing to the hazy concept of possibly having a child one day was one thing, actually being pregnant an entirely different reality. He went quiet for a few days. Digestion mode. And then, I think not entirely in jest, he mentioned a trek he had always planned to do, walking between temples in Vietnam . . .

On the phone to Ruth, I joked that he might just keep on walking and we would only receive word of him, from somewhere in Iceland, when the baby was starting high school.

Back in Sydney, editing the story, the morning sickness hit with a vengeance, waves of it all day and night. We were editing in a tiny airless booth on a floor they were refurbishing. The toxic stink of glue as new carpets were laid and the fumes of fresh paint only made things worse. Harley, the editor, would say, 'What do you think of putting that shot there?' And I would say, 'Hang on', and rush to the toilet and vomit, then come back and say, 'Yes, that would work well if that shot followed it.' He has three kids, so he understood.

Long days editing, long nights scripting in my motel room, dry-retching into the ice bucket and pressing hard into my eyeballs to force them open. I read somewhere that morning sickness is a sign of a strong pregnancy, so I am actually happy to be feeling like the arse end of a mongrel dog.

Arrived home to find James now excited, in a quiet sort of way, about the baby. He likes the fact that telling people makes them happy. Loves that his mum and family are overjoyed at the prospect. I'd forgotten the joy that news of a baby can elicit. It's beautiful to be in that bubble of warm wishes again.

Life or Death?

knew that anxiety and fear would be my constant companions in this pregnancy. Even so, I felt anxious about my anxiety, fearful of so much fear. There seemed only one sensible solution and that was to embrace it all. Fully. Make these emotions, if not my friends, at least amiable acquaintances. *Ah yes, there you are*, I'd say when they rose to torment me. I would breathe deeply, letting the fear play itself out. I wanted to be free but knew it was impossible. Pregnancy was asking me to surrender again to the possibility of life or death.

James stayed open, and could listen to my anxiety with a calm I envied. 'It won't happen twice,' said friends, trying to reassure me. I wanted to growl at them. How did they know? How can they know the future? I had read so many stories of parents who had faced multiple losses. Tragedy could strike again. But secretly I told myself it would not happen again. I prayed that it would not happen again. I meditated on it not happening again. And forced myself awake from yet another dream about a dead baby.

I had an obstetrician in every port, Brisbane, Sydney and Byron, and I decided to have an amniocentesis to rule out another avenue of anxiety. The results were sent to my Brisbane doctor. 'It's all good,' he said. Hugely relieved, I asked him about the sex. I needed to know.

'Okay,' he said, 'I'm going to staple shut this piece of paper and you and your partner can sit on the couch tonight and open it together.'

James wanted a boy. I suppose deep down in my heart I longed for another daughter. I couldn't bare to look, held my breath as James pulled at the staples. 'It's a boy,' he said, grinning.

I can't lie. My heart leapt and sank all at once. There it was, a boy, just as the psychic had said. There was something right about the news. *A boy. Good, good, different from Layla. I can't even pretend that it would be her. A boy then. A son. I would have a son.*

My hope grew stronger as each week passed without mishap. I was growing larger in spirit and body. Talking myself into it. Healing each day, and yet still the tremor of anxiety. Wondering how much I could let myself love him. *What the hell. If he dies too, I'll love him just as much as Layla so I might as well cast caution to the wind and let myself fall in love.* I collected clothes for a boy and cried as I sorted through the pile of clothes collected for Layla, passing them on for other little girls with a heavy heart.

Contemplating labour again, I felt my body constrict with fear. I talked to my doctors about options and trawled the net for answers, statistics. We decided to have him by Caesarean in the hospital with the biggest neonatal intensive-care ward in the state, the Royal Hospital for Women in Randwick. I was sorry that a rude awakening into a cold and brightly lit operating theatre would be part of his birth experience but I was desperate to do everything I could to make sure he lived.

'Your first?' said a man at the pool one day, noticing my bump.

I eyed him, made that split-second decision. 'No, it's my second,' I said, acknowledging Layla.

'Ah, you know what you're getting into, then,' he laughed, and I smiled like I did know.

I never wanted to deny Layla but neither did I want to go into the story with just anyone. Always that momentary weighing-up. Was I up to explaining? How would they react? I didn't want to throw my darling pearl before a swine. In the changeroom an older woman asked the same question. She was kindly and we were both naked, so the truth seemed appropriate.

'It's my second, but my first baby didn't survive.'

'I'm so sorry,' she said. 'My daughter lost a baby.'

And then it was on, *the conversation*, the exchange.

Acknowledging Layla's loss connected me to a surprisingly vast army of people who had experienced reproductive loss, their pain as invisible as the children they have lost.

JOURNAL FEBRUARY 2002

Layla's second anniversary coincided with a visit to Sydney. I invited three girlfriends and my two sisters to meet me at Mum's house for a small ceremony. I asked them to bring photos of their own children to place in the circle. I needed to honour the day with these dearly loved people, but more than that, I needed a safe harbour after another year at sea, grieving for her alone. We all cried. It was moving for me to hear how Layla's death had affected them. How it had brought life and death closer together, for better or worse.

'I just don't know how I'd cope if Marcus died,' Bec said through her tears, pushing a picture of her blue-eyed boy into the centre.

'After Lulu was born,' said Michele, 'there was all the joy,

265

but when I heard about Layla everything sort of changed. I felt so sad for you that instead of rejoicing in Lulu, I cried every day for months.'

'I look at the girls sometimes,' said Annie, 'and I feel a kind of survivor guilt.'

'I know what you mean,' added Amanda. 'And sometimes when I look at Liam now, I feel this awful terror that something might happen to him.'

Somehow, hearing their empathy was a vindication of my pain. It was a strange relief just to have a space to sob without reservation or apology. Mum led a meditation about feeling gratitude in our lives and then we all ate lunch and talked of politics and Sydney real estate and other people, *and could you pass the salad and anyone for more wine*? Life resumed again, Layla relegated to her status as a sad memory. But for a while, she had been right there in the middle of the circle, as real and alive as the other children in the photos.

When people heard I was pregnant, they would inevitably ask, 'Are you doing a sequel to the documentary?'

'No,' I would say firmly. 'I'm leaving the camera behind for this one.'

My boss, Deb Fleming, had also raised the question of doing an *Australian Story* follow-up, but it felt too hard to contemplate, as if making another film might jinx things. I knew that people were asking for a happy ending to a sad story, and I felt irritated. How could there be a happy ending when Layla was dead?

After a public speaking engagement in my eighth month, three women rushed up to me. 'I think so many people were traumatised by your film that it would be beautiful to see something happy after such a sad journey. You owe it to us,' one stated bluntly. Something about her words, her insistence, made me bristle, laugh, then relent. In the end I decided I would make an *Australian Story* episode, to celebrate my son's place in the world, and to make the point that having a live, healthy baby does not take away the grief for the one lost. The loss lives on for parents, no matter the joyous events that might follow.

Even so, I didn't feel driven to do it. Rather, I felt almost embarrassed to be calling attention to myself again. *Losing Layla* had a message to give, but this time I wondered if I would be simply satisfying people's curiosity to find out what happened next, as if we were characters in a soap opera.

We didn't begin filming until my ninth month, just a few scenes of James and my heavily pregnant self wandering a beach and an interview about the pregnancy.

During the weeks leading up to the birth, I felt anxious that he would just up and die inside me. 'Hang on,' I would whisper to him, and feel relief every time he prodded and poked me. *Just one more night now – hang on.* James and I had rented a motel room near the hospital, and we were both lost in our own worlds. I was anxious, he was uncertain. We were tense, a little irritated with each other.

I tossed and turned all night, unable to sleep.

Lifeforce

It was a spectacular winter dawn: brushstrokes of deep orange and pink splashed against inky blue sky. James and I paused in the hospital's carpark and held each other, marvelling at nature's heralding of our momentous day.

'Hang on, little one,' I whispered as I showered and filled out forms. 'Just a few more hours.' I wanted him out and breathing.

Once again I was on a trolley, waiting for an operation. But this time everything was calm.

We had a top anaesthetist, but something went wrong with the epidural and it didn't work. Out came the massive needle and another was inserted. Time passed. The new block didn't work properly either. I was beginning to feel sick with whatever drugs they were pushing in there. The anaesthetist told me the next day that I was dosed to the edge of toxicity.

Then we are off to the operating theatre, crowded with staff and ABC film crew. My eyes roll back in my head. I want to vomit. Feeling odd sensations, the sense of my flesh being pulled and cut, the anaesthetist standing by to knock me out if the pain gets too bad. Wanting desperately to be conscious for the birth, I breathe deeply through the pain. The smell of burnt flesh, pulling, tugging, even being told to push. Thinking, *There just is no easy way to get them out.* James beside me, staring fascinated over the drapes at my insides. And then the whoosh as he is pulled from me. I hear a cry, a shocked bellow, and they lower the drapes and someone helps me lift my head and there he is, pink and slimy and outraged, letting go an almighty howl as he is lifted and held aloft like the magnificent trophy he is, his outrage the most blessed noise. James and I look at each other and laugh with delight.

Then he is taken from sight and I can breathe out. James goes to be with him, anxious to hold him close at the first opportunity, cuddle him tight.

The nurse calls out that he is healthy and well, Apgars excellent. Finally I can let go of my heavy load of anxiety, the fear that he would die inside me. And in the same moment I feel all the echoes of Layla's birth, and I can't help it, I am no longer in control of any part of myself and I hold my hands over my face and sob for the pain that has been my heart these two and a half years.

I got to hold him properly for the first time in Recovery, this little bundle of newborn glory. His eyes lazily wandered, his mouth opening and closing with his first tastes of the world. The nurses propped me up and opened my nightgown and placed him within reach. The euphoric surprise of his vacuum seal over my nipple, the strength of his gummy grip, his determined lifeforce making me gasp and laugh with delight as he began what would be his favourite pastime.

Upstairs, my mother and sisters are lined up, James's sister, everybody crowding around to meet him. The tiny hospital room is jammed with family and friends and film crew, celebration in the air, relief. I want to laugh and cry and hold him and sleep for two days straight.

James and I had agreed on his name, our very first choice. Raphael, for the archangel who comes to earth to heal, an immense task shouldered with innocence. Raphael. Raf. Raffie. It worked for a prime minister, an artist, a small child, an angel of healing.

Over the next few days people arrived smiling and overjoyed, clutching useful presents instead of consoling flowers. Everything was as it should be after the birth of a baby. Learning to change his nappy and bathe him. Learning how to attach him to the nipple. Waking through the night to feed him, cuddling a squirming bundle. I could hardly believe that he was breastfeeding, that his nappy had poo in it. His gurgles and cries a symphony of sound that would make me smile.

I was filled right to the brim with the extraordinariness of this most ordinary event. I felt like I was living some kind of amazing miracle, even though I knew it was being repeated in rooms up and down the corridor, had been repeated billions of times on the planet. I was high on painkillers and Raffie and ordinary life, lived finally as it should be.

On the third day I crashed and burned, hormonally charged blues colliding with the realisation of everything that I had missed out on with Layla. A nurse sat with me as I choked on the sorrow, the pain of the past rising and falling within the joy of the present. But with Raffie in my arms, and the hilarious sight of the six-foot James crammed quietly into a chair knitting, I rejoined the world, and it was a marvellous place to be.

The tears came again at the thought of leaving the security of hospital walls. How to keep Raf safe in the world? Placing him in our car seemed the most treacherous thing we could do. A great rage filled me, at all the careless, dangerous drivers on the road, hurrying, running yellow lights. There was shame, too, for my old self who skipped blithely through the traffic. I wanted to protect his tiny fragility from all the dangers of the world, to protect my own heart as well, powerless with rapture for him.

We stayed at my older sister's place for ten days, and I gorged myself on visitors' admiration for our little fellow who slept all day amidst the mayhem of family life and was awake much of the night.

One day, feeling brave, I bundled him up in the pram and set out for a long walk through the crisp winter sunshine. I knew I was an ordinary sight, a woman negotiating a pram along a suburban footpath, but I felt triumphant. I was Persephone back from the underworld. Demeter turning the earth to spring. Ulysses sighting home after his epic journey. And I was a mere mortal – I walked too far and my stitches began to hurt. I had to call my sister to come and collect us in the car.

The day we flew home to Byron, our friends gathered to greet us. I will never forget the sight of their beaming faces, arms aloft, forming a guard of honour through which we carried Raffie as he slept in his capsule. I didn't know whether to laugh or cry at their beautiful welcome.

And then life with a new baby began and the reality of this ordinary miracle hit us with the force of a tornado, sucking us up and dropping us into the foreign land of the newly born and their newly bewildered parents.

There are just enough stories about new babies who sleep well, wake to feed, gurgle a bit and then fall off to sleep again to give every expectant parent some hope that they will win the lottery. But for many, that hope is noisily extinguished by the first plaintive cries of a colicky, unsettled baby.

It was an El Niño winter, dry and mild, the warmest people could remember. The days settled into the routine of no routine as Raphael slept, woke, fed, became overtired and cried relentlessly into the evening. We paced the floor with him for hours, trying to settle him. I became intimately acquainted with all the moods of the night, feeding and soothing him back to sleep.

Once again we were enfolded by the loving arms of friends and community. People rallied to help, making an ad hoc roster to bring meals and hold the crying baby. But the mind-numbing exhaustion was relentless, and never getting more than three hours sleep in a row sapped my reserves.

JOURNAL JULY 2002

Sometimes I used to feel like Superwoman. I can remember striding down corridors at work and feeling a sort of power surge through my veins. I did a job that was hard to do and a certain smug satisfaction would rise momentarily, in between the waves of mild panic as the next deadline loomed. But I was generally confident and in control. And then I had Raf . . .

Right now I feel so out of control, so vulnerable.

He is trying to sleep, trying to sleep, but no sooner do I finish reading another novel, rocking him off, than suddenly the little legs pull up and pain hits and he's awake again, crying. Pacing the floor with him, singing ridiculous made-up verses of 'Hush little baby don't you cry, Mama's gonna buy you a uranium mine.' I pause under the windchimes and make them tinkle with my head and he stops crying for an instant to listen, and then it's back on, all night, on and off. The next day, both of us delirious, a photographer arrives to take pictures to accompany a magazine article about Raffie's birth. The make-up lady spoons concealer over the dark bags under my eyes and all afternoon pictures are taken – Raffie being overfed, overhandled, missing another sleep, until he is hysterical. James and I pose with him, the photographer asking us to keep the smile plastered on our faces so he can snap the instant Raffie draws breath between one scream and another.

He was inconsolable from four till nine at night, when James took him for a drive and I lay before the fire, catatonic. All the drive did was clam him up for half an hour. A shot of baby Panadol, a shot of Mylanta for the reflux, Rescue Remedy. Anything . . . Still crying. I rang my friend Lynda in tears.

'Strong alcohol,' she said.

'For the baby?' I asked, alarmed.

'No, for yourself. A big nip of Scotch.'

At least it calmed me down. We gave him his second bath of the day to relax him and he cried again until eleven p.m. and then fell into an exhausted sleep but woke again at three a.m. I pushed him in the pram around the living room until four a.m.

'Any ideas?' I said to James.

'Maybe another bath?' he suggested, as perplexed as I was. In for the third 'relaxing' bath of the day at five a.m. Finally a fitful sleep, for an hour, at six a.m.

Lynda arrived in the morning and gathered Raffie in her arms, sending James and I out to a cafe. Black Monday will forever be etched on my memory. It is perhaps the most unbearable thing, to endure your child's screams of pain and not be able to soothe them. I understand now how parents and carers can get to the end of their tether and shake a baby or do them harm. Once or twice I have had to do what the baby books suggest and just lay him down safely, still crying, and walk outside and take some deep breaths. I would never harm him but even feeling the flicker of an urge gave me an enormous shock. Parents' helplines were either engaged or wanted you to leave a message so they could call back in office hours. This kind of support is underfunded and underresourced.

I have resources and support, he is desperately loved, and still I am finding it hard to cope. What of the babies of people less equipped to cope, under greater stress?

Joanne, the naturopathic, homeopathic angel of mercy, came the other day and suggested I cut wheat and dairy, and about thirty other foods that might cause wind, from my diet. That finally seems to be working.

I am overwhelmed when I have to take him out into the world. The other day I was contemplating appointments I had to keep over three days, and honestly, if someone had told me to get on a plane and fly to Mogadishu and film in a cholera-infested warzone, I would have felt less anxious than I did at the thought of taking Raffie out and have him miss a sleep and set up another tragic evening of crying and sleeplessness. I will never again scowl at a screaming baby on a plane or in public. I will let the mothers go before me in queues and help them up stairs with their prams. You never really understand the sheer vulnerability of the early days of this parenting journey until you go through it yourself.

One reason there is not a great deal written about what it is like to be the mother of a new infant is that there is rarely a moment to think of anything else besides that infant's needs. Endless time with a small baby is spent asking, *What do you want? What do you want?* Until I've satisfied her need, my brain is a white blur. I lose track of what I've been doing, where I've been, who I am.

Louise Erdrich, 'A Woman's Work'

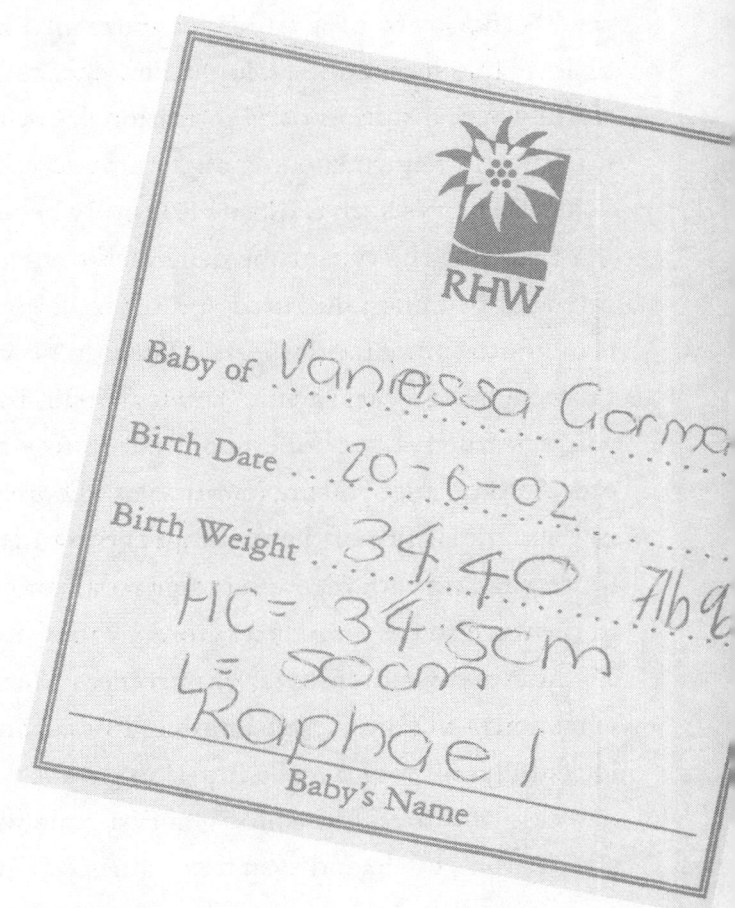

RHW

Baby of *Vanessa Gorma*

Birth Date ...20-6-02

Birth Weight ...34.40 ...7lb 9

HC= 34.5cm

L= 50cm

Raphael

Baby's Name

Mute

giving birth to Raffie and mothering him sent me into another dimension. The excruciating tiredness was superimposed over the blissful joy of his darling presence, my heart beating in waves of love and tenderness. I loved being in this mysterious underworld where intuition rules the rational, but heading out into the wider world felt threatening and strange. Feeling so wide open, so defenceless, was both exquisite and overwhelming.

I am not the type to be dependent, but now I needed to feel cared for by James, nurtured and tended to with the same effort I brought to caring for Raffie. But I couldn't communicate properly. I remember Michael saying, 'You won't slip back. You'll take what you've learned about honest communication and apply it to whatever circumstance you are in, whoever you are with.' But somehow, in the dark silence of the night, in the exhaustion, I found myself mute, shaking with rage and indignation at not being taken care of in the way I so desperately wanted.

And in my muteness lay the problem. How was James to know what to do if I didn't tell him but instead fumed silently? I had locked myself within a silent prison. It was partly to do with the newness of our relationship. The first time we lived together was after Raffie's birth, and even then James was away a lot, rehearsing with his group. I felt to ask much from him was unfair. Already he had given me this greatest gift, upending his life in the process.

Both of us were adjusting to new roles, but James, like many new fathers, was still trying to work out exactly what his role should be. Although his heart was open to Raffie, he too was coping with a crying baby – and his partner's metamorphosis from lover to mother. Perhaps his emotions could be summed up in one line, *Oh my God, what have I got myself into!*

And then the sun would be shining and Raffie would be asleep on James's shoulder and my heart would be full of love.

'They don't tell you about all the joy,' said a friend with a three-month-old. 'I had him on the change table the other day and I was looking down at him and I just wanted to cry, I felt so much love for him. They don't tell you about the good bits.'

I knew exactly what she meant. Just as I'd felt like a cracked record when I told people how much I missed Layla, I was now the same bore telling anyone who would listen how much I loved Raphael. I wanted to shout it from the rooftops. He was the liberation my shredded heart had longed for.

The joy bubbled up and threatened to suffocate me, so that I would have to laugh to release it. He was in danger of suffocating from my hugs and kisses. I loved the caress of his silky hair grazing my face as he snuggled into my neck, the feel of his body nestled next to mine in the bed, the sweet smell of his milky breath. The wandering eyes as they came to rest on my face with a look of surprise that someone was watching. The fierce chomping as he got the milk flowing, the fluttering quivers around the nipple as he fell asleep. I was breathless with mother love and full to the brim with gratitude for the salvation he offered.

Towards the end of October, the *Australian Story* sequel to *Losing Layla* aired, and we got another huge response. It was so intense, having our private lives broadcast again, but the responses let me know that we were serving a higher purpose. Layla's life continued to amaze me.

Name: Tanya
Remarks: Regarding Raphael on Australian Story

Dear Vanessa Gorman & *Australian Story*
Two years ago when the Layla story went to air, my first child (son Bailey) was a mere few weeks of age. I was a first-time mum suffering from sleep deprivation, hormones running wild, not wanting to do the whole mum thing any more. I wanted to give up right there and then, I had had enough. I found myself watching *Losing Layla*. I absolutely sobbed throughout the whole documentary. From that evening/moment on . . . you had changed my life forever. I now cherish every moment I have with my son (who is now 20 months old). Also from that evening, my life as a mother became more rewarding and meaningful, because my attitude had changed. Now my positive thoughts would change my family life forever. My son started sleeping longer through the night, I found breastfeeding a breeze, our new lives together as a family just became a delight rather than a burden. It's amazing how it all just seemed to make sense and everything was put into perspective. I just want to thank Vanessa as she made a difference to my life, for which I am forever grateful. I was so happy to see your program last night and I am so happy for Vanessa.

Vanessa, you have a lovely man and son. I hope all your dreams come true and more. Enjoy your beautiful family, as I am.

Tanya Newell

Frumpy and Flanneletted

*I*n an interview for the *Australian Story* sequel, James was questioned about how having a baby had changed our relationship. 'Well,' he said, with the apologetic laugh of someone about to reveal an unpalatable truth, 'you go out with a very sensual, intelligent woman and you end up with a frumpy, flanneletted, weepy mother.'

I laughed too. 'Make sure you put that grab in the story,' I told producer Claire Forster. Because it was true. Flannie pyjamas were my new couture. I might be out of them by, say, early afternoon, but by sunset I was eyeing them off again. Postpartum frumpiness comes with the territory. The hormones and the love leave you weepy. And yes, I'll admit it, sponging vomit off my shoulder was the extent of my grooming regime.

I attended a breastfeeding class at the hospital a few days after Raffie was born. In wandered an assortment of new mothers in nighties and dressing gowns, some limping and hobbling with rearranged pelvic bones and stitched-up perineums that they lowered gingerly onto rubber inflatable rings. Our breasts were enormous, engorged and leaking milk, stomachs hanging in folds, blood-soaked maternity pads wedged into underpants, arses padded from pregnancy weight, hair dishevelled and faces devoid of cosmetic enhancement.

I wanted to laugh. This was woman in the raw – swollen, rearranged and sore, but real and true. The earthy, mysterious underbelly of the goddess.

Motherhood demands surrender. These were not the females their men had wooed or married: nubile, slim, groomed girls. They were women now – frumpy, flanneletted, weepy mothers nursing their hardwon bundles of new life. I thought of the supermodels and actresses we see in the magazines looking slim, tanned and fit just six weeks after birth. *Kate back in prebaby form! Liz wows them at christening!* These women have nannies and personal trainers to help it happen. They're not allowed to experience this natural metamorphosis but have to fight against all their body needs to do to nurture a new baby.

As any healthcare professional will tell you, losing weight too quickly after birth, through exercise and dieting, is detrimental to breastfeeding and unhealthy for a body recovering from childbirth.

I knew that in a few months' time, most of the women from the class would be striding out, leaner and groomed again. Their breasts would settle into manageable shape, their flab would be toned, hormones under control. But I want to say, 'Rise up!' We need to own the frumpy, flanneletted, weepy mother, for she is beautiful beyond words and her job the most sacred on earth.

Overwhelmed, I fed my way through that first three months. If he cried, I fed; if he squirmed, I fed. When he was tired and should have been sleeping, I wept with frustration and fed. Suddenly I turned around and he was no longer a newborn. My apprehension diminished as I begun to relax and get a handle on this baby-raising business. My old confidence returned and I strode down the street feeling like a superhousewife.

There is a rhythmic timelessness to caring for a baby. Breakfast, playtime, sleep, lunch, a walk in the pram, sleep, play, bath, dinner and bed. Tuesdays Babyswim classes, Wednesday's playgroup, every second Thursday mothers' group, and suddenly another week, another month has passed. Before, my home was only a brief pit-stop between work engagements. Now it was my sole domain and I began to enjoy the gentle undulations of the days and weeks like some guilty secret.

> . . . love of an infant is of a different order. It is twinned
> love, all absorbing, a blur of boundaries and messages.
> It is uncomfortably close to self-erasure, and in the face of
> it one's fat ambitions, desperations, private icons and urges
> fall away into a dreamlike *before* that haunts and forces itself
> into the present with tough persistence.
>
> Louise Erdrich, 'A Woman's Work'

JOURNAL FEBRUARY 2003

After Raphael's dinner we hop in the bath together. The sun is shining through the palm trees and they wave gently outside the windows.

Raffie likes to stand in the bath now, leaning over the edge, banging the tiles and grabbing whatever he can get his hands on. I wedge his sturdy little legs between me and the edge and hang on to one thigh, feeling with delight his chubby, muscly little form. He makes noises as he bangs his plastic spade around. Singing noises, gurgling noises, blowing bubbles and raspberries happily as he experiments with the vibrations a mouth can make. When he's had enough, I pull him to me and he lies on top, his bottom wedged onto my pubic hair, his head resting between my breasts as he chews on his duck and gurgles and I sing to him, the vibrations of my chest relaxing him as he looks out at the dappled sunlight.

And then he's up straddling me and he pulls on my pubic hair and laughs as I jump in mock pain. We're laughing together and he's lunging for my nipples and we both know it's a game and while he's all stirred up for a laugh, I grab him and force my mouth under his chin, his tickly spot, and he bursts into a manic giggle and I blow a raspberry on his stomach and the laughter gets more uncontrolled, until he just can't take any more. I turn him so he's facing away from me and he bangs the water, watching the droplets fly, sucking in his breath as they shoot up his nose. The sunlight catches the flying water and he is all motion and dripping wet, a picture of joy and concentration.

He turns suddenly and his mouth makes for my nipple. I support his head in the crook of my arm as he suckles happily, warm water and my body cradling him. I wonder if there's greater bliss for either of us as we look out at the wondrous world together.

And for a fleeting moment I remember again what I have lost with Layla, but I am calmer about this than I ever thought I could be. I simply let gratitude forge its healing path and thank all of existence that I have joy with Raphael.

Letting Go

Our parents' generation understood self-sacrifice as being among the highest forms of love. It was not uncommon for people to stay in an unfulfilling relationship for the sake of the children or to uphold the sanctity of the marriage vow. There is nobility in this, but it's a notion that has lost favour in this day and age. My generation has been influenced by the New Age notion of placing honesty to oneself as the cornerstone of a successful relationship.

I discovered in my time with Michael that there is both pain and joy to be found in this honesty. Our competing needs had seen our paths diverge – I had travelled through grief, while Michael walked on with a heavy guilt. But we still had a strong connection, a friendship, even if our love was no longer played out in the bedroom or kitchen. We did our best to honour each other's new life, to respect our new partnerships. Even so, I avoided him when he was out with his new girlfriend.

James had run into Michael in a cafe one day and they had established a respectful friendship. We asked him to be Raffie's godfather, in part to keep him in the family and forge a closer connection between Layla and Raffie. He had decided to leave Byron and move back to Sydney. His father had recently died and his relationship had ended. Change was again in the wind, as it so often was in his life, and once more he was following the siren call into the unknown. On the phone he spoke of his unease about the move. 'I need to get things happening with my life businesswise. I don't really want to leave Byron but I think I need to be in the city. I'm contemplating buying some real estate so I'm in the middle of that research. Things feel in a state of flux.'

He took a deep breath and found the philosophical stillpoint. 'It's happening and I'm just trying to sit in the middle of it.'

We had lunch the day before he left, sitting under a poinciana tree in a courtyard cafe, Raffie jiggling on my knee, sucking my face or perched in his pram, slobbering over tidbits of our lunch.

'I'm going to pull back a bit from your life,' Michael said. 'I just think it's the right thing.'

'It's okay,' I said. 'I'm coping well now. I love seeing you but I don't need to see you.'

We talked of real estate confusion and Layla's approaching third anniversary and life in general as I gently rocked the sleeping Raffie in the pram.

'You brought me up here and now you're dumping me and running back to the city,' I joked.

'Just leaving you here with these awful people in this dreadful place,' he laughed, as we surveyed the courtyard filled with relaxed, gorgeous locals and laughing children playing amongst the rocks and ferns.

'You bastard,' I said, and we hugged goodbye.

The next day he rang. 'I know I said I was pulling back from your life,' he said in his most loving voice, 'but you know I miss you and I'll always love you and you'll always be a part of my life.'

'I know, I know.' I was picking up Raffie's toys from the verandah and bringing them inside. 'And you know I love you and you'll always be in my heart,' I added, meaning it, but also gathering the newspaper and dropping it on the recycling pile.

'I'll miss you. Call me any time you need to talk,' he said, and a picture of Lisa Marie Presley on the back page caught my eye. I glanced at the first paragraph of a story about the release of her first album. Apparently it was getting good reviews. I thought, I can hear all this and say all this and my heart is barely moving. I must be healed from him.

We rang off and I gazed at the debris on the bench next to the phone, the bench he hated to see messy, and I breathed out and smiled, thinking, I still love him but I have let him go.

JOURNAL 21 FEBRUARY 2003

Layla's third anniversary has come and gone, slipping by without the earth cracking open. But it's been a catalyst to contemplate the nature of healing.

It is actually quite hard to say the words 'I am healed' after a death like this. I want to say 'I am healing', that I am still susceptible to the lash of deep grief. But the truth is, I know that some part of me is healed. Not that a deep sadness won't always be there, but the scar tissue is strong now and will no longer tear under all but the most intense pressure.

I have also come to understand the healing that has happened around Dad's death. Often when I cried for Layla, I cried for him as well, enough to feel his presence now as a gentle, ghostly benefactor.

But those words 'I am healed' are hard to say. They mean letting go of all that sympathy and support. The fading ecstasy of grief. The relinquishing of Layla's loss as the central event that defines me. I am not sure if I can utter the words yet to another person, what that might mean. Will people think I have forgotten her, that I am failing her in some way? I fear the word will spread, *she no longer needs our sympathy* . . .

I am not 'good as new'. I move on differently now, scarred, wary, opened to love and pain alike. But I am no longer moving in a state of deep grief. I feel deep sadness sometimes but not that tearing and renting of the soul, that black ache. Pain rises but I can weather it now. I know that as it rises, it will also fall.

Raphael has been my saviour, flooding me with so much delight that it's hard for the grief to get a foothold. I dwell more in the present because the present with him is infused with happiness. I count my blessings moment by moment. I pray for the healing of those unable to have more children after a loss. I know I am one of the lucky ones.

Soiled Blessings

*R*affie and I load up his little yellow cart with the dirty washing and he pushes it around the verandah to the laundry with me, humming the way he does, feet splayed like Charlie Chaplin, tottering on his chubby thirteen-month-old legs.

I turn on the washing machine and let the water run, bending down to give him a big green peg. He smiles at me like I have just given him the crown jewels and crawls to find the hose nozzle, another of his jewels. A bird flits through the trees, catching his eye. He turns, using the clotheshorse to haul himself up, waving his treasure for the bird to admire – standing unsupported, a new trick. I smile and crouch down, urging him to walk towards me, and he seizes the moment, tottering with glee, like a drunkard, making for my outspread arms. He falls into my embrace and wraps his arms around my neck and we melt into one another, his head nestling on my shoulder, his silken crop of blond hair grazing my cheek, his body cuddling the length of my torso. We sway like that for a minute or two. And so great is my joy, I whisper a thank you to God and James and to the universe. I drink him in: his weight, his smell. I hum back his small sounds of pleasure.

This is the gift of Layla's passing – knowing how precious this moment is. I close my eyes and feel it all. The loss, the sadness of her three-and-a-half-year absence, and the deep, deep joy at what is here, now.

He pulls away from our embrace, because he's a busy boy, and I stand and sort the whites and the colours, because there's laundry to be done. I glance over to where he is 'watering' the potplant with the hose and smile, dropping the bibs and washers and playsuits into the machine like small, soiled blessings.

Wading into Shark-infested Waters

Not long after giving birth, I was surprised by friends and colleagues asking when I would place Raf in childcare and return to work. Their questions left me wondering if the choice to stay at home is any longer considered a valid option for women with opportunities in the workplace.

Many parents feel intense anguish on being separated from their babies and small children on a regular basis. Yet we expect parents to accept this anguish, to set aside their guilt, frustration and sadness. For women in particular, it is as if we cannot afford to feel vulnerable lest we derail our professional ambitions. But many of us are having children later in life. We are used to economic independence and the recognition that careers can bring. Yet many of us also long to be transformed by motherhood. It seems that we face an inevitable loss, no matter which path we tread.

I remember one afternoon when Raphael was about nine months old. I had a few pressing tasks at hand but Raf was grizzly, so I forgot my to do's and took him out on to the verandah. The afternoon sun dappled through the poinciana overhanging the railing. Perched on my hip, he stared wide-eyed at the dazzling sunlight playing amongst the branches. In turn, I was mesmerised by his enchantment at the beauty of life. His natural ability to be totally in the moment brings me there, too, and in that space all my agendas drop away.

I think of the working mothers who are up in the morning and rushing their babies and children to childcare and school, hurrying to jobs and to the supermarket and home to do the second shift. I wonder if they have time to take these moments with their children, to stop and see the world through the eyes of wonder and move at a child's pace.

Many of us don't have a choice – we have to go out and earn enough money to put food on the table. But being absent from our children for long stretches means we can't *fully* give them the trust and tenderness they need. We are not able to *fully* meet their emotional and psychological needs. I wonder if we are not only thwarting our children but our own deep desire to nurture them well. We worry about how separation will affect our children, but rarely do we speak of how it affects our own sensitivity and connectedness, our effectiveness as a parent.

Learning to be a good parent takes time. My relationship with Raffie unfolded gradually. We move in a subtle dance of initiating and responding to each other's moods. I feel myself flowering not only as a mother but as a person, learning to interpret his signals, to respond flexibly and interact creatively. And if things don't go well, if I lose my cool, I want the time to repair the damage and learn from my mistakes. Through all this, he is learning and growing, but so am I. To be separated from him five days a week would mean stunting that mutual growth and exploration.

I can't pretend it isn't hard letting go of my ego, letting go of the respect and recognition that work can offer. Forgoing the gratification of material goods and services is also hard. I have had to step back and look at what I can live without in these few crucial years.

Since Raffie was born I have not held a job. With the exception of a few small freelance projects done from home, I have lived with some help from the government and some money I had managed to save. All his clothes and most of his toys are hand-me-downs from friends or op shops. I no longer eat out, I rarely go to the movies. My social life consists of dropping in to visit friends. This is not a tale of woe but an example of the choices I have made to keep in close contact with Raf in these early years. It's a choice I feel at peace with. Having the time to nurture Raffie at home brings me real happiness.

And yet and yet. Many afternoons, when he woke from his nap, the hours ahead would stretch into an eternity of mind-numbing boredom. His need for stimulation competed with my own. Isolated in the hills, it was a trek to the beach, shops or a set of swings. Some days I experienced the irritation and frustration of achieving nothing more than keeping a child unsoiled and happy, and getting a few domestic chores done. I craved time to engage in my own creative work and when I began writing this book, I looked at the daycare option. I placed him for two short days with a carer who looked after three other children. He was nearly two, an age, I reasoned, when interaction with other kids would be a positive thing.

Driving from the carer's house that first morning, I felt both guilty and exhilarated to be free for a few hours. Why had I thought it would be any other way? The one thing that mothering Raf had taught me was that nothing is simple or straightforward.

Eros Interruptus

My libido went missing off the radar after Raphael was born. Sleepless nights did it, along with the feeling that my sexual organs had been rearranged. A still healing Caesarean scar was tender and breastfeeding seemed to dull desire even more.

It is Sunday morning and James is away. Raphael comes into the bed at four a.m. and we toss together for an hour. He wakes me at five for a quick feed and at 6.30 he has a gnaw at 'the udder one' and slowly we both come out of that dozy place of half-formed dreams. He raises himself on all fours and looks at me, tousled hair framing an impish grin. He laughs and launches himself across my body and we snuggle together, cooing. He straddles my body to gain maximum contact and I feel the thrill of my attraction for him. He fossicks at my pyjama top, finds a nipple and settles himself in, gazing up at me as I smile down. Another thrill passes through me. It comes from the same place as sexual attraction but it is not that. It is part of an expanded sexuality, a mother's primal attraction for her young. Beautiful and thrilling. There is not a spare cell of my body that doesn't adore him. Loving him expands the boundaries of my existence. I could bore you with it for hours.

James moved to the other end of the house to sleep two nights after Raphael came home from hospital. I'm not sure which fool coined the expression 'sleep like a baby', but at least James slept, while the real baby could barely manage more than three hours in a row for many months. Still, this meant that I could sometimes grab a morning sleep-in while James looked after Raffie.

James would have liked to make love three or four times a week. I would have been happy with a twice-a-year arrangement, to keep my hand in, as it were. This disparity caused a rift, but nothing more than what is played out in any house harbouring a new human being. When I did acquiesce, I was tense, anxious that I was losing even more precious sleep. He understood, but missed the slow, languid afternoon lovemaking sessions that went on for hours. I missed feeling like a normal human being.

'Afternoons then,' we agreed. 'When Raf is sleeping.'

We got a whole hour in on one Sunday lunchtime, revelling in the old surge as our bodies exploded against one another. Mid-penetration, from the other end of the house, we heard the familiar cry.

'Hang on,' I said, and padded, tousled and slightly dizzy, to get the boy. He was about fourteen months old, still passionately attached to the boob. It was a warm afternoon and I took off his nappy so he joined us in our nakedness. I lay on my side as Raphael latched onto a nipple and James and I resumed our union. Slowly we moved, our moans a chorus that Raphael joined, even with his mouth full. His innocent enthusiasm to join the fray made us laugh. James rose above me, preparing for a missionary coupling. Raphael straddled my body, his mouth moving to the other nipple. Again I felt James fill me and together the three of us moved in an ancient dance of mother, father and child.

293

I closed my eyes. We might have been beside a fire under bear skins, in wigwams, mud huts or igloos.

Keeping our deep contact, we lay on our sides, facing each other. Raphael fell into the space between us, still firmly attached to his nipple. Raf would often caress my skin as he fed, feeling the contours of my ribs and shoulders, the rise of the other breast, the texture of spare nipple. His tiny hands followed his father's over my skin. As they stroked me, James kissed the back of Raffie's head and looked lovingly into my eyes. We grinned with tender lasciviousness over our son's wild sleep-tangled hair. Raphael stuffed his chubby legs between our entwined thighs and slowly we undulated, sweat mingling with sweat, awash in milk, saliva and the moisture of our union. He has been in the bed with us through our lovemaking from his very earliest days and nothing about the energy or motion was alarming to him.

When he'd had enough of the boob, he climbed on us, straddling his dad and bouncing up and down with demented glee. He was everywhere, filling the gaps between our entwined bodies, insinuating himself into crevices and laughing like a maniac. Eventually he wanted up and slid off the bed, leaning on the mattress as he bent to pick anything off the floor that he could throw on us.

We knew we didn't have long now and James came to orgasm, a languorous, deep sigh. Raphael dived on his head, disrupting his postcoital bliss, and we lay him between us again. There would come a time in the near future when we decided it was no longer right for him to join us like this. But right now, for just a few moments, our little family was still, exploring each other's hands in a gentle caress of discovery.

JOURNAL 16 FEBRUARY 2004
LAYLA'S FOURTH BIRTHDAY AND ANNIVERSARY

All day a blanket of fierce, wet February heat settled over the
house, causing the iron roof to pop and spit.

I cleaned and rearranged Layla's altar in the morning. A
few friends rang. The day itself is always easier to live through
than I anticipate. Rolling waves of sadness have washed over
me these last weeks, thinking of my girl as a four-year-old.
I imagine her as curious and talkative, with a mind of her
own and a loving heart. Preparing for preschool, asking mad
questions, laughing at the wondrousness of the world.

In truth I now welcome the sadness as the gossamer
thread that pulls me closer to her. She feels sometimes so far
away. This is perhaps the saddest feeling of all, that she is no
longer close enough to tear me apart.

In the late afternoon James and I took Raffie down to
Tyagarah Beach. The grey skies threatened a change but the
gentle breeze was still moist and warm. Sand, water and sky
seemed to melt together in the heat, the magnificent coastline
taking my breath away.

Tyagarah Beach being 'clothing optional', a naked
fisherman, comic in his portliness, stood at the shoreline, his
rod a giant phallus. One or two disrobed couples lounged
on the sand and lolled in the shallows. A few solitary figures
walked the shore. We stripped off, laughing at the play of
the now cooling breeze over our clammy skin. Overjoyed to
be at his beloved beach, Raffie ran down to meet the waves,
bottom wobbling, stocky legs hurling him forward as his arms
windmilled the air. Watching him, a great wave of delight rose
in me and a prayer of gratitude, *Thank you for both my children.*

The water was warm but chilled enough to melt the heat. We dived under, laughing, loving that we lived in paradise, the sorrow giving way to the joy of the moment.

James has blossomed into the most tender and delighted of fathers, playfully encouraging Raf's boisterous side, delighting in his antics and company. I left them giggling in the ocean, gathered what I needed and set out down the beach.

I had asked James for this moment alone. I'd imagined myself walking for miles and thinking about Layla. But time was suddenly short and I knew I did not have long for contemplation.

I wanted to be with her, remember her, thank her. But as I walked, my head was suddenly full of trashy gossip from women's magazines. *Liza Minnelli and that Gest bloke's marriage is breaking up. They only just got married and now they're suing the pants off one another. What kind of people are they? Oh my God, what am I thinking this for? I'm supposed to be thinking of Layla . . .*

A couple in white strolled along the sand, lovers young in their affair, melting into one another like they had just emerged from days of lovemaking. She was a rounded redhead, he a tall, angular Japanese. I thought about a curious survey I'd once read of Japanese businessmen and their top ten fantasies. The most common involved making love on a deserted beach. Murdering their boss was number two on the list.

Layla, think of Layla . . .

I sank down on the sand and pulled out of my bag a pale pink rose, past its prime, that had been gracing Layla's altar. And a little silver box of her ashes, which I had scooped from her urn. I walked down to the water's edge and opened the

box, touching the burnt charcoal. A tiny white bone shard.
I picked it up. Perhaps it was from one of her fingers or toes,
so delicate. The tears rise at this tiniest morsel of her. So little,
so precious. I cast it into the water, then the ashes, which the
breeze whipped into the waves. I scattered the rose petals,
crying healing tears as the grey and pink reminders of life's
impermanence were swept away.

I set off homeward, weeping behind my sunglasses. The
lovers were now naked, straddling each other in the shallows.
In the distance I could see James stooping down to Raffie
and they became one figure. My heart leapt for them both.
I quickened my pace, drawn back to the land of the living.

James pointed to me and Raffie began to run. I spread out
my arms and his face broke into a smile as wide as the ocean.
I scooped him up and hugged him tight, letting him down only
so I could hug James, who held me as I wept.

'I love you,' I whispered.

And we took to the wild ocean again to wash off the sand
and the tears and the four long years that Layla had not been
on the planet.

The Ubiquitous Terror

*T*oday I passed a naked Raffie as he piled crackers into the unplugged microwave and gaily pressed the buttons. I thought, *Oh my God, I can't believe my luck*. And then my heart caught in my throat on a hook of anxiety.

I feel the fear of losing him in thousands of fleeting moments and understand with a terrible shudder how utterly devastating that loss would be. Worse than losing Layla, now that I have so many moments to grieve. I have heard the phrase hundreds of times, *The death of a child is a parent's worst nightmare*. I haven't met a parent who has not voiced this most ubiquitous of terrors.

Fear can make us wrap our children tight in cottonwool. Our fear can deprive them of the right to explore the world. I try to keep my son safe while allowing for the adventure of a physical childhood. Beyond that, I have to accept that there is much about the world that is out of my control.

Where are parents to put this fear? I say let's put it centre stage. Instead of pushing it underground, I try to let the fear give me a deeper appreciation of Raf, to remind myself to give him an extra cuddle, an extra moment of love, to be willing to surrender to his agenda. If the worst ever happens, I will know I have loved him to the very best of my heart's capacity.

The only other thing I can do to contain the fear is pray. I enter the half-gloom of the bedroom where Raffie and I sleep and pull back his insect net to tuck in his blanket. Not every night, but often, I stand there and call for his protection. I call on Jesus and the Buddha and Mohammed and all the prophets and all the saints to protect him. I call on all the guardian angels and great beings and all gods of any persuasion. I call on the force of the universe and the great Mother herself, knowing as I do that they are all one and that Raf and I are of that one. But still I ask for their protection. Then I climb into bed next to him and with a gentle sigh lay down my hopeless fear and love and fall into the fog of sleep.

Michael's Postscript

Michael lives in Melbourne now but we maintain regular
contact. He is still single but now feels ready to enter into the
commitment of a relationship.

Dear Vanessa

Thanks for the manuscript of your book. As I read it I felt something
between a deep sadness and soft fondness at the memory of it all.
Even though some of it dates back many years, it was such a
momentous period that I feel a strong need to respond.

It's almost a bit embarrassing to see myself back then. I
was always so torn between staying and going, it was exhausting
just reading it! I've heard this push/pull conflict in me, and my
unwillingness to have children, described over the years as many
things . . . too many things! As much as I love and stand behind the
many messages about grief and love and honesty that we expressed
in the documentary about Layla and our relationship, when
something goes public like that, there's always going to be a lot of
criticisms and opinions! Personally I found that hard at the time and
no easier as the years have passed.

I suppose that's why I wanted to write and at least attempt to explain things more from my viewpoint. When we met, eleven years ago, I was just out of an empty and painful seven-year marriage and I was willing to risk whatever it took to find another possibility. Whatever it took. I was in an extreme or you could say extremely determined state and I needed to experiment. Simply said, we had, at our core, a strong pull in very different directions. You wanted children and commitment and I wanted to feel alive, with no definitions or restrictions. I wanted that regardless of the risks and the loss of so called safety. We both, in essence, wanted to love deeply and that's partly why our connection was so powerful, but the difference in how we thought that should look was huge and eventually we were going to have to face that.

The next leg of our journey was to bring that to a head . . . a painful one. I was once more in a live-in relationship and feeling frozen . . . and I was having a baby without ever having the desire or having made the choice to do so! I felt like I had lost all sense of control in my life and had given up on something that felt essential to me. We had moved on without ever really resolving our differences.

Before I go on, I just need to get something off my chest about the topic of children. This idea that my not wanting children was somehow immature or that it was about me 'not being ready' is something that has driven me crazy over the years, the implication being that if I was a 'full male' I would be ready, and that 'although men may kick and scream' they all love being parents in the end. There is, in my opinion, too much being said about children as a necessary rite of passage for either gender. Why is it that it is considered empowering for a woman to choose not to have a child but weak for a man? Whether we have them or not, ALL of us, men AND woman, have lives of equal importance and value. The choice to not have children should not be seen as a statement about spiritual or emotional size.

Regardless of the rights and wrongs here, we never found a combined 'yes' or an agreed upon 'no' to the idea of children and we suffered because of it.

After Layla died THAT morning in February and we separated eight months later, I was thrown into quite a long dark period too, but quite different to the one you were in. I think in many ways I went numb in the aftermath. I knew I wanted to support you in the deep grief you were feeling and, in retrospect, I probably needed you to grieve for me too. Somewhere deep inside myself I was very confused. My body was grieving the loss of a child I hadn't really wanted, and the loss of you opened a big hole in me . . . despite the fact I'd chosen to leave. Everything was a contradiction. I started feeling both an ongoing kind of guilt about Layla and almost everything that had gone wrong with us, and a strong, unspecified anxiety. Two years after we separated I moved house close to twenty times between Byron, Sydney and Melbourne. I think, looking back, I was searching for some relief, as if it could be found in a geographical place.

Something that I feel gets easily missed in the tragedy of the story and its aftermath is how strong my love for you actually was. And just how difficult that made my decision to leave you. I don't think I've had to make a harder, more excruciating or more widely misunderstood decision in my life. I was sadly but fully aware of where that decision would leave you, but it felt true for me. It's still a decision I believe was the right one but at the time it felt like it was only a choice between different flavours of the worst possible wrongs.

You were a great love, Vanessa. Someone I still respect, love and treasure in my life today . . . So in a way, whatever we did in our loving, it has survived. That is something not only rare but a testament to how many things we did well. Layla, via your documentary, has ended up having such a powerfully healing voice in the world. I can only feel proud of her and of us too. Out of our connection and the eight hours of her life, I feel there is something very lovely that has remained here and that I treasure with you. Any story about us would be incomplete without that ending. Which is, in a way, not an ending at all.

So much love.

Michael

Nothing that begins does not end.
We see that all we love will be pulled beyond
even our most tenacious grasping
by the ongoing flow of time.

Quote on the mirror of a Blue Mountains cabin, author unknown

JOURNAL DECEMBER 2004

I have had to loosen the taut control I had over life before my child came. Sometimes I still want to be one of those people whose lives run like well-oiled machines, smooth and efficient, everything in place. Even that is an illusion – everyone has their wounds, their travails, their parts imperfect. But still I feel a stab of longing when I see those shiny surfaces. My own life seems altogether messier, frayed around the edges. I know that some of this mess is the legacy of Layla's death.

James and I have our turmoils, our differences, our confusing ups and downs. Nothing about our relationship feels fixed or sure. All I know is that we are united in the desire to become the best parents we can be.

The optimism and dreams of my thirties are tempered now – life isn't quite how I imagined it would be. Here instead is the chaos of everyday existence. I am trying to work out when to step forward, when to let go, when to stand still amidst the chaos. Sometimes I fall flat in my own mess. Other times, when I leap off that cliff into the unknown, I soar. Occasionally all on the same day.

But today's one of the ordinary days, only eight sleeps before Christmas. *Shit, better start the Christmas shopping.* My mind is full of end-of-year anxiety, the need to tie up the loose ends. *Bloody hell, get the car in for the brakes, book that doctor's appointment, rice noodles . . .*

Friday mornings are Raphael's swimming class in an indoor aqua-therapy pool nestled in a small valley outside Mullumbimby. I park the car and Raf runs ahead. I have been bringing him here since he was four months old. He's two and a half now, and like a mad performing seal in his watery element. He yells out, 'Come on, Mumma. Svimming!!' And his excitement makes me erupt with pleasure.

I have this urge to celebrate my love for Raffie often and to anyone who will listen. Yet this mother love is an ordinary thing, duplicated in millions of hearts worldwide. Why should it be anything more extraordinary in my case? Yet it is to me. Something extraordinary. The tender wind that propels the boat of my existence now. That fills my day with unexpected glee and makes me pause often to offer up my gratitude to life.

I want to urgently grasp the hand of younger women who do want children and say, 'Don't put it off for too long, it is too treasured an experience to miss out on. Re-organise your priorities and procreate.' The message I wish some woman had passed on to me. Not to bolster a falling population rate but for the health of your heart and soul. For the understanding of what in the end is one of the most sacred connections life has to offer. For the sheer flaming joy of it.

But this morning I am preoccupied. *Change that airline ticket, take the library books back, ring Alex and see how she's doing.* And then suddenly I feel it, that first strong kick from inside. Not a flutter or a twitch but a definite *I am here now* kick. The kick of a baby. The gods are smiling on me. Allowing me one more chance.

The sun is shining after days of rain. The landscape glistens, and there is nothing for it but to drop all the lists and the worries and the dramas and say, 'Fuck it! This is it. Reap this happiness right here, right now. This beauty, these blessings, this simple, complex confluence of nature is as good as it gets.'

There are the regrets and griefs of the past, the worries and hopes for the future. But this is the gift, the simplicity of the present. I am just this moment. Free now to heed the call, *Lord, make me an instrument of your peace.*

And then the next moment claims me . . . *Call Bill about the pump, remember to buy insect repellent* . . . and I laugh at myself and hurry down the hill to swimming class.

Dear Layla

Today I had two little girls here. They climbed together to the top
of my garden stairs, defying their parents' call to hop in the car
and go home. Both in fairy costumes, dancing their little dance,
wands pointing skyward, underpants sagging beneath pink tutus.
I narrowed my eyes and through the blur of my tears I could feel
you there with them, dancing your dance. But I knew your spirit was
large enough to have danced the earth. And I felt again the particular
desolation of your absence.

I still struggle with the sadness of how much I do not know
about you. Whether you would have been a fairy princess or perhaps
a tomboy, scared of the dark, bossy, loving, shy.

One of the only ways I have left to know you is through what you
have given me, how you have changed me, what I have learnt. And
that list is endless.

So five years on, I have come to accept the unlikely gifts of your
passing. This surrender to grief, letting it rise when and where it
chooses, has given me an understanding of the rise and fall of life itself.

Despair rises and also falls. Joy rises and also falls. Allowing
one allows the other, until they merge in a river that runs through
the cracks of any broken heart. I have felt my primal despair and

longing spring from the same source as love. To close off from the grief would be to close off from the love. This river flows steadily towards the ocean, a grand unity, the source of all beginnings and the destination of all hearts.

And of all your legacies, this one that dances underfoot, shining light on my life, this is the greatest. My son. He would not have been born had you not died. And if all goes well, another child to raise. Two of the greatest of consolations.

So I lay this tale down now, even as I know it is not the last time the ache of wanting you back will fill me.

But at least when I am crying I can feel you close, like a gossamer kite flying above me. At least when I am crying I am connected to you, and to all parents who have held their own kite strings and felt the pain and love of that unbearably distant tug.

All my love

Your mother

BIRTH NOTICE

Vanessa and James are delighted to announce the arrival of
Francesca Grace
5 May 2005
A sister to Layla and Raphael
Thanks to all the wonderful staff at Royal Women's Hospital, Randwick,
and our family and friends for their support and love.

Resources

SANDS (Stillbirth and Neonatal Death Society)

SANDS promotes awareness and support for families following the death of a baby from the time of conception through to infancy.

www.sands.org.au

QLD   (07) 3254 3422
VIC   (03) 9899 0218
SA   (08) 8277 0304
TAS   (03) 9517 4470

SIDS AND KIDS (Sudden Infant Death Syndrome)

SIDS AND KIDS raises funds for research and provides bereavement counselling services to families who have experienced the sudden and unexpected death of a child up to six years of age. (Incorporates SANDS in some states.)

www.sidsandkids.org

NSW   1800 651 186
VIC   (03) 9822 9611 or 1800 240 400
ACT   (02) 6244 2372 or 1800 138 300
SA   (08) 8363 1963
TAS   (03) 6431 9488
WA   (08) 9474 3544 or 1800 199 466
NT   (08) 8948 5311

THE COMPASSIONATE FRIENDS

THE COMPASSIONATE FRIENDS is part of a worldwide self-help organisation offering friendship and understanding to parents, siblings and grandparents grieving the loss of a child of any age, from any cause.

www.thecompassionatefriends.org.au

QLD (07) 3254 2657
NSW (02) 9290 2355
ACT (02) 6286 6134
VIC (03) 9888 4944
TAS (03) 6261 4250
WA (08) 9486 8711

Acknowledgements

For a wonderful introduction to the world of publishing I wish to thank Viking executive publisher Julie Gibbs, who always believed in *Layla's Story*, editor Sandy Webster for a sensitive hand, and designer Debra Billson for making a beautiful book. I also want to thank my agent Jane Ogilvie for her enthusiasm and support. For early critiques, many thanks to David Leser and Rebecca Gorman. Thanks to my mother, Anne, for showing me what is possible, and to Alexandra, Austin, Henry and Rebecca for their undying love. Thank you also to Kamal and Elizabeth for their beautiful childcare.

I have great gratitude for the people who have allowed me to write about them. Special thanks to Michael Shaw for his love and generosity in letting me expose a difficult period of his life, and to James for his forbearance and love during the writing of this book. Thank you to those family and friends who held me with loving arms during the darker days and beyond. Lastly, thanks to Raphael and Francesca for the joy. And to Layla, my muse and teacher.

Vanessa's website is: www.vanessagorman.com

For permission to quote from their work, the author wishes to thank the following authors and publishers. The excerpt from 'A Kiss is Still a Kiss', by Edwin Dobb, is Copyright 1996 by *Harper's Magazine*, all rights reserved, reproduced from the February issue by special permission. David Malouf's *An Imaginary Life* is published by Chatto & Windus, reprinted by permission of the Random House Group Ltd. 'Loving the Wrong Person', by Andrew Boyd, is taken from *Daily Afflictions: The Agony of Being Connected to Everything in the Universe*, and is reproduced by permission of W. W. Norton & Company Inc. The quotes from Nathaniel Branden's